MANAGEMENT
Success Factors
—— *of the* ——
XXI CENTURY

Lessons I've learned from a lifetime of Creating and
Leading high-performance teams in a technology-driven
multi-cultural work environment

CHAKIB ABI SAAB

CONTENTS

CHAPTER 2

INTRODUCTION

If you took a snapshot of the workforce today, you would see a drastically different picture than you did two generations ago. Today's workplace is diverse, with personnel ranging from women to immigrants, Millennials to Baby Boomers. However, managing diversity in the workplace poses difficulties. Employees arrive at work with diverse expectations, demands, and skillsets.

Diversity is not merely a marketing buzzword. Managing diversity in the workplace enables firms to leverage all employees' experiences, abilities, and skills.

Making adjustments entails 'creating or becoming something different'—you are introducing something new or adjusting an existing item.

Changing something requires you to step outside of your comfort zone. You have grown accustomed to doing things a specific way and for certain reasons, and when this pattern changes, you tend to resist, claiming that 'but we've always done it this way and it works perfectly. However, do you truly understand how or why the changes occurred? Change, when applied intelligently, can be a wonderful thing, as this chapter will explain.

We are always changing—both professionally and personally:

Changes in technology influence us differently; consider how we operate now with business equipment such as computers, the internet, email, ATMs, and online conferencing.

They promised us a paperless office (which has not yet materialized!)…we now have mechanisms in place to save our information on a microchip the size of a thumbnail. Formerly, the same amount of information was stored in a file cabinet. Additionally, computers have made reserving services and keeping track of people and inventory much faster and easier.

We can save a lot of time and money by conducting business online. It saves time, effort, and money (envelopes, paper, and stamps), plus it's quick and convenient.

To ensure that change occurs efficiently and with the least amount of disturbance or stress possible, you must address the issue methodically:

You (or your supervisors) must:

Identify the need for change—what is currently occurring and why is it no longer working?

Conduct research on what needs to be done—consider the steps necessary to get from where you are now to where you want to be (in a logical order).

Identify potential issues with the new procedure and work to resolve them.

elicit comments and input from appropriate personnel in a range of department-mplement the change—educate all stakeholders about the new plan, process, or system and offer any necessary training to staff. Evaluate the change's efficacy—iron out any kinks and determine if the new process or system is performing as intended.

In the United States, we currently have four distinct generations coexisting in the workplace. It was easier in the past when there was less diversity and a firmer set of norms. The older employee was the boss, manager, or supervisor, while the younger employees were subordinates who "obeyed" their supervisor's rules.

Older workers remain in the workforce for longer periods of time (whether by choice or necessity). Business is becoming more globalized, technology is transforming the way people work, and the skills required are changing. These factors contribute to the amended, dropped, or adjusted regulations, highlighting the importance of effective communication, management, and leadership.

When we engage with customers, it becomes evident that generational differences can impact every aspect of business, including the how's, why's, and where's of recruiting, team building, dealing with change, motivating, managing, and sustaining and growing productivity. Consider how generational disparities in communication styles may cause misconceptions, high employee turnover, trouble recruiting and retaining staff. We know that people communicate in ways that are influenced by their experiential and generational histories.

Each generation has its own unique set of attitudes, actions, expectations, habits, and motivators. Learning to communicate effectively with different generations can help avoid many significant workplace clashes and misunderstandings and great outcomes.

These distinctions can result in four strikingly diverse employee kinds. While we do not advocate for "stereotyping" someone based on their age or generational group, it is beneficial to grasp the broad generational disparities.

So how should organizations begin managing workplace diversity?

Take a cultural temperature. Make no assumptions about your company's present cultural environment based on a hunch or guess. Utilize an employee satisfaction survey to get employee feedback on workplace diversity.

Create a framework for workers with minimal or no English proficiency. If these people densely populate the work environment, decision-makers should begin managing workplace diversity by addressing linguistic challenges. While organizations cannot enforce a uniform language policy, management may explore the following strategies:

Determine which types of business documents may require translation. This may include employment regulations, anti-discrimination/harassment procedures, and information about health insurance. This technique for managing workplace diversity will go a long way toward decreasing employee and coworker confusion.

Without due study, do not implement an English-only policy. Banning a foreign language is a surefire way to alienate the personnel that makes your organization run. Additionally, the EEOC establishes tight criteria for English-only regulations. For instance, the policy must be targeted precisely and narrowly to legitimate business goals. It cannot prohibit the use of non-English languages during breaks, meals, or other non-work time. Consult an employment lawyer or human resources specialist before implementing an English-only policy.

Employees should be educated on harassment and discrimination issues. Team members may be unaware that culturally appropriate complaint mechanisms should be used. In most cases, the American workplace relies on employees asserting their rights by filing a complaint.

Complaining about coworkers or superiors is considered impolite in several cultures. If you employ employees from diverse cultural backgrounds, collaborate with them to create a mechanism in which they feel comfortable making a workplace complaint.

Recognize that you may face resistance to change. If the organization has never been diverse or if diversity rules are new to the workplace, resistance to the reforms is not uncommon. Begin addressing workplace diversity opposition by explaining why changes are occurring and how they will benefit employees and the organization.

Establish attainable, quantifiable objectives. Best-in-class organizations do not enter a new market or develop a new product without establishing a clear vision for where they want to go or where they need to be. Establish sensible, attainable goals and benchmarks if you want to manage diversity in the workplace successfully.

The genuine meaning of success in the workplace depends entirely on your interpretation of the term. You need to create a list of the professional goals you want to attain and build your success around those goals.

CHAPTER 1

MEETING EMPLOYEE EXPECTATIONS

Employees are the lifeblood of any business. We invest considerable time in recruiting, screening and interviewing them. We spend additional time training, coaching, and monitoring them after they are hired. And we like to believe that we have contributed to the company's future and helped weave the company's fabric.

After that, there is another category of employees. The Obstacles are the individuals who make us question why we became managers. The true reason we are compensated.

Perhaps you inherited them, hired them, or managed them into the unhappy swarm that they have become.

Four of those individuals are highlighted below, along with some strategies for dealing with them.

However, there is the first rule. You are powerless to change their attitude. They own it; it is internal, and the only way for it to alter is for them to think differently.

What is the Definition of an Attitude? Before we proceed, let us define it.

This is a term I like; see if you disagree.

An Attitude is a state of mind. It reflects how individuals react to their external surroundings on an interior level.

Emotions, acts, reactions, events, and people affect one's attitudes. They can be quite delicate or incredibly robust.

And they are constantly changing in some individuals.

Now that we've established a working definition let's look at four of the most common problems for employees.

The Grinder of Axes. This individual exists in every business. They are the ones who have suffered an adverse event during their employment and believe the company or manager was complicit. It could have been a missed promotion or being forced to work overtime due to "inadequate management."

Rather than concentrating on a solution, they would rather focus on how "messed up" the company or manager is. (Similar to the Schleprock, but with increased range and defensiveness)

Instead of entertaining coworkers with their private philosophy and "management style, they prefer to carry their sad story around, never offering a solution, instead of entertaining coworkers with their individual "management style" and "personal ideology." If I were you, I'd do the following. If allowed to continue with their Axe Grinding, they can become quite bitter towards the company and other coworkers.

The Remedy. It is a three-step procedure. To begin, determine the primary problem or issue confronting the Grinders. It can be extremely difficult to get to the bottom of the problem, as most Grinders list things wrong. You must work with repairable and addressable items. If you attempt to address every item on their list, you will become bogged down in "once" or "he did" or "they said" and will never get around to truly discussing what is wrong.

Second, solicit their assistance in resolving the issue. This is the initial investment. You cannot proceed to step 3 until the Grinder certifies that the solution you agree on resolves the issue satisfactorily.

Third. Identify the steps you want to take to accomplish your goal. And the behavior you anticipate from the Grinder going forward. I made no reference to "altering their attitude" or "shaping up." If you want them to refrain from speaking to anyone about the incident or whatever occurred, inform them that this is a condition of the agreement. One final thought is that they agree to bring other issues to your attention before escalating, and they have a solution they believe will resolve the issue.

The Setter of the Agenda. These individuals have a point to make. They are entirely focused on achieving something for themselves, frequently at the expense of others or the company. They're not interested in collaborating as a group and don't respect anyone's interests except their own. They have been known to sabotage other coworkers in order to obtain what they desire.

They are frequently outstanding at what they do. Numerous businesses rely on their performance. The numbers generally have the potential to make or break a month or even a quarter. It becomes a matter of managing the least of two evils for many managers. Each business requires performance, but each business also requires cooperation and harmony to succeed.

Does this person have the authority to run roughshod over my division in performance and numbers? Neglect your coworkers? Perhaps even become so arrogant as to disobey management openly?

The Remedy. This entails identifying the individual's conduct and establishing some boundaries for them. By informing them that you will not allow them to set the pace or tone for your department, you also establish the bar for their continued employment.

Inform this individual that you appreciate their efforts and will continue to assist them in carrying out their responsibilities. Simultaneously, inform them that you require cooperation and that they may have to find another band if they wish to perform their music. Solicit their assistance in developing the department or business. Solicit their assistance in training and supporting other team members. In some circumstances, they are actively seeking greater responsibilities and a chance to contribute to the business's growth.

They leave if they are unwilling to follow the regulations.

Bombers insanity. These are the people who keep to themselves. They are rarely verbal. They can be aloof to unfriendliness (in public) (sometimes).

Now, some of you may ask, what difference does it make? At the very least, they are remaining silent and performing their duties. What else do you require?

I understand your point of view. This is the issue with these individuals. They walk into your office one day and say, "I'd like to file a complaint," or "I've taken a new position," or other bombshells.

Due to their lack of involvement with the company and its personnel, they never inform you of developments and exhibit little loyalty. They frequently detonate bombs due to years of feeling "stepped on" or "unappreciated."

The Remedy. Request their comments frequently. Involve them and engage them in conversation about their activities. These individuals will demand additional MBWA time but will open up if you demonstrate a real interest in them. I've learned more about a company by conversing with quiet employees than loud employees. They are, on the whole, excellent observers.

Assist them in becoming more active participants by including them in more daily activities. Consider starting a Toastmasters or public speaking club at your place of employment, as these individuals will benefit from public speaking.

Assure their decision-making and policy development involvement by openly soliciting their input and suggestions.

Paycheck. These individuals are here for financial gain. As with everyone else, they perform their duties admirably. Regardless of their rank. But they rarely go above and beyond the call of duty.

They never volunteer yet are always first in line for food at the corporate picnic. You can rely on their attendance at work, but not much else. They lack loyalty and frequently change jobs or locations.

Additionally, they are the "first" complainers. They whine and extend their hand whenever something new occurs or involves a little more work than before. In some instances, they may become "malicious obedience" or "selective obedience" employees. They never do anything explicitly that might result in their dismissals, such as misconduct or poor performance, simply teeter on the precipice's edge.

The Remedy. This is also a three-step method.

To begin, inform the Paychecker that their performance is "average." Assist them in understanding that reaching basic standards only ensures that they will receive minimum wages.

2nd. Identify shared goals that the Paychecker can meet and accomplish that will result in greater levels of production and remuneration. Assist them in seeing the vision of who they aspire to become.

Third, schedule a monthly review with them for the first 90 days to assess their progress toward their goals. They will begin to come around if they see that you are genuinely interested in their accomplishments.

If they maintain minimum standards, assign them assignments and tasks that reflect those standards. If they aspire to stay a "Paycheck" in perpetuity, they are unlikely to remain in your job for long, as they are constantly on the lookout for the BBD. (Better, Bigger Deal) Universally applicable answers don't exist. It demands some significant consideration on your part, well-designed implementation, and ongoing monitoring. You cannot hold one meeting and expect that everything will run smoothly from that point on. That is not how it works.

And, along the way, recognize people who do things the correct way, day after day.

The Workplace's Expectancy Role

Victor Vroom's 1964 Expectancy Theory uses a simple equation to explain human actions in the workplace. According to the notion, an individual's behavior or performance of a task is closely related to the outcome the individual anticipates. If an individual has cause to believe that their expectations will be met, their behavior and performance will improve.

The entire theory is summed up in the following equation:

Motivating Force= Anticipation Instrumentality Valence

Expectancy refers to an employee's belief that completing a task will result in specific desired and expected outcomes. This is typically determined by prior experiences—whether the employee's expectations were met or not met in similar situations in the past. Additionally, the employee must be convinced that they have some control over the outcome of their work. If a person has no say in the outcome, they will be less motivated to perform well. Similarly, if the goal is set excessively high, expectations and motivation to perform well will be low.

Instrumentality refers to the employee's belief and certainty that they will be rewarded for completing a task successfully. The reward could be a promotion or a wage increase, just recognition and admiration for a job well done, or the opportunity to take on more challenging responsibilities and duties. If employees are not recognized for their efforts, their drive to perform properly will be quite low. Instrumentality is primarily reliant on the employer-employee relationship. The employee should have confidence in the organization's ability to reward them appropriately after completing a task. Again, prior experiences and a measure of control over the outcome contribute significantly to sustaining a high level of Instrumentality.

The term "valence" refers to individual aspirations and the value they place on the promises and rewards. If an individual is rewarded insufficient raise for them or a promotion that is insufficient for them, this has a detrimental effect on their 'valence.'

According to the Expectancy Theory, performance in a professional situation is directly tied to the task's expected outcome. If managers aim to improve performance, they can do so by developing an appealing and equitable compensation system.

Employees must be encouraged to strive for greater heights and seize every opportunity to learn and improve themselves. Employees' satisfaction or unhappiness can be ascertained by frequent contact, whether through meetings and personal interviews or questionnaires and self-reports. The reward system and the sorts of goals and opportunities available to employees

The Expectancy Theory Equation demonstrates that if any of the three variables (Expectancy, Instrumentality, or Valency) is 0, the Motivation Factor is also, all three variables should

In the 1930s, Harvard University researchers conducted productivity tests at Western Electric's Hawthorne facility, demonstrating how management attention results in immediate productivity gains. However, sustained, long-term productivity is promoted when management consistently conveys to staff that they will perform to established criteria.

These data suggest that by expectations, even when their perceptions about their talents are low. This fact may have a substantial impact on an individual's performance.

Managers must understand that if they freely exhibit their belief in an employee's competence and worth, the person is more likely to be effective and enjoy their job more. Managers reinforce this approach by encouraging and responding to their staff, assigning them more difficult tasks, and providing additional guidance and support.

As the phenomenon is frequently known, the Pygmalion Effect emphasizes that achievement is more closely related to expectations than individual aptitude. The self-image of an individual has an effect on their performance. This concept establishes the parameters for individual achievement. Its core tenet is that people can work up to and beyond their apparent capabilities by rising to meet their superiors' expectations.

Managers can influence overall performance by increasing their employees' self-confidence and self-esteem. These activities have an effect on performance by broadening individuals' personal beliefs of what they are capable of.

Due to the nature of business, employees must cope with everyday stress and the inevitability of errors and failures that affect their self-esteem and confidence. Managers may assist their staff positively by remembering the Pygmalion Effect. They can instill confidence in employees that they will easily overcome setbacks and continue to work toward achievement.

Additionally, a manager's attitude toward their staff has an effect on their performance. They are frequently astounded to realize that individuals demonstrate far more potential and ability than the management anticipated when allowed to prove themselves.

The second factor in enhancing productivity is managers' degree of attention. Attitudes, expectations, and attention all influence what and how is accomplished. The Hawthorne studies demonstrate that management's time and attention are directly proportionate to results. In the majority of enterprises, time is the most precious resource. Employees recognize that when their manager is visible to them, they invest a significant personal resource in their performance. As a result, a visible manager is a more effective manager.

When most people consider leadership, they believe it exists only at the highest levels of an organization. However, successful leadership occurs on a one-to-one basis. Managers engage closely with their direct reports to develop their competencies and personal commitment to producing favorable results. A single manager's attitude, expectations, and attention can have a more dramatic effect on productivity and positive results than anything else.

Organizational changes occur mostly at the personal level. Successful managers recognize that progress develops gradually but steadily, one modest adjustment at a time. While each adjustment may look insignificant in and of itself, the impact is huge when assessed over time and an entire workplace.

When managers have a favorable effect on their employees' performance and incrementally raise their productivity, they begin to contribute regularly and successfully toward the organization's goals. Each tiny victory contributes to long-term commitment.

Global transformation occurs due to everyone having the opportunity to commit and contribute. Progress is the consequence of several small changes—not huge management choices.

What do your employees anticipate from you?

There are numerous books on leadership and management—former/current leaders are usually happy to share what made them successful. While each individual has a unique perspective, style, and enthusiasm, it ultimately boils down to three things.

Yes, employees have three expectations of their bosses.

Coaching in Fair Communication

While the concepts may appear straightforward, mastering them can put you well to be a great leader. Incorporating these elements into your style and philosophy may demonstrate an authentic leadership style that your colleagues will admire and follow.

Fairness. This is about holding every employee to the same standard. For instance, do not accept one employee's unpleasant behavior while disciplining another for the same. The inverse of this example would be to expect all employees to perform at their best—not to tolerate substandard performance.

Communication. Inform, educate, and demonstrate to your employees where the firm is headed, what you hope to accomplish, and what your customers anticipate. The structure and tone are all up to you; what matters is that you share and do not leave them guessing or, worse, allowing the rumor mill to take over. Occasionally, this will include giving unpleasant news, demonstrating empathy and understanding, and they will respect you.

Coaching. Others may prefer the terms guiding, performance feedback, or expectation setting. Whichever title you use, the goal is to assist your people in working more effectively, performing at a higher level, and treating your customers properly. This can be accomplished through training, one-on-one meetings, or a formal evaluation procedure—the method is entirely up to you.

They sound straightforward to implement, but if you are not accustomed to working in this manner, it will take intentional effort and dedication to integrate them into your daily leadership.

Performance—Achieving Objectives and Exceeding Expectations

Performance is defined as the accomplishment of objectives and the fulfillment of expectations. On the other side, performance management is defined as a continual cycle of job performance improvement through goal setting, feedback, coaching, awards, and positive reinforcement.

The goal-setting theory is founded on two fundamental principles, both of which are validated by research:

+ Individuals who set explicit difficult goals ('stretch goals') do better than those who set easy, imprecise, or 'do your best' goals;

+ The more accomplishments a person has, the more satisfied they are.

According to research, the strongest link between objectives and performance occurs when employees are committed to their goals, provide input, and receive rewards and feedback.

Thirdly, the management must select which performance components will be monitored, typically defined by job analysis and description; it must attempt to incorporate all employee contribution areas to minimize demotivation. Employee morale is likely to decrease if a component is overlooked, as employees who excel in that dimension will not be recognized or rewarded.

Following that, actual performance is compared to established criteria, with discrepancies noted. In other words, performance assessment is concerned with determining whether objectives have been fulfilled and whether individual and organizational goals have been cascaded down, vertically aligned, and attained.

The management must determine whether to use performance indicators based on traits, behaviors, or outcomes.

The attribute method has dwindled in popularity as it has become more personality-driven. It is possible to monitor and quantify behavior more objectively; it is also more legally enforceable to document activities. Appraising predetermined results versus previously established goals is becoming increasingly popular since it easily compares the organization's strategic objectives and enables management to exercise control.

The next stage is to discuss the appraisal with employees, as it has a great deal of emotional weight and significantly impacts employee self-esteem. It is far more convenient for both appraiser and appraisee to convey positive news than to deliver the bad news that performance fell short of expectations. In the former situation, compensation may shape cash or positional benefits. However, in other instances, the desire for recognition and belonging may be significant motivators for employees' groups and teams to achieve above and beyond expectations.

The final phase is to determine what needs to be done to improve the employee's current performance. Corrective action should ideally address the underlying causes of substandard performance rather than merely the symptoms, as this is more advantageous in the long run.

Meeting Employee Work Expectations: Effective Strategies for Reducing Turnover

According to workforce experts, the cost of replacing a worker is 1.5 times the worker's annual wage. Employers must look beyond wages and benefits to avoid turnover costs and retain a productive environment.

When your employees' work expectations are met, work may be a satisfying and rewarding experience. While salary and perks are the apparent compensations that an employee expects from their employer, there are a variety of intangible rewards that might contribute to job satisfaction. Whether you're considering a recruit or attempting to keep existing staff, four critical characteristics can contribute to a pleasant work experience.

Environment

Many employees anticipate working in a pleasant atmosphere. Nobody wants to awaken each morning dreading going to work. Do your employees prefer a low-stress, friendly environment? Perhaps you should give projects that demand collaboration and interpersonal connection. However, many personalities anticipate varying work environments. Certain individuals do better under duress and relish the opportunity to be tested. Allowing employees to share their ideas in a work environment that prioritizes results over personal relationships may satisfy them.

Structure vs. Individuality

For some employees, the structure is a vital aspect of the workplace. Perhaps they appreciate the knowledge that some resources are available. Providing explicit timelines, methods, or directions to employees may aid them in finishing a project or resolving a problem. However, some individuals anticipate working independently. They may wish to establish their priorities or apply their problem-solving techniques. Allowing staff to take on new responsibilities or streamline existing procedures may be a strategy to keep them pleased.

Personal Life vs. Work

The majority of employees anticipate a certain level of balance between work and personal life. They have obligations outside of work and believe that work should not obstruct their ability to fulfill those obligations. Assure your staff that you appreciate their dedication to their families and extracurricular activities. Assure them that work will not interfere with their personal lives but that you want them to perform at a high level.

Career Advancement

Career development is critical for many people in today's culture. If your employees take pride in their work, devote significant time and effort, and achieve success, they expect to be rewarded. The reward does not have to be monetary; occasionally, a new job title, additional responsibility, or other incentives will give the desired positive reinforcement.

Career-minded individuals are likely to seek new experiences and expand their set of professional abilities, so increasing their marketability to prospective employers. Assuring your staff of promotion chances may help keep them content and loyal to your organization.

Once you've discovered the factors that contribute to an enjoyable work environment for your staff, it's critical to maintain open lines of communication. If your employees' work expectations are not met, they may never be pleased in their existing employment. You, as an employer, are fully aware of this substantial expense associated with staff turnover.

If you want to keep your employees, you must first understand their job expectations and then take steps to improve their job satisfaction by making work a pleasurable experience.

Raising Expectations, Accountability, And Recognition

Many bosses move around their offices as though everyone is mind-reading. This is not correct. While many concepts may seem intuitive to you, they may not be to your employee. How often have you wondered why Tim does not send out reports of his staff meetings? or "How come Nicole does not respond to e-mails while on conference calls?" While these may seem like conventional practices to you, they may not be to your employees, and you have no right to expect them to be followed unless and until you advise them of your expectations.

Establish Expectations

Examine the areas where your staff falls short of your expectations and ask yourself, "Have I conveyed this expectation?" If the employee responds "no," schedule a meeting with them to discuss your expectations. If you believe you have communicated the expectation effectively, it may be worthwhile to have another chat with the employee in which you inquire whether he recalls discussing the expectation. Attempt to ascertain why he is unable to meet it.

They are assuring that expectations are well established and communicated aids in the smooth operation of your department or project. Employees are also more content when they know their supervisor's expectations. It's a relief to work each day knowing precisely what will satisfy your boss and ensure your success; when your employees feel this way, their productivity increases due to their lack of self-doubt.

Maintain Accountability for Them

Setting an expectation and never following through is a sure-fire way to build frustration within your department. When an expectation is not fulfilled, the view is that it was never essential in the first place. Despite the fact that we'd all like to believe that we can set an expectation with an employee and have it met 100% of the time with no follow-up, this is unlikely to happen. This is not because your employee lacks respect for you or is obstinate.

Typically, this is because the expectation is not ingrained in her and thus is not a natural part of her workday. She has a backlog of expectations to meet and is unsure where this one ranks on the priority list. Whatever the cause, the most straightforward method to guarantee your expectations are met is to follow up. This demonstrates to the employee that you took the requirement seriously and that it is significant to you.

If your expectation is not met even after following up, it is vital to hold your employee accountable. Holding an employee accountable is not about playing "I've got you" or attempting to catch the employee in the act of wrongdoing. Accountability fosters team to trust. It communicates to the entire team that you adhere to performance standards.

When keeping someone accountable, I propose meeting with the employee and inquiring whether the person understands your expectations. If she does, inquire why she is having difficulty meeting the standard. You may be able to remove an impediment for the employee to ensure the expectation is satisfied in the future. After determining why, discuss with the employee what you can do to assist in meeting the expectation in the future.

This demonstrates to the employee that you care about her achievement. Finally, after the talk, communicate that you will follow up to ensure the expectation is met and that failure to do so cannot continue.

Express Your Appreciation

A significant morale destroyer, a productivity destroyer, is when a supervisor establishes expectations and fails to recognize his people when those expectations are satisfied. While expressing gratitude for sending out the meeting recap may seem trivial, it is critical if you want the habit to continue. By expressing gratitude, you demonstrate to the employee that you noticed he followed through on your request. It gives the employee the impression that you are not present to yell orders and direct him. It is especially critical to recognize an employee if you have previously had to hold them accountable. Recognizing an employee for doing something correctly when he previously fell short demonstrates to the employee that you will not just correct him when he is off track but will also recognize when he is on track.

Employees perform better in an environment where expectations are explicit, where they are held accountable for their performance, and where they are recognized for their efforts. Concentrating on these items will help alleviate frustration and improve department performance. Communicate your expectations clearly to your personnel and reaffirm their significance through follow-up and recognition. It is far more straightforward than convincing your colleagues to read your mind.

E-Learning Can Help Strengthen The Human Resources Department: Strategies For Meeting Employee Expectations

Today's corporate environment is fraught with rivalry. While people compete for the job of their dreams, firms work hard to retain talent. Employees in today's corporations have a lot of expectations of their employers. Additionally, organizations recognize that the human resources function should try to increase employee engagement to ensure that people give their all at work.

It is self-evident that the more engaged an individual is at work, the more likely they will be to give their all—thereby enhancing performance and overall financial and operational results.

To ensure that employees are adequately engaged at work, we must consider the following: What do employees most desire from their workplace? According to a major study, learning and development opportunities are among the top expectations that corporate employees today have from their employer, alongside income, job stability, and career advancement.

Thus, the human resources function must identify acceptable routes for training and development that enhance employee abilities and give growth prospects. Some may question the long-term influence of training not necessarily conducted within the workplace limits. However, we must recognize that employees today desire to perform better both within and outside of their given positions. Thus, they're more open to new ideas and willing to learn as long as it benefits their ability to perform better work or obtain better career possibilities.

Utilizing technology-based learning to create and deliver staff training is beneficial to everyone—notably the human resources function.

It is easier to offer appropriate courses and track learner progress on a technology-enabled platform. The effort required is negligible, as the procedure is completely automated.

Because learners can enroll in courses according to their schedules, there is no need to schedule training around the schedules of all employees.

Reports on learning retention and built-in assessments can be created automatically and used to plan the employee's benefits and compensation package.

However, adequate procedures should be in place to ensure that the training is effective and that the technology-assisted solution provides both exciting and effective learning.

Most employees are dissatisfied with corporate training because it lacks color or warmth and is frequently didactic in tone. It is true that the majority of these training deal with important themes and are thus frequently text-heavy. However, technology-enabled self-paced e-material courses must capture the learners' attention without overwhelming them.

Even if the courses are dense with information, there are ways to make the subject engaging and intriguing. For example, we can pique learners' interest by providing some information via an instructive visual or perhaps a little animation and then posing thought-provoking questions about the subject. This ensures that the student gets 'hooked' on the subject—by providing some basic knowledge and prompting them to think more deeply.

Another source of employee unhappiness is that courses frequently fail to hit a familiar note and fail to connect with the subject. Because the topic stays unknown and there are no connections made inside the course to what they already know, the course fails to have the desired impact.

To do this, scenarios can be created to acquaint learners with the subject and contextualize it to better comprehend and relate to it. The scenarios might use real individuals and their stories to help students develop a stronger connection to the subject. Learners may now connect what they already know and what the course wants them to know through relevant situations.

E-courses do not have to be entirely textual or visually focused. Interactivities can be incorporated into a course to serve as a potent tool for increasing learner engagement. Numerous interactivities can be incorporated, ranging from basic slide transitions to audio-visual interactions. In an attempt to make the e-course appear slick, developers often include excessive interactivity, which might make the course too complex and overwhelm the learners. When building interactivities for e-courses, the golden guideline is to keep things simple.

Additionally, technology-assisted learning solutions must be sustainable to ensure learners can extract relevant information for long-term usage—even when their initial enthusiasm wanes. A frequent method of ensuring the sustainability of an e-learning program is to incorporate job aids into the course. These publications can be downloaded for convenient and quick reference—depending on the learner's needs. The job aids can be accessed and used even after the learner has completed the course.

Today, corporate learners demand a certain amount of freedom regarding access and choice of learning content—both in classrooms and on technology-assisted platforms. A range of courses can be created on the corporate learning management system—both bespoke and off-the-shelf content.

Two distinct versions of a course can be generated in custom courses to accommodate novice and advanced learners. The version for rookie learners can be detailed, while the expert learners can benefit from skimming introductory material and focusing on newly introduced material.

This ensures that rookie learners are well-informed and that advanced learners are not bored with previously learned information. This seemingly straightforward technique can deliver tailored learning for a diverse group of learners while meeting their individual needs.

Employee expectations are realized when learners are fully engaged and connected to their work—an ideal state of work excellence. The human resources function seeks to accomplish this, and it is a constant process. It is now possible to give learning opportunities that enhance the job and provide knowledge/skills for career growth. Through strategic thinking and the incorporation of creative concepts, the human resources staff may develop learning solutions that impart information and contribute to overall employee happiness.

Personnel Management Techniques

1. Be clear about the expectations of your staff. This begins on the first day you hire an employee, but it's never too late to repeat this strategy with current employees, and in fact, I strongly urge it. It's as simple as scheduling some one-on-one time with new employees to review your company's standards and expectations, regardless of whether you have written policies.

    You should have fundamental company policies available on your website or in a handbook for you and your employees. More essential, be extremely explicit about your employees' expectations to avoid misunderstandings.

2. Make meetings with personnel, whether one-on-one or in groups, a routine aspect of your work. It's tough to encourage and lead staff when you're unfamiliar with their work or the obstacles they confront.

Therefore, let us be clear: comprehending the job performed by your staff and being able to undertake the task yourself are two entirely different things. And I'm not advocating that being able to assume the function of your direct reports is a best practice, although it may be necessary depending on the firm with whom you work.

I'm arguing that to succeed in employee management, you must be able to discern the issues your employees encounter and provide them with the tools and support they desire and require to succeed. Bear in mind that your employees' performance directly correlates with your own and your company's success.

It is critical to meet with your employees frequently to stay informed about their job and provide encouragement, direction, and support. Make the error of believing that it is a waste of time. It is, in fact, a critical tool that will assist you in becoming a successful leader.

3. Avoid being a contributor to the problem. So what exactly am I referring to? Therefore, avoid being the stumbling block that hinders your staff from performing the tasks you engaged them by micromanaging them. Empowering employees by allowing them to make decisions that do not require your permission upfront and only as necessary is critical. This is critical because empowered employees think their professionalism is valued.

4. Inform staff whether they are performing well or not. Your team wants to hear whether you believe they are doing a good job or if there are any areas where they could improve. After all, who wants to believe that everything is going swimmingly only to discover that there are

issues or concerns at an annual performance evaluation? Additionally, positive reinforcement will assist in motivating your employees and increasing their job satisfaction. Additionally, it saves you time, frustration, and, in some situations, money by preventing your employees from wasting time on errors caused by a lack of knowledge of what you truly expect from them.

5. Avoid burying your head in the sand when confronted with challenging job challenges. While it may appear easier to simply ignore terrible behavior or hope it will magically disappear, the more likely effect of ignoring poor workplace behavior is losing clients, customers, or even your best employees. They are upset by their work environment.

You must address issues as they arise and be candid about your worries. Inform your employees of your expectations for the future and the repercussions of workplace difficulties recur. And, of course, these types of interactions are always held in private.

Engagement of Employees

You are calling all Executives and Managers! Are you engaging your employees' hearts and minds"? "This sentence has been used so frequently that it has become a cliché," you're probably thinking. Naturally, I am!" However...are you truly?

Gallup's study indicates that 29% of employees are engaged, 54% are disengaged, and 17% are actively disengaged. According to Gallup analysts, the reduced productivity of actively disengaged workers loses the US economy approximately $370 billion each year. With employee disengagement at an all-time high, could it be that managers just do not comprehend what it means to "engage the hearts and minds of our employees"?

Rational engagement often referred to as "mind engagement," refers to individuals' intellectual commitment to their organizations. It is their comprehension of how they may contribute to their organizations' success. And it's about appreciating the benefits to both the individual and the organization.

Engagement in rational discourse is conditional. The conditions of a new assignment are determined by the expectations you establish with your employee at the start of the task. These expectations are renegotiated with each assignment and with each change in direction within the business.

On the other hand, emotional engagement is about something more fundamental and deeper. It's about your employees' instinctive attachment to your organization. It's how your personnel feel about the task at hand. They may not express their emotions, but they significantly impact your organization's performance.

Emotional engagement is self-sustaining. Your relationship with your staff shapes their expectations. Your relationship becomes a prism through which your employees view your business.

The following is a true story about a manager who believed her people were extremely engaged. What are your thoughts?

Diane was a project manager at a large retail organization's information technology support group. She described her leadership style as "tough yet fair." The project lead and her six coworkers were nearing the end of a six-month project. They had obtained user approval and were preparing to implement the new program that evening.

The users were delighted that the project was nearing completion and that their system would be available for them when they returned to work the next day. The project team had worked late nights updating the software in response to changing user requirements. Users had voiced their gratitude to Diane for the project team's efforts, particularly the project lead's "going above and beyond."

Diane did not communicate their feedback to the team. She believed that the team members were not performing to their potential and that if she provided them with user input, they would likely slack off even more than they already were.

The organization had not performed as well as projected, and layoffs were rumored. The crew had become aware of the rumors and conveyed their concern to Diane. She stated that she had heard them and that they should not be alarmed since no layoffs were planned. In actuality, Diane had been aware of impending layoffs for several months.

At 3:00 p.m., the IT Operations Manager approached Diane. He had only recently become aware of the impending implementation. He inquired whether they had tested the software on the newly installed equipment put into production earlier that week. Diane was stunned for a brief period—she had not heard of any new device, much less tried its software. She informed the Operations Manager that they would do a test immediately and then proceed with the implementation.

Diane convened a meeting with her team and briefed them on the situation. She stated that the Operations Manager had failed to inform her about the new equipment and that the team would be required to work late until testing and implementation were completed. As Diane had anticipated, the team members grumbled and whined, but they agreed. "I'll stay and assist you," she stated.

At 4:30 p.m., Diane received a call from her daughter reminding her that it was parents' night at the school. Diane had forgotten about it entirely. She left the office around 5:00 p.m., requesting her project lead to notify the team and call her mobile phone when the system was installed.

The squad reassembled following her departure. What occurred? They conjectured. Diane did not get along well with the Operations Manager. According to one team member, the Operations Manager "set her up—there is no love lost there." Another individual stated, "To be fair, she deserves it. Here we are—once more. And where has she gone?" "Ignore it—let's get this over with," the project lead intervened.

The project team initiated the test. They met numerous difficulties. By 11:00 p.m., they had determined that they would be unable to complete the work that evening. They would complete it the following morning.

Diane was hailed upon her arrival at the office by the Vice President of Information Technology, who invited her to visit him in his office. Her project manager was already present. He shut the door behind him and demanded to know what had occurred. His phone was constantly ringing! Diane instantly accused the project lead of failing to contact her and the team for failing to complete the assignment. "They are plain untrustworthy," she stated. "Get them all in here!" exclaimed the Vice President of Information Technology. Diane gave the nod and gathered the squad.

The Vice President stated, "We were going to discuss this further tomorrow, but I figured I'd inform you now. You are all going to get laid off. We're planning to outsource our information technology support." The whole project team was taken aback, except the project lead, who responded, "Given that you've laid your cards on the table, I will work. I am departing. I've stayed on till now only to see the project through '". Diane was taken aback.

What occurred here?

Two critical components of a relationship that contribute to emotional engagement are trust and respect.

Trust is built in three distinct ways:

Openness—Keeping your staff "in the loop" by giving as much information as possible about your organization's direction and the critical nature of their jobs.

Diane failed to keep her team informed of positive user feedback or organizational concerns.

Honesty—Responding genuinely to questions, except in cases when your organization's confidentiality restrictions apply.

When Diane was questioned about the layoffs, she gave an untruthful response. This is one of the most difficult topics for a manager to respond to, as they may be bound by an organizational order not to discuss layoffs. Rather than that, a guideline to follow is to state, "When I have the knowledge to give, I will notify you."

Integrity—Keeping your word by carrying out your commitments.

Diane had stated that she would remain and assist, but she did not. Under normal conditions, she had a valid excuse, but these were not usual circumstances. As a project manager, she was ultimately accountable for the project's success. If she had stayed, she might have been able to avert the crisis.

Respect is earned by treating your employees in the same manner, you would want to be treated by your manager.

In her meeting with the Vice President, Diane expressed open contempt for the project manager and the team.

What's the bottom line? Diane and her colleagues had not "gone to the heart of the situation." How are you doing?

Is Technology Capable of Improving Employee Engagement?

Global research indicates that employee engagement directly affects staff performance and, subsequently, the bottom line. Employee involvement has been shown to be associated with organizational performance and corporate performance.

Some Quotes on Engagement (from articles in professional journals)

Work itself never kills a person; its absence (unemployment) has claimed numerous lives.

Idleness is not inherent in human nature.

Nobody enjoys avoiding work if there is clarity about what has to be done and how it will be evaluated.

Inactivity breeds pessimism, which has a detrimental effect on team performance.

Engagement occurs through engagement; when people are emotionally invested in their task, they perform better.

Delaying personal decisions increases tension and diverts an employee's attention from work.

The absence of engagement is a risk factor for workplace discontent.

Unless you know someone deeply, you cannot successfully engage them.

Managers must maintain a high level of engagement to keep their teams engaged.

A manager who is empowered is a breeding ground for staff engagement.

Employee motivation increases levels of engagement.

Transparency fosters trust, which in turn fosters involvement.

Leadership fosters engagement; managers who lead from the front aggressively engage their task force.

Encouragement on an as-needed basis always promotes engagement.

Commitment results in engagement.

Attitudinal transformation establishes a temperament conducive to productive involvement.

Numerous firms have benefited from increased employee involvement.

What does it mean to be an engaged employee?

Engaged employees consistently display the majority of the following characteristics:

Excellent understanding of the company's operations.

Complete understanding of one's function and job deliverables.

Always meet or surpass specified goals; frequently go above and beyond expectations.

Ready to go the extra mile to get the job done.

Disassociate personal performance from rewards and recognition.

Maintain a nice and tidy work area and take good care of task tools.

Constantly on the lookout for new information.

Maintain a high level of energy at all times.

If in a supervisor/manager position, extremely conscientious about information.

Never declare, "This is not my responsibility."

Take up extra responsibilities willingly.

Possess an exemplary record of personal discipline and attendance.

Self-accountable & highly accountable: never have a backlog of tasks.

Always willing to assist others; contribute willingly to the team's success.

Have a track record of consistently good performance.

Never succumb to pressure: they are always calm and adaptable by nature.

Unconcerned excessively with work-life balance.

Flowing with fresh ideas: take pleasure in trying.

Rarely do individuals begin complaints or concerns.

Improve processes that obstruct work on a conscious basis.

I am extremely allergic to folks who are slow and sluggish.

Always lead by personal example.

What Factors Contribute to Employee Disengagement:

The major issue organizations face the requirement for increased productivity without fostering an environment favorable to employee involvement at all levels. Several diseases have been observed, including the following:

Management lacks awareness of modern human resource technology to foster a healthy work environment.

Managers/supervisors lack empowerment.

Human resource technology for fostering a healthy work environment

Between 20% and 30% of an employee's time is spent on personal matters, such as the following:

Leave/loans & advances/claims & reimbursements approval.

Pay/promotions/increments/tax deductions-related inquiries.

We are obtaining copies of company policies, procedures, and forms.

They are pursuing the appropriate employees for responses to their inquiries.

It is tracing personal cases that have been misplaced, withheld, or neglected.

These factors contribute to heartburn, stress, and a lack of accountability. Today's technology enables online tracking of all cases launched by an employee. Automated work-flows expedite request processing. Numerous forms of 'Help Desks' enhance cross-functional interaction and increase the account-ability of decision centers.

'Employee portals' allow access to pertinent information regarding company policies/processes. An employee can access and edit their personal information, read their job description, and view a live view of their attendance record. An employee can manage all his difficulties by investing only ten minutes daily. What an enormous energy savings, and what a great method to demonstrate that "Someone cares"! Thus, technology increases motivation for labor.

Employee Involvement on an Emotional Level

To cultivate a work environment that encourages productivity, a sense of well-being, and a sense of belonging. On the part of employees, firms must assess if their current human resource operations are backed by technology that permits the following:

They are making human resources policies and procedures accessible to everybody with the click of a mouse.

Process requests for Leave/Loans & Advances/Claims & Reimbursements, etc., online, with constant status monitoring.

Address employee concerns/questions online using various types of help desks.

Provide simple-to-use 'Information Kiosks' near workstations for blue-collar employees (workers) who are not authorized to use personal computers.

Provide employees with the ability to see and update their personal information online.

Allow each employee to view their Work Description (J D) interactively and become familiar with job responsibilities.

Each employee's career path is apparent in a connection between their J D (in the current job position) and the J Ds for subsequent higher-level job positions (open for employee advancement). Additionally, information regarding the additional credentials and Skills/Competencies required to be eligible for these higher-level positions are available online.

On-line goal-setting capabilities ensure that objectives and performance targets (or KRAs and KPIs) are properly stated. This requires the presence of a ready-to-use 'Performance plan.'

To assist newly hired employees in developing SMART goals, access to the Goal Sheets (without performance information) of their predecessors in the same Job Position is available.

Employees receive automatic reminders to periodically register their accomplishments for each objective so that performance may be tracked.

At all times, performance appraisal reports and any counseling conducted by the manager/supervisor are available.

Employees can access their 'Development Plan' and enroll in training sessions.

There is an option to share all ideas and creative contributions produced by an employee on the 'Knowledge Platform.'

Employees can communicate critical information/suggestions to management without going via the reporting channels. This provides a direct access platform without the need for intermediary filters.

Human resource technology that empowers managers

Managers are frequently frustrated, especially when their employers fail to provide automated tools to supervise their employees. As follows, modern technology assists Line Managers in their people management responsibilities:

Empower them with online access to their subordinates' records, including their pictures, Job Descriptions, career pathways, growth profiles, performance records, disciplinary records, attendance and leave information, and remuneration structures.

Empower managers with online information regarding team members' overall unavailability during the week to assist them in approving leave requests. This enables job planning by balancing work obligations and subordinates' demands.

Allow Line Managers to complete the Goals/Key Performance Indicators (KPIs) establishing process with the active participation of team members.

Enable members to examine their Goal Sheets and align them with the organization's objectives.

Enable tracking of progress toward completing the goals provided to each team member.

Allow for creating counseling records for subordinates who fail to meet their targets on time. These records are accessible to employees and management at all times and serve as a reminder to enhance performance.

Allow managers to launch online award recommendations when performance consistently exceeds expectations. Keep track of all such instances and automatically transmit pertinent data to employees' records.

Managers can initiate training recommendations and keep track of all team members' key situations. These are displayed automatically when the performance appraisal reports are initiated.

By providing each manager with 'Bell Curves' for their team's performance, we can instill a score normalization culture at the initial reporting level. Managers get increasingly invested in understanding their direct reports as they evaluate their respective performances.

How does technology impact the level of engagement of human resource personnel?

It provides an opportunity for fresh graduates from business schools who choose HR professions to exercise, study, and develop their theoretical understanding of automated human resource principles, improving their degree of job engagement.

By honing the skills of HR teams to manage their operations more efficiently, the technology eliminates the need to hire additional HR staff to satisfy organizational growth objectives. A few team members can accomplish more work by employing the resources given. As a result, increased engagement levels contribute to cost savings in human resource services.

Distributed data input, which enables employees to update their personal information online, and automated workflows for managing employee services, performance appraisals, training and development, and other human resource operations relieve HR of routine effort on tedious tasks. As a result, they get naturally connected with professional issues, providing valuable input to the organization's decision-making process. Additionally, the environment perceives increased transparency when human resource activities are automated.

Additionally, the availability of time with HR broadens their connection with other functions and Line Managers. They can do this by actively reviewing and enriching various job positions across the organization. This results in workforce rationalization and workforce resizing. These collaborations have aided organizations in lowering their overall workforce expenditures.

Human resource professionals now have the time and energy to focus on strategic concerns, transforming them into active business partners.

Platforms of Technology Preference

Today, the global trend is to purchase technology platforms that:

Facilitate the online functioning of the organization's entire human resources procedure.

Enhance the Line Managers' people management ability.

Provide self-service facilities to employees to increase their availability on the job.

Integrate all human resource operations to enable the automatic flow of information to the employee database, enabling the firm to make strategic decisions about various talent management concerns.

Measuring Employee Engagement An HR technology platform equipped with the characteristics above will enable the following modalities of assessing employee engagement levels:

Employee engagement survey based on instruments developed in-house and tailored to your specific surroundings. A repeat poll every year should reveal patterns in employee engagement improvement.

The annual increase in the percentage of employees who 'Exceed Expectations' in completing their goals is a proxy for employee engagement.

As measured by staff attendance records, reduced absenteeism is a sign of increased engagement.

Reduced grievances/complaints and disciplinary cases are additional indicators of engagement.

Attrition rates over time provide insight into the level of employee engagement.

Increased profits/revenue per employee is viewed as a proxy for engagement by certain firms.

Retention of Employees

Despite changeable economic conditions and greater globalization of American jobs, most firms have difficulty retaining qualified employees. Today's employment market reality is that employees expect more from their employers and are not afraid to leave if their expectations are not satisfied.

According to persuasive evidence from the Society for Human Resource Management and others who monitor workforce trends, forward-thinking firms must invest time in analyzing their retention issues and ensuring that their most important employees are not looking for brighter pastures.

How can outstanding firms sustain low turnover rates and high employee satisfaction levels? The solution can be summed up in a single word: culture.

Employers with strong retention rates focus on developing four unique cultures that keep employees focused on the firm and its goals. This article examines these four cultures and makes practical recommendations for cultivating them in your business. Effective retention cultures emphasize opportunity, balance, development, and care.

Today's employees seek flexibility in their methods to do a job, the advantages they receive from their employment, and the times and places they report to work.

We've seen an expansion in the variety of employee benefits offered by firms over the previous two decades. Telecommuting and flextime have gained growing favor. Innovations in human resource management are defined by their instruments, their strategies, and the acknowledgment they receive. In summary, we are always learning about employee engagement and the relationship between empowerment and retention.

Do your staff have daily options? Otherwise, they may soon use their right to leave.

The Balanced Culture

Businesses report high workplace stress levels despite greater acceptance of flextime and work/life balance programs. Employers with low turnover acknowledge the growing importance of work-life balance and are addressing it through proactive programs that assist employees in finding fulfillment at home and on the job. This trend is fueled by an increasing number of women entering the workforce. The trend is anticipated to continue, with young women expected to exceed men in obtaining professional degrees.

Progressive firms will identify these trends and look to their growing female population to help them maintain a balanced culture. And while some firms have already reacted to this demand, those in traditionally male-dominated professions may discover this is a growing concern in attracting and maintaining employees. For instance, in the historically male-dominated area of professional accounting, firms have demanded a high level of billable hours and little vacation time.

Certain businesses now realize the value of cultivating a balanced culture by increasing the number of mandated vacations each year. When combined with flexible hours and family-friendly perks, these businesses recognize the value of balance-focused work culture in retaining top workers.

The Developmental Culture

High retention rates are inextricably tied to the level of attention paid to the employee's professional development and advancement. When employees believe their career aspirations have been recognized and are still pushed on the job, they are more inclined to stay. Employees who feel stagnant, unappreciated, or bored will begin looking for new options. Thus, how do outstanding organizations foster development cultures?

A development culture can be cultivated through a variety of tools. This culture is shaped via training, mentoring, and defined career routes. However, the first-line supervisor fosters the most robust development culture and interacts daily with the employee. Each supervisor and manager has the chance to demonstrate their interest in an employee's growth and development by asking the appropriate questions and gaining an awareness of the employee's professional goals.

Managers and supervisors should conduct regular "stay" conversations with each employee in which the following topics are discussed:

- What educational opportunities can we foster?

- What types of employment difficulties would "light you up?"

- What can we do to assist you in becoming more fulfilled at work?

- What is going to keep you here?

Simply by asking, managers and supervisors can begin to foster a development culture, resulting in increased retention.

A Culture of Compassion

"In a strict sense, the type of motivation that we should be discussing in today's world is inspired, not induced." Employees will stay put and perform at a better level if they feel cared for and care about their work. In other words, employees must be inspired to devote their complete attention to their everyday activities.

According to a study, employees find inspiration in their professions at businesses with a high retention rate and a low turnover rate. This inspiration could come from a desire to contribute to the larger good. It could be a dedication to the team and its objectives. Following a devoted and ethical leader can inspire. Employees must be motivated to care about their work and the organization, regardless of how inspiration is generated.

How can one cultivate a culture of care? The research was recently conducted with personnel of a small city government. Employee polls revealed low morale and that many staff, even long-term employees, were considering leaving the business, searching for better possibilities. Indeed, turnover was higher than in previous years. In a small organization like this one, with fewer than 30 employees, frequent turnover has a detrimental effect on the organization's production and reputation in the community.

Further investigation of the survey data through one-on-one interviews revealed that employees were unsatisfied because they felt unheard by the new management. Certain staff expressed a lack of respect. They said that a newly promoted boss frequently trivialized their abilities and failed to acknowledge their daily accomplishments. Following a thorough study, the following conclusions were reached:

- Leaders, especially managers and supervisors, directly impact the organization's culture and sense of care.

- The leaders were unaware of their practices' effect on the workforce's morale.

- To enhance morale and retention, the leadership team, many of whom were new to the organization, needed to address their views and abilities as leaders.

In this scenario, the level of empathy and attention demonstrated by the organization's first and second-line leaders directly affected retention and overall employee happiness. Today, the interaction between these key individuals and employees plays a significant role in employee retention.

Organizations will undoubtedly face difficulties attracting and retaining competent and engaged staff. It's time to get serious about this inside the four retention cultures. Utilize the following questions to get information about your organization's four cultures:

- Does your organization provide adequate opportunity for employees to express themselves during the workday? Do employees believe they have control over their daily work lives?

- Is your organization aware of employees' growing desire for work-life balance? How can you ensure that this priority is communicated to employees?

○ How is your organization developing a development culture? Apart from the more traditional development tactics such as training and tuition reimbursement, how does your firm promote a continual learning and development culture? How do supervisors and managers contribute to the development of this culture?

○ Do your staff have a sense of being "cared for?" Have the organization's executives instilled a sense of commitment in their employees by demonstrating their concern?

With the average length of employment in the United States hanging around one and a half years, it makes sense to investigate how to maintain and build a committed workforce. While retention is frequently viewed as a function of economic conditions, it is increasingly viewed as a long-term strategic objective for firms that appreciate its benefits.

HOW TO DEVELOP A FIVE-STEP EMPLOYEE RETENTION STRATEGY

The most effective way to increase employee retention is to develop a strategy that you can implement consistently and address all of the critical factors of staff retention. There are five critical topics to include when developing a retention plan. We don't intend for this to be an all-inclusive resource article on each stage but rather a summary of some of the key considerations for each.

1. Attractiveness

Consider yourself single and putting your best foot forward to attract a date. The more appealing you appear as an employer, the more qualified applicants will be interested. The more applicants, the more options you have and the higher your chance of selecting exceptional candidates.

The question is, how appealing do you think you are? It makes no difference how attractive you believe you are. What are others' perceptions of you? What is your employer brand (reputation)? Most firms lack a brand because they do not attempt to develop one. Size does not have to impede developing a brand as an employer of choice. The days of solely marketing your goods are over.

Additionally, you must consider promoting your employer's image. You may have the nicest place to work globally, but if no one knows about you, you will fail to garner the attention you seek. Determine what you want to be recognized for first, and then devise a strategy for spreading the word. Numerous businesses are taking novel steps to improve their 'attractiveness.' Not one of them is posting a job advertisement in the classified section.

2. Recruiting

The hiring period is defined as the period between an interview and signing a contract. Often, we believe that the hiring process is limited to those hired, but in truth, anyone who interviews for your firm is included in this phase. Consider the hiring step like having numerous guests over for supper one after the other.

You're going to have many more guests than seats at the table. One will eventually be chosen. What about the other five individuals who sat with you? What will they say about you when they leave your house? How you handle rejected applications has a significant impact on your company's reputation. I heard of one corporation that offered movie tickets to everybody who came in for an interview. It's a small gesture, but it has an effect.

Interviews function similarly to first dates. Both parties want to impress the other, and with so much at stake, candidates have their inner radar set to detect any defect, imperfection, or disarray. Ascertain that this method is orderly, well-planned, and professional. Your hiring process hasn't been looked at in a while. Objectively identify methods to make it more effective, efficient, and compelling?

3. Embarkation

The first 90 days are all about building relationships. Numerous studies demonstrate that a new employee can decide whether or not they will stay for the long haul within the first week. This is your opportunity to entice them. While most businesses do an excellent job of delivering individuals with the knowledge necessary for their jobs, they fall short when it comes to the more critical connections, such as relationships.

For a new hire, emotional relationships must be established quickly. You want to ensure that they understand the function of the team, their manager, and the organization. For some, these linkages occur naturally, but they require some assistance for most people.

In my retention session, I detail establishing an onboarding process that can help cement new hires to your firm. The trick is to develop a step-by-step approach that assists recruits in establishing those critical ties early on.

4. Duration of Stay

This is the actual period of an employee's employment with your firm. Your objective is to extend each employee's length of stay. The ultimate goal is for your organization to serve as its final stop before retiring.

This is where the majority of your retention efforts should be concentrated. It is always more efficient to focus your efforts on staff retention than recruitment. Take good care of what you've got. This is the primary emphasis of my training. You want to build an engaging workplace, and you do it through the leadership of outstanding individuals who understand how to manage people and projects.

You want to ensure that your organization has a healthy culture that values difficult and fascinating work, fantastic teams, incentives and recognition, training and development, and fun. Inspiring leaders understand how to communicate and build a compelling vision; they actively seek input; they are enthusiastic about their roles; they set excellent examples; they foster an excellent culture and genuinely care about their people. Equipping mid-level managers to build engaging workplaces should consume most of your training time.

5. Disappearance

Your entire organization will disband! Including you. The ideal situation is for people to retire. However, for the rest of us, how we say farewell has a significant impact on the first point, we covered—Reputation! When an employee decides to quit a company, the decision is never simple.

There are numerous worries and anxieties associated with terminating an employee's employment. You may be upset, furious, bitter, or even joyful as a boss. The critical factor is emotional regulation. If you ever want to see them return, let them go on a positive note. If you don't want them to return, let them depart on a positive note.

Every person who quits your organization on bad terms is terrible advertising for you. They can act as a poison that seeps into the talent reservoir you're yearning to tap. Establishing a process that assures practically everyone leaves on a positive note is rather simple.

You'll also want a mechanism to communicate with people who have departed. Consider them alumni or extended relatives. If you can communicate with them regularly via email, news bulletins, or other ways, you can maintain your organization in their minds. This is especially advantageous if their new workplace is causing them distress and you manage to write them a cheerful email on the same day!

Keeping alumni on good terms after they leave your firm is akin to having unpaid recruiters out in the field for you. When a position becomes available, you can reach out to your alumni to see if they know someone who could be a referral for the position. By including some form of monetary reward for recommendations, you may create a powerful force that is constantly replenishing your pipeline of new employees.

If you can develop a strategy that eventually encompasses all of these stages, you will notice a significant increase in your retention rate. As more employees stay longer in your organization, you will see an extraordinary shift in morale, culture, productivity, and overall enjoyment. First, choose an easy issue to handle, such as a strategy for those departing, and then on to some of the larger, more challenging issues. Give me a call if you need some suggestions.

Employee Incentive Programs

Each employee has certain organizational expectations that he believes must be met. When an organization falls short of its expectations, it develops a sense of dissatisfaction or discontent. This emotion is called a grievance. Disagreements arise as a result of mismatches between employee expectations and management actions.

Employees should be free to voice their displeasure with their work, whether it is a minor annoyance, a significant problem, or a disagreement with their boss regarding employment terms and circumstances. There must be an established mechanism for venting discontent.

Personal administrators must support line executives in resolving employee issues, particularly forepersons and supervisors. They must investigate and analyze grievances within the plant, department, and persons involved and the kind and trend of grievances. This is so they may assist top management in developing policies, processes, and programs for grievance handling and teaching supervisors and other line executives in grievance handling and dealing with unions.

Employee grievances concern the interpretation and implementation of collective bargaining agreements, labor laws, various personnel policies, rules and regulations, past practices, code of conduct, and code of discipline.

Thus, grievances have a limited scope and are primarily concerned with interpretation and implementation. They may be directed towards a single employee (individual grievances) or a group of employees (collective grievances) (group grievances). Unions play a minimal role in the grievance process.

Conflicts arise between employees and employers over personnel policies, compensation levels and benefits, award agreements, codes of conduct, codes of discipline, and laws and regulations. Collective bargaining is used to resolve conflicts. As a result, disagreements have broader policy ramifications.

When an employee is unsatisfied with their employment for genuine or factual reasons, such as a breach of contract or any other reason that can be ascribed to management or any variation in implementing organizational policies, they have a factual grievance. Thus, when legitimate requirements are not met, factual grievances occur.

Dealing With An Employee's Inadequate Performance Or Misconduct

Dealing with an employee's poor performance or misconduct effectively can make a significant difference in ensuring a positive outcome for your organization and the individual. While certain instances of misconduct are terrible, dealing with them forcefully, fairly, and professionally can significantly impact everyone involved.

Defining what constitutes poor performance or misconduct comes down to the employee's intent. In most cases, poor performance indicates that the job is not being completed to the standard required by the employer.

This could indicate that the person is not a perfect fit for the work— or that they are struggling to perform their obligations satisfactorily through no fault of their own. However, misconduct generally indicates that a rule has been violated. Serious misbehavior indicates a flagrant violation of rules, resulting in immediate dismissal.

Both poor performance and misconduct can be damaging to an organization's culture. However, while bad performance can affect results, it is easier to address poor performance than wrongdoing (i.e., misconduct) because retraining, clarifying their responsibilities, or careful supervision can sometimes assist in achieving the desired end.

Inadequate Performance

In instances of poor performance, what needs to be defined are the required standards of work and their reasonableness. For instance, certain criteria may be unreasonable if an employee is expected to perform at a specific level (which they are typically capable of) but never has enough time to complete their job.

From the initial interview, an employer should have a good picture of an employee's talents. If the employee was candid about the areas in which they may require training, it is the employer's responsibility to provide retraining, assistance, and, if required, counseling in these areas. Employers can initiate a formal process only after they have been allowed to meet their standards.

Everything must be clearly defined for both the employee and employer during a formal process: what is expected of the employee, the repercussions for failing to improve standards and a clear and acceptable opportunity for the employee to express their concerns or ideas on the topic. Both parties may need to take action to reach an agreement. A follow-up meeting between the two parties may also aid in smooth running.

Employee Indiscretion

To be called misconduct,' an employee must commit an act that may be regarded as 'deliberate.' If an employer is unsure whether the behavior was intentional, it can easily fall under the 'poor performance' category.

It may be tough to tell whether an action was planned or accidental in some instances. For instance, an employee providing an excessive amount of change to a customer or failing to charge them for something maybe a grey area, as it could be considered carelessness.

If the employee's negligence is due to their inability to verify items, this might be deemed misbehavior; yet, if they were exhausted from working long shifts without breaks, it might be unreasonable to anticipate zero errors.

Another example is whether the employee intends to act in a certain way; for example, if they are not meeting the standards you set during the interview process, it could be because they lack the necessary skills or require additional training—or it could be because they don't want to put out the effort it takes for the job. If the latter is true, this may amount to misconduct.

If an employer believes there has been misbehavior, they must clearly outline the steps they intend to take and convey them to the employee. Employers may choose to suspend an employee during this period, but this is not required. The first step is to indicate clearly that there has been wrongdoing and that disciplinary action may be taken.

Employers would have to warn employees that disciplinary action may be pursued. This would entail providing them with access to any documents, setting up a meeting, and informing them of the attendees. An employee must have time to prepare for the meeting.

To ensure a fair (and lawful) procedure, the employee must also be allowed to justify their conduct during the discussion. Additionally, it is probably helpful for both parties if recordings of what was discussed and the consequences are retained.

There will be instances where no further action is required—either the meeting served as a warning or clarified a misunderstanding.

Naturally, making a decision will also depend on other considerations, including the length of an employee's tenure with the organization, their prior performance, the amount of training or advice provided, and their current circumstances.

People like those who have been with a firm since its inception for many years may be granted further tolerance if their record is otherwise spotless. It's worth mentioning that an employer may also choose to warn employees at their discretion—even if substantial wrongdoing has occurred, the employee is not required to be terminated if an agreement has been made.

After concluding, the employer must describe what they feel occurred, their decision, and its reasons. If someone is to be dismissed, a reasonably compelling case must be supported by reasonable evidence. If the issue is handled properly and thoroughly and the employee is allowed to respond, the dismissal will almost certainly be simpler for everyone involved.

What Employees Desire the Most

Employee satisfaction and contentment are more than financial considerations. While people desire to be treated fairly, studies reveal more concern with other factors. And it is those other factors that significantly impact talent retention, whether in the corporate or charity environment.

Individuals must feel, act, and be certain to maintain their current position and create at their maximum capacity. Consider the following ten personnel requirements in today's workplace:

1. Employees must feel suitably suited to their jobs.

A good match takes education, talents, interests, financial commitment, and personality. A bad fit often results in decreased productivity, behavioral issues, and voluntary or involuntary termination.

2. Employees must feel appreciated for their efforts.

For the majority of individuals, simply performing their work is insufficient. They need to know their supervisor values their abilities, technical expertise, interpersonal skills, and desire to go above and beyond the call of duty.

3. Employees must see tangible results from their work.

Continually switching from one isolated job to another degrades the work experience. Individuals grow best when they understand how one procedure or meeting contributes to or builds upon another.

4. Employees require growth opportunities.

Professional development is typically accomplished through scheduled activities such as targeted reading, seminars, work-shops, conferences, webinars, e-courses, and college programs. We set people up to fail, remain stagnant, or lose interest by omitting these possibilities.

5. Employees must view their supervisor as a source of information.

To perform at their best in the job, employees must feel com-fortable approaching their employer for additional informa-tion, precise instruction, smart advice, or a safe sounding board. Bosses who lack credibility as a resource communicate one of three things to their staff: they don't care; they don't know or want to find out.

6. Employees must feel confident in performing their jobs competently and on time.

The vast majority of employees despise and even despise micromanagement. As long as employees have the skills nec-essary for the task, supervisors should set realistic, unambig-uous objectives and deadlines and then enable them to work independently.

7. Employees must feel true collegiality among their coworkers.

When employees believe their colleagues do not genuinely care about them, they are less likely to seek partnerships, work successfully in teams, or develop personal ties. When there is genuine collegiality, everyone benefits—including the organization.

8. Employees require timely and constructive feedback.

Any supervisor owes this to their staff. Employees should not have to make educated guesses about their performance. They deserve to be informed at least monthly, if not more frequently.

9. Specifics are required of employees.

Individuals must understand precisely what they are expected to perform and by when. They also need to understand why they are falling short of supervisory expectations in this case. They must be informed on policies and what is and is not permissible. They require direction on improving their abilities, behavior, approach, and style.

Employees require security.

Individuals require a sense of security in the workplace. Protection against physical harm, bodily harm, sexual harassment, and verbal abuse. Additionally, they need to know they have a job if certain conditions are met.

Keys to Retaining Employees for a Longer period

It's one thing to hire the individuals you desire and require to move your vision forward, but quite another to ensure those employees are productive and fulfilled to the point where they stay with your company long enough to make the impact you wish. The employee-employer relationship is mutually beneficial.

The employer meets all required standards, while the employee focuses on key performance areas to achieve outcomes commensurate with the advantages associated with their name. An issue arises when there is a discrepancy in expectations and delivery on either side, friction is unavoidable, frequently culminating in the early termination of the partnership.

I'm writing about common keys that are part of what I've encountered in the corporate sector, both as an employee and employer, throughout eight years. I've left employment for one of the reasons listed below, and I'm sure some employers have lost staff due to a failure to observe or execute one of the keys listed.

The longer you retain your staff, the better, as you avoid continually training new employees, as existing employees who have the business DNA continue to pass them on. I've written about how critical it is to retain customers, but as critical is the truth that you must retain every employee you hire.

Several keys to retaining an employee's happiness

1. Keep your promises—Employers frequently make the error of overpromising and underdelivering. Suppose an employee joined because you, the employer, promised certain perks and advantages. Any discrepancy between the promise and the reality on the ground is instantly rejected (almost automatically).

   You'd rather underpromise and overdeliver than entice folks with lucrative contracts that don't deliver on their promises. The days of laborers clinging to pies in the sky are over. Meet the promises you made and observe the level of retention.

2. Recognize and reward superior accomplishment—Every human being is born with an innate yearning for recognition. You will notice that some consistently meet deadlines are on time for work, are correct, and are committed to their work. Take the time to determine which employees contribute the most to the business's success. Make it a habit to publicly recognize and reward exceptional accomplishments. Instill a sense of rivalry in employees.

   Maintain an unbiased incentive system if they are all doing well, including a celebration lunch or party on Friday. When employees feel appreciated, they will stick with you through difficult times. Promotions must be made based on merit, not proximity to the CEO or departmental leader.

3. Provide possibilities for personal improvement and career progress—Employees would rather work for a constantly innovating business than for one stagnant in learning new skills. When everything gets routine, when they can perform the work in their sleep, people constantly seeking fresh knowledge feel restless and want to flee quickly.

   Arrange for some short courses, seminars, and other activities to increase employees' effectiveness in their work settings. Employees must be able to see their place in the organization after putting in additional effort. Which work opportunities are available to them as they improve academically and earn the necessary experience?

4. Sell vision and hope to them consistently—As the organization's leader, you must constantly communicate and paint a vivid image of its future to your employees. Once employees share their visions for the organization with

you, retention will skyrocket. Never assume that you and your staff are communicating well. The assumption is the lowest level of knowledge and hence should be avoided.

5. Provide job security—When employees see the company expand, they gain confidence that their job will be available the next day. They are not leaving home wondering if they will be with you tomorrow.

   Constantly provide assurance and confirmation. When leaders become so focused on "today's issues," they lose sight of the bigger picture, so their dialogue becomes negative. Employees consider jumping to the next ship, which does not appear to be sinking anytime soon despite having a few lower values. They want security from people in authority.

6. Pay employees fairly and on time—Very few employees come to work as unpaid volunteers. Indeed, if they are volunteers, they do not expect to be compensated. However, the majority of employees wish to be paid on time. When payday becomes a guessing game, people cannot organize their lives accordingly; their budgeting process becomes a jumble, forcing them to discover alternate means of meeting family demands. If you do not pay well, they will disregard your utterances.

   They will simply leave without providing you with adequate notice. This is the primary reason why individuals change jobs. Certain individuals may tolerate difficult and demanding jobs as long as their pay is adequate and always on time. Only a few employees form bonds with their coworkers based on their perception of potential in the leaders and the organization.

7. Be fair and just in your interactions—When double standards are applied to discipline, employees will constantly seek a better situation. They are constantly monitoring your actions for "tomorrow's sake."

When Peter steals $100, his employer immediately fires him. At the same time, a secretary takes $500 and only receives a warning; it is evident that there is no established pattern for how justice is administered in the workplace. Nobody should be immune to the mechanisms that you establish. You cannot be deemed discriminatory regarding regulations applied to different groups of persons inside the organization.

8. Provide an appeals process—An employee has every right to speak with their employer about work-related difficulties. The policy of open doors must become a reality. Once employees feel empowered to contribute without fear of retaliation, you've established a positive family culture in which everyone's perspective is appreciated. When they believe a decision has been made incorrectly, they can come to you and discuss it with you.

If the door is locked in their faces, they are left with no choice except to plot their schemes behind closed doors (since you have set the pattern that people deal with issues in their own closed offices). If they cannot speak with their CEO, they will resort to other methods of appeal, such as strike action, to garner attention. Rather than that, make yourself available to hear for yourself before the issue becomes one the press would want to cover. When employees believe they contribute value to the firm, they develop a sense of belonging and stay.

9. Credibility of the core leadership is critical—The people at the top shape the culture and framework of the business. Are they men of their word, who mean what they say? Do they always keep their word? Is it possible to rely on someone's promises? Credibility enables employees to feel comfortable, satisfied, and confident in their leaders. Once credibility is lost, there is a complete disrespect for leadership in the workplace, laying the groundwork for the organization's demise.

10. Increase Transparency and Trust—It is incorrect to isolate personnel from the realities of the business. When a business is doing well, employees must be informed. When things are not as expected, employees deserve to be informed since they are critical stakeholders and occasionally the bearers of the very remedies we so sorely need. Be forthright about what is occurring. Confidentiality erodes confidence. If they are forced to hypothesize and draw conclusions based on assumptions, do not criticize them if they conclude that proceeding is the best course of action.

CHAPTER 2

MOTIVATING A MULTIGENERATION TEAM

Have you ever wondered why your team members do not appear as motivated as you are? Or why do some people approach their jobs with zeal and vigor while others barely make it through the day without frowning?

You are not alone in this. For hundreds of years, the subject of human motivation has been studied. As a result, it's a subject we're quite familiar with. Regrettably, it is not frequently taught to managers during their training.

Working with groups of people, whether as a member of a larger group or as a team leader, or as a manager of multiple teams, is a critical component of a manager's remit. Teamwork is rapidly gaining popularity in many organizations as traditional corporate hierarchies give way to flat, multi-skilled organizational structures. Using the information in this area can help you become a better leader. Expert teams cover topics such as defining the skills necessary to complete a project, establishing trust among team members, and optimizing the team's performance. This section is required reading for anyone involved in teamwork, whether as a novice or a seasoned team leader.

In this chapter, we will discuss:

1) An understanding of how teams function

Recognize How Teams Work

Collaboration is the bedrock of all successful management. Managing teams effectively is a significant and stimulating challenge for any novice or experienced manager.

1) What Constitutes A Successful Team?

A true team is a dynamic force that is constantly changing and evolving in which a group of people comes together to work. Team members discuss their objectives, evaluate ideas, make decisions, and collaborate to accomplish their goals.

A) Collaborating

All successful teams share the following fundamental characteristics: strong and effective leadership; the establishment of precise objectives; the ability to make informed decisions; the ability to act quickly on these decisions; open communication; mastering the necessary skills and techniques to complete the project at hand; providing clear objectives for the team to work toward; and—most importantly—finding the right balance of people to work together for the team's common good.

B) Examining Team Assignments

Successful teams can consist of two to twenty-five or more members, but shape—the pattern of work into which team members settle to perform their assigned tasks—is far more important than size. There are three fundamental approaches to accomplishing a task:

Repeated tasks and familiar labor demand that each team member have a defined function that they fulfill autonomously, as in assembly lines.

Creative projects demand that team members have defined responsibilities and operating processes and operate in unison, as when developing new items

Work involving regular creative input and personal contributions necessitates strong collaboration between individuals. This is a common way of functioning for senior management.

Collaborating Effectively

A manager's team discusses a fresh idea proposed by a team member. All team members are welcome to participate in the debate. The input will be evaluated later by the team leader.

C) Realizing One's Potential

A good team's potential is limitless. When confronted with an "impossible" assignment, team members will boost one another's confidence as they work to make the "impossible" a reality. Collective innovation is more powerful than individual innovation because a team's aggregate brainpower exceeds any individual's, regardless of size. By harnessing this force, a team can make more than incremental improvements; they can achieve true breakthroughs. For instance, an engineering team at one corporation was tasked with double machine reliability. They believed it was unachievable but created a plan that jeopardized performance.

Towards Comprehension

Encouraging open communication and information flow within a team guarantees that each member is fully aware of the group's talents and expertise.

Note:

Bear in mind that team members must support one another. Break down long-term goals into smaller, more manageable projects.

D) Being Aware of Team Objectives

Once a team has been constituted, the next critical step is to define its objectives. There is little value in having an energized team if members pursue divergent goals. The goal of a team may change over time: for example, if a new product is being released, the team's first objective will be to conduct market research on its competitors. If the objective is to increase customer happiness, the first objective should be to identify ways to give a higher level of service.

Teamwork objectives may include the following:

Increasing a manufacturing company's productivity rate;

Enhancing the production quality;

increasing job satisfaction by including all employees in decision-making processes;

Examining working processes and practices to minimize time waste;

Collaborating with customers to develop stronger ties to understand market needs better.

Strengthening Performance

The American Association for training and development discovered that teamwork resulted in a significant increase in performance in key areas following a survey of 230 personnel executives.

Cultural Distinction

Cross-functional, multidisciplinary, interdepartmental teams are gaining traction in the west after years of success in Japan. In some British firms, managers already spend half their time working in such teams, and the democratic attitude of many North Americans has aided their adaptation to this mode of operation. Continental Europeans are still more at ease with traditional hierarchical structures. Still, increasing competitive pressure and the need for speed-to-market compel managers in various industries to change.

Nota Bene: Assign a distinct deadline to each of your initiatives.

You can do several things to influence the number of energy employees is willing to invest in their jobs. The following are five critical points to understand about motivation.

1. We are incapable of motivating others.

We do not 'do' motivation to others. It must originate from within. All we can do is foster an environment conducive to motivation. As a result, we are partially absolved of responsibility. Our responsibility as managers extends only so far; once that point is reached, it is up to the individual to join.

2. Certain individuals will never be inspired.

This is something that I believe we can all agree on. Certain individuals are simply in the wrong place and have no interest in functioning as part of a team or working harder than necessary. It can be extremely difficult to supervise these folks' performance, especially if they are barely getting by. Typically, the approach is to incorporate behaviors and attitudes into the requirements for performance. Then their attitude is transformed into an actual performance issue that can be coached and managed via the performance review system.

3. Certainly, one size does not fit all.

The enjoyable aspect of motivation is that we are all unique, necessitating diverse tactics and approaches. Different generations, different periods of life, and varying professional requirements all affect what people desire as a motivator throughout their lives. The simplest method to determine what motivates people is to ask. The majority of folks will gladly inform you. And if you're looking for some inspiration, here are eight:

1. flexible Hours of operation
2. Opportunities for training
3. A work-related difficulty
4. Public or private acknowledgment

5. Possibility of working from home
6. Technology advancements
7. Gift certificates for movies/dinner
8. A chance to be compensated for great performance

4. The difference is in the management style.

People do not quit jobs; they quit bosses. If team members appear to be lacking motivation, one of the first places to look is at the manager's style. Because people do not respond well to being told what to do (at least not for an extended period), authoritarian, controlling, elitist, and dictatorial styles will result in dissatisfied and demotivated employees.

Developing a collaborative style is critical for building an environment that motivates and engages individuals. The majority of managers are utterly oblivious of their impact on others and frequently overestimate their abilities. Therefore, provide training for your managers and assist them in developing the abilities and mindsets necessary to have a good impact rather than a negative one.

5. Boring jobs cause people to disconnect

Certain occupations are inherently monotonous and uninteresting. Make every effort to inject interest and variety into various jobs. Cross-training, job rotation, multi-skilling, and project work all contribute to keeping people's minds stimulated. If there is no way to spice up the task itself, you must give possibilities for an interest outside of work. A pleasant and comfortable work atmosphere will significantly mitigate the impacts of repetitive labor.

Numerous additional factors influence people's levels of motivation. For instance, if you pay peanuts, do not expect employees to leap for joy every time they report to work. If you can grasp these five principles, you will be well on your way to establishing the environmental factors that contribute to a highly motivated workforce.

ONE WORKPLACE FOR FOUR GENERATIONS

As business owners and managers, we are constantly looking for methods to improve the workplace and boost profitability. We've discussed the importance of becoming acquainted with employees' and coworkers' communication styles to match their abilities to specific roles in the workplace. We recognize that individuals possess various abilities depending on their culture, upbringing, and life experiences.

As business owners committed to obtaining the best performance from our employees, we make an effort to learn as much as possible about the people who work for us. Another extremely useful set of defining characteristics is the generational circumstances that shaped the individual.

Until now, this has never happened in the recorded history of the traditional workplace; four generations are attempting to collaborate to operate as a single entity. While I believe that generalizations are not always accurate, a little knowledge about the work styles and influences of each of the four generations can be beneficial in determining what motivates an individual.

Each of the four generations exhibits distinct traits, work styles, and characteristics. Consider what they are and how we can most effectively leverage the talents of each generation.

The Traditionalists (1909-1945)-This generation has seen hard times turn to prosperity. We are seeing fewer of them in the workplace, but many of them that are in the workplace hold prominent positions. Traditionalists are self-disciplined and maintain a strong sense of corporate loyalty.

The Baby Boomer Generation (1946–1964)-

This generation requires little explanation, as they continue to comprise the lion's share of the workforce today. This generation is comprised of individuals who are diligent and competitive. They accomplish tasks. They occasionally expect others to do things their way and are not always tolerant of others' work styles.

Generation X (1965–1978)-This group of former latch-key children is dependable and self-directed. They desire autonomy but still require affirmation that they are doing a good job. This generation is known for focusing on their individual career development and sometimes struggles to balance their independence and the goals of the organizations that employ them. They look for fun in the workplace and prefer a more laid-back atmosphere. This generation will never accept "that's just the way we have always done it" as a reason for anything.

Generation Y or Millennials (1979—)-

This workforce's newest generation frequently receives a negative rap. They are an entitlement generation. They frequently arrive on the job with the expectation of becoming CEO and have little interest in picking up trash. They do, however, possess enormous strengths that make them valuable team members. They are quite technologically sophisticated. They will give recommendations that will help streamline operations. They are not afraid of change, excel at multitasking, and thrive in a team environment.

Each generation brings its own set of abilities and talents. As a business owner or manager, one of our primary goals is to identify and capitalize on each employee's strengths. This has always been a win-win strategy, as an employee who works to their strengths will be more productive and happy.

Knowing the general characteristics of each generation also gives employers the tools they need to match work style to specific tasks. Some of these differences can present frustrations, and when that happens, we have to look for ways to understand, work with and benefit from those differences.

Employers can gain valuable problem-solving skills by studying strategies for dealing with these generational differences and assessing how to achieve the desired results. Resources are available, including workshops and specialized training to help employers and employees become familiar with these techniques. Examining the generational characteristics is just one strategy for gaining insight into bringing out the best in that individual.

X, y, or z—does an employee's generation matter?

Throughout history, each generation believes it is smarter than the one before it and wiser than the one who comes after it.—George Orwell

Different generations working side by side has become commonplace in the modern working environment. While this is unquestionably a positive development, it begs an important question-is there really a generation gap in today's workplace?

The simple answer is "not really." The primary differences in generational interaction in the workplace revolve around a lack of communication and slight differences in expectations. Every generation relates to situations based on their own cultural experiences, whether they are Boomers, Gen-Xers, Millenials (also known as Generation Y), or Generation Z. This can cause friction if not properly addressed.

Despite these differences, most employees, regardless of generation, share similar values. Mixed-generation workplaces can be both positive and productive employment experiences for all employees with the proper guidance from management.

Expectations and Communication

Communication is critical to ensuring that all employees have a great work experience. Employers may improve work environments by understanding how individuals of different generations communicate, enhancing employee job satisfaction and overall productivity.

Over the years, generational opinions on labor have altered numerous times, and each generation brings new ideas and viewpoints to the table. Historically, younger employees were considered subordinates to older, more experienced employees who had been with the organization for an extended period. Today's younger employees are challenging these roles by leveraging different employment experiences—such as volunteer work, internships, and entrepreneurial endeavors—to advance to more prominent positions sooner in their careers.

Values That Are Shared

Regardless of their differences, generations share certain values. Finding common ground in multigenerational workplaces is critical for employee retention. While technologies evolve, employee needs remain relatively constant, including a desire to be respected and a sense of belonging. This significance is communicated through opportunities to be heard and the possibility of receiving public recognition.

Whether the subject is new technology or evolving business practices, employees of all generations value the opportunity to learn. Employers invest when they express an interest in passing along information pertinent to an employee's position. When employees are given these opportunities, they can see their value to the company and are more likely to feel satisfied and a part of a team.

Utilizing the Intergenerational Workplace's Potential

Intergenerational work environments can be excellent experiences for everyone as long as management is capable of facilitating communication and meeting common needs. By balancing learning and leadership opportunities, such as intergenerational mentorships, multigenerational teams can be formed that enable persons of all ages to contribute their strengths. These interactions foster a sense of respect and value for each employee, resulting in harmonious intergenerational work experiences.

As is the case with so many other facets of a successful work environment, it all begins with effective hiring, training, and management methods.

Each generation advances further than the previous one because it stands on the shoulders of the prior generation.—Reagan, Ronald

MULTI-GENERATIONAL
WORKPLACE SHARING

Is corporate America the same as it was a quarter-century ago? No. Is your belief system the same as it was ten years ago? Most likely not. Consider, for example, someone who is currently 20 years old. Do they have different perceptions than someone currently in their 60s? Most certainly, yeah. These disparities in attitudes, values, beliefs and even ways of working together and communicating are "generation gaps." Generational differences can lead to misunderstandings and conflict in the workplace.

For the first time in history, businesses must manage four generations. This can create complications! Would you be startled if you noticed his mother accompanied him while greeting a job candidate in your lobby? This occurs at businesses across the country as recent college graduates compete for their first job.

Instead, how would you respond if you were a recently hired manager and requested a 30-year employee enter the information you just discussed into an Excel spreadsheet and email it to you. The person looked at you as if you were from another planet? This is also more prevalent than you may believe.

The Generations Have Been Defined

We'll refer to the generations as Matures, Baby Boomers, Generation X, and Millennials. Each generation has a distinct past that shapes its attitudes, values, beliefs, work habits, and communication styles. Naturally, generational descriptions and periods should be taken loosely to avoid prejudices. However, certain commonalities do exist due to the life events that have influenced each group's values and ideas of work.

Matures (born before 1946) often show a healthy respect for authority and compliance, raised in a conventional family environment. Their dedication to duty is unwavering. Honor and nation. This generation endured adversity before achieving riches. College was a pipe dream for them, and they communicated via rotary telephones and handwritten letters sent by US Mail. Tom Brokaw, Jack Nicholson, Herbie Hancock, and Senator John McCain are all mature. Matures make for approximately 5% of the workforce.

At work, these employees exhibit a strong work ethic and a team attitude of "sacrifice me for us." They are not looking for individual recognition but desire to blend into the group. For them, a job well done is sufficient compensation.

Baby Boomers (born 1946–1964) are optimistic, even though they grew up when the conventional family structure disintegrated. College was a given for them. Communication was conducted via touch-tone telephones, and letters were prepared using word computers and transmitted via the United

States Postal Service. Numerous Baby Boomers define themselves through their profession, expected to pay their dues.

They began working for large corporations and gradually but steadily ascended the corporate ladder. As a result, this generation now accounts for the lion's share of company leaders and supervisors in the workplace. Bill Gates, Chairman of Microsoft, IBM's CEO, Sam Palmisano, Oprah Winfrey, George W. Bush, Hillary Clinton, and Madonna are all Baby Boomers.

Among the tips for managing Baby Boomers is valuing the team concept and providing them with face time. They may not require individual comments on their achievement, but they welcome public acknowledgment in plaques, prizes, and diplomas. Bear in mind that Boomers may struggle to report to younger employees who have not "put in their time" or "are only interested in the outcome."

Employees from Generation X (born 1965–1979) are more comfortable challenging authority than their elders, maybe because they have experienced the public humiliation of political and commercial leaders who disregarded the rules.

They are taught that happy endings are not always guaranteed from an early age. Many grew up with two working parents and saw college as a "means to an end." This group interacts mostly through the use of personal computers and cell phones. Tiger Woods, Angelina Jolie, San Francisco Mayor Gavin Newsom, and Google co-founders Sergey Brin and Larry Page are notable Generation X members.

Generation X does not work to live; they live to work. Unlike their elder counterparts, they believe they own their time and lease it to the corporation. Generation X employees rarely retire with a firm to receive the gold watch but frequently change companies to develop a portable repertoire of skills and experiences. Their greatest fear is being stagnant.

When managing Generation X personnel, assign them numerous projects and communicate the ultimate objective rather than devoting much time to process. When given the required resources and an opportunity to prove themselves, Generation X personnel perform admirably. Delegate the outcome to them rather than the specific actions necessary to achieve it.

Millennials (born after 1979) are outgoing and gregarious; they grew up in blended families and frequented shopping malls. They perceive education as too expensive, and most of them are only familiar with cell phones, instant messaging, and the Internet.

This generation has lived through terrorist strikes in the United States of America and high school shootings. They are neither adults nor adolescents but are in the adolescent stage. The "future" is a relative concept for Millennials. Millennials include Mark Zuckerberg, the founder of Facebook, Justin Timberlake, Britney Spears, and LeBron James.

They thrive in collaborative work environments and may seek friendships with their supervisors. They are incredibly digitally adept and creative, and even as adults; they keep strong relationships (some even say too strong) with family. They are hungry for feedback and want to understand their place within a business.

When managing Millennials, consider that many of them grew up in a menu-driven environment where they may make choices without conducting research. They may believe that "since it's on the Internet, it must be true, and if it isn't, I'm not going to use it for my term paper."

This has resulted in a deficiency of critical thinking abilities taken for granted by other populations. As a result, delegating specific duties may result in improved performance. Prepare to articulate your organization's principles and culture and how they contribute to the big picture.

How Can the Gap Be Bridged?

Managing a department or team comprised of four distinct generations may necessitate at least four distinct management styles. For instance, a Boomer manager may be irritated by a Millennial employee who leaves work on time every day since the Boomer manager expects long hours on the job and the Millennial employee is seeking work/life balance. Several pointers for managing today's multigenerational workforce include the following:

- Managers are no longer able to operate within their value system. Rather than that, you must manage according to the value system of each employee.

- When disagreements emerge, it is necessary to lay aside personal prejudices. Maintain objectivity, understand each person's communication and work style, and manage appropriately for the issue and the people involved.

- Keep in mind that an employee's prior experiences are irreversible, regardless of whether the individual is mature, millennial, or somewhere in between.

+ Managers should develop an appreciation for and acceptance of each generation's values.

+ However, how a manager encourages their personnel can be altered. A Generation X employee may desire time off for doing an excellent job, but a Baby Boomer may desire a plaque or other form of public recognition. Inquire about your employees' motivations and then reward them appropriately.

+ Leverage the strengths of each generation for the team's benefit. For instance, teach and mentor Matures and Boomers to Generation X and Millenials. Their institutional wisdom is priceless, and their personal experiences will provide vivid practical examples. Encourage Millenials and Generation X to assist their more older coworkers with technology.

The effective motivation of a multigenerational workforce enables a manager to leverage all of their team's strengths. All team members must collaborate and keep focused on the same goals. Additionally, it is critical to recognize that others' opinions are not superior or inferior but simply different. After all, individuals with diverse perspectives may always contribute unique thoughts and ideas to a team. The ultimate output can be significantly superior to a more homogenized group.

TRAINING AND THE WORKPLACE
OF MULTI-GENERATIONS

If you tell me you haven't heard anything recently about the multigenerational workplace, I have to say you've been living under a rock. Pay close attention…you'll hear a lot of chatter about the millennial generation entering the workforce. Additionally, you'll learn about the tremendous departure of retiring baby boomers. While the oldest boomers hang up their boots and retire, many younger boomers choose to stay in labor.

The youngest boomers will not retire for another two decades. Additionally, data indicate that some traditionalists remain in the job, and many baby boomers who are eligible for retirement are staying put. Instead, they prefer to continue working alongside Gen Xers and Millennials for various reasons ranging from the state of the economy to avoiding boredom.

While we are focused on Millennials entering employment, it is important to remember that there are already three coexisting generations in the workplace. Additionally, with the arrival of Millennials, we will begin to see changes in workplace dynamics that cannot be ignored and must be addressed if we are to remain competitive.

Is it possible that the fact that four generations coexist in today's workplace affects training? What information do managers and trainers need to know about generational differences? Do these distinctions have a discernible effect on employee relations and productivity? Each group has distinct values and experiences that impact their behaviors and beliefs.

To comprehend the implications for training, managers and training experts must first grasp each generation and its distinctive workplace characteristics. According to a paper published in the Journal of Pension Benefits: Issues in Administration by Sarah Simoneaux and Chris Stroud (2010), Bridging the Generation Gaps in the Retirement Services Workplace, the generations are described as follows:

The Radio Babies were born between 1930 and 1945. This generation is also known as The Silent Generation and Veterans. (In certain other periodicals, they may be referred to as The Traditionalist.) This group is defined by their dedication to their work, respect for those in positions of authority, and seriousness about their profession. They may have difficulty thinking about how to make work enjoyable. They view employment as a crucial component of providing for their families.

These employees are typically devoted to the organizations for which they work, and it is not uncommon to discover some of them with more than 30 years of service. Radio infants are notorious for being quite set in their ways and have difficulty adapting to change.

Due to their hierarchical character, they have difficulty accepting direction from younger generations. When they were children, technology consisted of a radio and a rotary phone. As a result, people are often intimidated by modern technology, and their knowledge of it is restricted to what they allow themselves to study at work.

Between 1946 and 1964, the Baby Boomers generation was born. This group's attitude toward work is quite different than that of their Radio Baby parents in that they are not just hard workers but also workaholics. Their hard ethic and thirst for success define this generation. Because this generation of workers believes that one must work to live, they frequently lack a sense of balance between work and life.

This generation is extremely concerned about status and recognition. They place a high premium on titles and the chain of command. They believe in teamwork and champion team players. They are far more social than their Radio Baby parents and are significantly more adept at developing and sustaining connections. The Baby Boomer generation grew up with technology and came to view it as a helpful tool for increased productivity and a reliable source of knowledge.

The GenXers are a group of people born between 1965 and 1980. They are also known as Generation X, Xers, and Busters. This is the generation of latch-key children who saw their parents work long hours. Thus, in contrast to their workaholic parents, GenXers strive to balance work and life.

They value efficiency and determining the most effective method of accomplishing a task. They are career-driven but prefer not to mix work and personal life like their Radio Baby grandparents. Gen Xers respect their autonomy and are frequently upset by micromanagers.

They value lifelong learning and actively seek out opportunities to improve their abilities. They comprehend and are reliant on technology to the extent that it facilitates work and keeps them linked to their peers and the rest of the world.

Between 1981 and 2000, the Millennials, the youngest of the known generations, entered the world. This generation of people is also known as Generation Y, Gen Why?, Nexters,

Echo Boomers, and Bridgers. This generation may be the most hopeful of the four. Their sense of accomplishment and entitlement defines them as gregarious and extremely social.

Millennials, like GenXers, demand a balance between work and life, but their definition of this balance is slightly different. Because they were born with technology as an integrated part of their beings, Millennials can multitask and believe that contemporary technology enables them to work from any location. They are prone to boredom and crave a meaningful job.

Additionally, they have a strong want to please and a desire to perform a good job but require constant feedback and monitoring due to their inexperience. They value collaboration, are gregarious, and are always prepared to lend a hand and pitch wherever assistance is required. (p.68-69)

Managers and training experts must be aware of these distinctions when planning for successful onboarding of new employees, continuing development of current employees, and knowledge transfer from retiring employees. Some experts argue that there are no generational differences and that all employees seek the same thing in the job.

Josephine Rossi (2007) discusses Jennifer Deal's book Retiring the Generation Gap in her piece What Generational Gap: Are Generational Differences in the Workplace a Myth in the ASTD training periodical T&D. She explains that all employees fundamentally desire the same things at work, as their value systems are identical. Employers must consequently "...pay strict attention to essentials for all employees, such as respect, recognition, the opportunity for growth, competitive compensation, and, you guessed it, learning and development," according to Deal. (p.11) From this vantage point, I must concur with Ms.

Deal's analysis and the conclusions drawn from her seven years of research. However, from a training standpoint, I must ask: Are we doing our employees a disservice by disregarding their preferred learning styles and pushing everyone to fit into a box simply because it simplifies our work?

The truth is that while we all desire the same things, we do not always desire them in the same way. Here is a straightforward illustration. Breakfast is about to begin for a family of five. True, anyone could eat scrambled eggs and be satisfied. However, how much more will each person love their eggs if they can order them over-easy, sunny side up, poached, fried, or scrambled to their liking? Everyone has eggs, but they are prepared uniquely for each person. It's similar to adopting the Burger King philosophy—we want things our way, and why shouldn't we when it comes to learning?

We are increasingly witnessing the need for a more mixed approach to workplace learning. Organizations that embrace a diverse range of learning styles will discover that their staff is more cooperative, productive, and generally happier.

A happy employee is more likely to be engaged, and engaged people contribute positively to the firm's bottom line. Employees in the twenty-first century are aware of their options.

Although our current economic position appears to reflect a culture of lay-in-waiting, employees understand that when things improve, they have the power to exercise choice. Industry patterns show that the majority will do so. Learning and development opportunities are crucial for the employee of the twenty-first century. As a result, let's find a solution to this problem. that will proactively benefit our entire work population. It is critical to our organizations' bottom lines.

THE DIFFICULTIES OF WORKING WITH MULTIPLE GENERATIONS

Have you ever overheard something like...

The younger generation lacks a sense of responsibility...

Senior management is a long way removed from reality...

She's phoning in sick one more???

You've almost certainly heard those and others if you work with people. For the first time in history, our workplace contains four separate generations; some experts assert that there are five. We have usually had two, occasionally three, but never four. And this presents us with an intriguing, if not perplexing, dilemma: how can we have such wildly divergent viewpoints and experiences while remaining focused on and devoted to a shared vision?

As with any challenge, the solution is not straightforward, but it is worth investigating. The first step is to comprehend the current state of affairs. Who are these generations that are today employed in our economy?

They are referred to differently by different experts and authors, and there are several variations, but the traits are essentially the same. I most identify with Thom Ranier's and Gary McIntosh's "Four Generations" concept, which includes the following:

+ Construction workers—born between 1910 and 1945
+ Baby Boomers—those born between 1946 and 1964
+ Generation X—(a.k.a. Busters)—those born between 1965 and 1984
+ Bridgers—(also known as Generation Y)—were born between 1984 and 2002.

Each generation brings unique perspectives, experiences, and value systems to the table, and each one deserves to be recognized and honored for them. The difficulty arises, of course, when the contributions of one generation are substantially different from those of another, and neither can comprehend, much less value, the contributions of the other. Take a glance at each of them.

Builders are people aged 63 and beyond, making them the smallest category. These are the traditionalists who value hard effort, dedication, and commitment to a cause or corporation. Their motto is "Whatever it takes," They will go to any length to complete a task. On the other hand, builders prefer things to remain as they have always been; what worked for them will work for others. They are unenthusiastic about technology and can be sluggish to recognize it as a benefit, let alone a necessity.

The Boomers (often referred to as Baby Boomers) are individuals born following World War II. It is frequently stated that there are two 'waves' of Baby Boomers, each with its distinct traits. However, this is the generation committed to progress, giving their children

They were raised by parents who endured the Depression and frequently scrimped and saved to get necessities. The Baby Boomers feel that they can climb the career ladder with diligence, education, and long hours, which is critical to them. They approach problems with an "I can do it" attitude and strive diligently to overcome obstacles. However, people are more likely to embrace change if it benefits them personally, rather than 'the whole.' They may be viewed as disobedient and a generation that bends the rules.

This generation is currently the most powerful between the ages of 44 and 62. This places them in the category of senior leadership positions. Thus, it is critical to recognize that many businesses and organizations are governed predominantly by Boomers today.

The Busters are the generation on which analysts differ the most regarding their age range, but they are currently between 24 and 43. Busters are extremely relational, and maintaining and protecting major relationships will take precedence over almost everything else. That is far more essential to them than output or completing a large task. However, they do not always view business executives highly, particularly when those leaders make decisions that appear to disregard individuals.

And the Bridgers would be individuals in the workforce who are under the age of around 24, i.e., those who have recently graduated from college, are presently enrolled in college, or are not currently enrolled in college. This group has grown up entirely in the computer age; they are your most technologically savvy group. With their extensive understanding of the internet, they constantly have information at their fingertips.

Because they have not been required to conduct any planning or problem solving on their own, and they are accustomed to being continually exposed to some form of technological input, their capacity to work quietly and alone is limited.

What is the point? How might this knowledge of the generations' traits assist you in your role as a leader of all of them?

First, what is shown here is a smattering of information about each one; much more material is accessible from various sources. Leaders in multigenerational teams should understand each generation's values, capabilities, and weaknesses.

Discover what each individual needs, how they define work, how they plan for the future, etc. Read what others have written; contact me for additional information and training on the subject; and, most importantly, ask crucial questions of each generation in your company and compare their responses.

Second, leaders must know that the Baby Boomers will embark on a huge departure. By 2018, 60% of our current leadership will have departed. Therefore, it is vital that deliberate succession planning occurs and that existing leaders learn how to participate in knowledge management and transfer plans, which entails much more than simply drafting up procedures manuals.

Third, realize that each generation shares some characteristics, e.g., none of us enjoys change, especially when it is not our choice; trust is crucial regardless of generation; everyone wants to be treated with respect, and everyone wants to feel important to the bigger vision.

Fourth, when you better understand the generations you manage, personalize your leadership style. For instance, builders prefer a personal touch; boomers value awards and recognition; busters require constructive comments, and builders gain from mentoring ties. Adjust your approach to each one to ensure that you're communicating in the same language.' Enhance each generation's strengths and mitigate its flaws.

Fifth, avoid encouraging homogeneity by attempting to fit all generations into the same box. Consider the following: "Are the individuals who fit in best today the individuals who will help the organization survive tomorrow?" "What will the organization of the future require?" "How can we, as leaders, ensure that we are prepared for the future?" The answers to those questions will provide you with an excellent blueprint for capitalizing on and celebrating your workplace's multiple generations.

CONNECTEDNESS ACROSS GENERATIONS—LEADING DIFFERENT GENERATIONAL SECTIONS TO GREATNESS

The entire trouble with the world is that fools and fanatics are perpetually confident of themselves, while wiser people are constantly filled with uncertainties.—Bertrand Russell Bertrand Russell is one of the most eminent

The days of engaging each employee in an organization with a broad, paintbrush-stroke approach as if they were all cast from the same mold are over!

The ability to connect, comprehend, appreciate (not necessarily agree or disagree!), and drive generational segmentation inside a company organization will be the defining characteristics of greatness and relevance. There is a clear and direct correlation between one's managerial-leadership style and age or generational division.

This is also true of the strategies used by managerial leaders today to manage, lead, and engage others in the business.

Centurions—Members of the 55+ demographic are more disciplined, formal, controlled, reserved, focused, loyal, long-term oriented, purpose and value-driven, and organizationally devoted.

Baby Boomers (and Eco Boomers)—This age group is less organized, more materialistic, more resistant to change, more loud and extroverted, commitment is conditional, more loyal to the industry than to a specific organization, title-driven, and more formally educated.

Generation X—Those aged 27 to 38 are more action-oriented, boundary-pushing, opportunity-driven, socialization-oriented, friend-oriented, entitlement-driven, change-tolerant, and more focused on rapid gratification.

Generation Y—The age group of 21 to 28 has open minds but shorter attention spans, requires a greater variety of stimuli, is change-driven, and is technologically proficient.

Generation MTV (or Mosaic)—The 17 to 21-year-olds seeking meaning and significance. Change is the norm, and they are relationship-driven, idealistic, technologically savvy, socially sensitive, and focused on the short term.

To improve one's ability to lead and connect with others, a leader should approach folks through the lens of their generational segmentation's preferred mode of operation.

Individuals often operate outward from their inside generational segmentation!—Magee, Jeffrey

A leader can achieve a greater degree of individual performance and group effectiveness by fluidly engaging individuals one-on-one or within group dynamics. By examining how individual segmentation functions, leaders can remove the mystery and anxiety associated with determining the optimal way to engage and motivate their team and significantly reduce, if not eliminate, micromanagement by simply meeting the bare minimum needs of each segmentation and achieving maximum performance!

HOW TO UNDERSTAND, MOTIVATE, AND REWARD YOUR COMPANY'S MULTI-GENERATIONAL TEAM MEMBERS

In the Workplace, the Mature Generation

The Mature/WWII Generation is 67 years old and was born before 1946. They are committed to their careers. They have a healthy respect for authority, are conformists, adhere to regulations, and believe labor is a duty. Job security is a significant priority for this age. Expertise and information are at their fingertips, and they produce high-quality work. Their parents endured the Great Depression of 1929, World War II, and the Korean War.

Receipts and Recommendations:

The Mature Generation appreciates receiving handwritten memos. You should provide them with trophies, plaques, and money as incentives as an employer. This generation desires to continue learning and improving, so remember to enroll them in classes that will teach them how to operate more efficiently and effectively. They are not retiring due to the current economic climate.

What about those Baby Boomers who are still employed?

The Baby Boomer generation is known as the workaholic generation. They are accustomed to working long hours to advance their careers. They are between 47 and 66, born between 1946 and 1965. Their parents instilled in them the value of hard work to achieve the American Dream. Baby Boomers grew up during the Civil Rights Movement, the assassination of President John F. Kennedy, and the Vietnam War.

Receipts and Recommendations:

Baby Boomers prefer to receive criticism in person and have documented performance documentation to back up their job. They desire to be rated and to have it documented. Baby Boomers desire financial compensation. They owe money on loans and credit cards. If your organization lacks the funds, give them promotion with a title and acknowledge them before the other employees during a ceremony.

Baby Boomers want to continue learning and growing, so be sure to enroll them in classes that will help them work smarter and continue to improve. Baby Boomers are not retiring in the current economic climate.

The Workplace of Generation X

The latch key generation is accustomed to working autonomously. They are between the ages of 36 and 47, born between 1965 and 1981.

Many of their parents were divorced, creating a household with two incomes because both parents worked. These children were accustomed to returning home, completing their homework independently, and performing their duties without being instructed.

Generation X desires a healthy work-life balance. This generation is eager to work hard and desires the successful marriages that eluded their forefathers and mothers. These are self-sufficient individuals with families they wish to spend time with, and they value money while purchasing a home. They also want to have a good time at work. They are adept at using computers, cell phones, and other forms of technology.

Criticism and Reward:

They want immediate straight input so that they can address any issues promptly. They are diligent employees who do not require supervision.

Generation X is eager to continue learning and improving, so be sure you enroll them in classes that will help them work more efficiently and expand their knowledge.

Generation Y/Millennials are the fourth generation of employees in the workplace. They are between 18 and 35 and were born between 1982 and 2000. They grew up in an age of technology and want work to be enjoyable. They are goal-oriented and seek meaningful work that contributes to the firm's success for which they work.

While some may believe Generation Y is the pampered and entitled generation, this is not the case. They require supervision and motivation in an organized and stable setting that provides rapid feedback and recognition. They desire to work in an enjoyable setting.

Generation Y members may have held up to ten occupations. Allow yourself to be disturbed by this. Numerous of these businesses have ceased operations. Generation Y is looking for jobs that match their abilities and interests. They desire meaningful jobs. Multitasking is a strength of this age.

If another employer offers them an additional 50 cents per hour, they will want to switch employment to get the additional money. Demonstrate the benefits of staying with your company and the opportunities for growth and development within your organization. Provide them with educational opportunities to help them develop their skills.

Numerous firms have hired Generation Y employees and schooled them on their first day of work on how they should dress, treat their clients, and use their businesses' safety equipment.

Recommendations & Accolades:

Generation Y requires supervision, as well as immediate feedback and recognition. It is critical to establish stability and organization to reassure and motivate this generation to work together. They are eager to be engaged and involved in your organization and make a difference. Contact them via text message, e-mail, or voice mail.

On Generation Y's First Day of Work, the Importance of First Impressions

When my friend's kid in Generation Y was 19, he became an electrical apprentice. On his first day of work, his electrical employer immediately provided him with a corporate shirt, hard hat, safety glasses, and other equipment. His employer promptly demonstrated how to properly dress and use his safety equipment to safeguard himself and the building where he would be working. Each new employee/team member was taught the regulations, proper attire, and the usage of their safety equipment on their first day, the minute they arrived.

For one month, the management of a local Brazilian steakhouse instructs its Generation Y workers and servers on how to dress, treat, and serve their customers. Additionally, each team member is taught how to safely operate any restaurant equipment to protect themselves and their clients. Once students begin working at the restaurant, they are evaluated regularly. Each table of guests is given a computer with a brief survey about how effectively the waiters and staff handled their meal.

Remember that Generation Y requires supervision and motivation inside a regulated and stable setting. Additionally, they require rapid response and appreciation. They want to provide meaningful work to your organization. Send them to courses that will teach them how to work smarter, faster, and with more knowledge. They desire to work in an enjoyable setting. Do we not all wish to work in a pleasant environment?

Four Generations of Team Members Collaborating Effectively

How will you manage a profitable firm with four generations of team members?

I drove my automobile to a Sears Tire Store due to a steady leak in my front passenger tire. I had just visited a local vehicle dealer for an oil change when they informed me, "You will require a new tire, which will cost $280 including tax, $140 for the tire, and $140 for labor." You will not be able to fix this tire again." I exited and proceeded to Sears.

I waited in line at the Sears Tire store to talk with an associate. J, a Baby Boomer in his fifties, spoke with a customer and his wife, Mr. and Mrs. Mature, both around 70 years old. When the employee checked this customer's record, he discovered that his tires were ten years old.

"He certainly got his money's worth out of those tires!" I thought.

Mr. Mature, a customer of J's, inquired, "Is the manager in?" "The Manager is in a meeting," Associate J stated.

After a few moments, the manager entered and smiled at this customer. The store's manager was a member of Generation X, roughly 42 years old. She addressed Mr. Mature in a polite, friendly tone and persuaded him to purchase four new tires.

The second associate was in his early twenties and was a member of Generation Y/Millennial. He was dealing with a Generation X customer who was approximately 44 years old.

Each colleague greeted their customers politely and genuinely desired to assist them. Each generation communicated with the previous generation without incident.

When my turn came, the Generation Y associate T requested my name, the year of my car, and my phone number and zip code. His fingers sped across the keyboard, and he could locate my information in seconds. T was a computer whiz. "Your tires were acquired here in 2009, and you purchased a policy on them," he smiled. Let's examine your tire and see whether we can double patch it. Triple-A of Tidewater and your car dealer both lack this capability."

We stepped outside to examine my front right tire, and he stated, "We can double patch it and rotate your tires." I inquired whether he believed I needed to replace it, as some of the tires had a minor bit of rust."

"When tires are exposed to the elements, it is unavoidable," T stated. This occurs when your tires remain in good condition. We will repair the tire and rotate it. It will be free of charge because you have already purchased the warranty."

It's worth noting that I am a Baby Boomer, having been born between 1946 and 1965. I'm really glad I purchased my warranty. I waited in the store lounge and devoured several articles on managing a multigenerational workforce. After reading two articles, TT entered the room beaming and stated, "Your automobile is ready." Consider the patch we removed. We repaired it twice and rotated your tires."

After completing the work, T stated, "If you go online and complete our customer satisfaction survey, you will receive a discounted oil change voucher."

I left the store and later that night, after work, filled out their Sears Tire customer satisfaction survey. I was blown away by how successfully this store manager handled her store with her multi-generational team members. Her staff was courteous, respectful, nice, accommodating, and informed.

I contacted and spoke with the store manager, Ms. L., a few days after visiting the Sears Tire Store. I complimented her on the fantastic job her multigenerational team accomplished. "That pleased her!"

By remembering and understanding the wants and needs of your four generations of employees, you, too, can learn to motivate and lead a successful team at work. Begin today by utilizing the principles and methods discussed in this book to develop a successful team of four generations of workers.

GENERATIONAL BLENDING IN THE WORKPLACE

While blending generations are supposed to boost productivity and employee happiness, firms need to satisfy the diverse demands of the workforce's distinct generations. Organizations that rise above mockery and preconceptions and work to comprehend varied generations advance better.

Demographic diversity is a feature of the workplace. The workforce is multigenerational. Dealing with generations and being able to communicate with their diverse features will provide a significant benefit.

Understanding what motivates and discourages members of particular generational groups enables you to modify interactions. As a result, workplace teams and groups become more productive. Concentrate on the comparable qualities and acknowledge that each generation brings something essential to society and the workplace.

Characteristics of several generations

Traditionalists: Individuals born before 1945

I was born between the Great Depression of World War II.

They place a premium on diligence.

Recognize their experience to avoid engagement failure.

Relationships are frequently considered a source of accountability.

Baby Boomers: Individuals born between 1946 and 1964

Born in the period of Woodstock, desegregation, and Leave it to Beaver.

They are idealistic, individualistic, and driven by a desire to make a difference in the world.

They value recognition of their contributions to avoid engagement failure.

Relationships are frequently equated with loyalty.

Born between 1965 and 1979, Generation X

They were born during widespread layoffs and with both parents committing their lives to work.

They place a premium on work-life balance. Since several children have been left to fend for themselves and their siblings, this group is frequently referred to as the generation that was forgotten.

They wish to carry out their plans uniquely and are wary of any engagement arrangement.

Relationships are centered on balancing family and work life.

The Millennial Generation (Generation Y): Between 1980 and 2000

She was born into an era of technological advancement, diverse education, and everyone receiving a trophy.

They are enthusiastic, self-centered, and adept at networking.

They value acknowledgment for everyday duties and are irritated by others who are less social or technologically savvy. As a result, disengagement occurs.

Relationships imply an entitlement to work-life balance.

Generation Z: Individuals born between 2001 and the present

I was born in the aftermath of 9/11, the internet, Facebook, and the Iraq war.

The group's motivation is still being developed.

When leaders acknowledge the emotional needs of several generations, they boost employee trust and engagement: all generations value reward, encouragement, and freedom of expression. By assigning value to each generation, a team and workgroup will get stronger.

Demographic diversity is a feature of the workplace. The workforce is multigenerational. Dealing with generations and being able to communicate with their diverse features will provide a significant benefit.

How To Integrate A Multigenerational Workforce

A growing challenge for managers and companies is efficiently blending the multigenerational workforce, composed of four generations: Traditionalists, Baby Boomers, Generation X, and Generation Y or Millennials. Each group has distinct qualities and ways of learning, talking, and working, resulting in generational conflict.

To manage and cohabit effectively, managers and employees alike must develop the ability to perceive and comprehend these various groupings' disparate expectations and characteristics. Here are five strategies for integrating the multigenerational workforce and fostering more harmony and effectiveness in work teams:

1. Notice distinctions—managers must recognize, comprehend, and accept distinctions. The manager is the leader, and it must begin with them to increase employee acceptance of differences. Set an example.

2. Bring the groups together and have them write down their views and preconceived notions about the other; this helps identify any preconceptions that may exist and stimulates conversation about the differences, which leads to their dispelling and the beginning of relationship building.

3. Collaborate on a project with people of different generations. This will foster trust and allow each party to appreciate the other's qualities. Elderly workers can impart wisdom and provide mentoring and coaching, while younger workers can assist in comprehending and utilizing the growing number of new technologies in the workplace.

4. Delegate responsibility for conflict resolution to employees; management should be involved only if there is no resolution. Again, this will "compel" each generation to communicate with one another, identify any preconceived notions they may have, and work collaboratively to develop solutions that everybody can live with.

5. Hold weekly team meetings to discuss work processes, resolve conflicts, and foster intergenerational connections. Meetings should be held over breakfast or lunch; provide a calm and supportive atmosphere.

COMMUNICATION ACROSS GENERATIONAL GAPS IN THE WORKPLACE

Where do you hear the scratching of fountain pens on paper and the buzzing of iPhones with incoming text messages?

In a normal office setting.

Today, four generations are at work:

+ Purists (born before 1946) loyalty and discipline are valued, as are hierarchy and authority.

+ Due to their goal-oriented, competitive, and work-centric nature, Baby Boomers (born 1946–1964) today hold positions of influence in the business world.

+ Generation X (born 1965–1980) comprises 55 million people in North America and is characterized by a critical, pragmatic, and self-sufficient mindset that values independence respects variety, and demands work-life balance.

+ Generation Y (born 1981–1999) comprises 80 million people in North America and digitally savvy optimists who value social responsibility, uniqueness and difference, rewrite the rules, and thrive on collaboration and kinship.

Per a Pew Research Center investigation from 2009, this generational combination can be explosive. Almost eight in ten respondents noticed a significant divergence between the perspectives of younger and older generations today. The Pew

Center's analysis confirms the findings of Randstad USA's 2008 World of Work survey, which found that the four generations rarely interact.

Due to this generational divide, managers and team leaders may face significant challenges in supporting productive workplace communication. On the one hand, traditionalists often prefer to communicate face-to-face and via formal typed or handwritten letters.

On the other hand, Gen Y employees prefer to connect via text, instant messaging, and email. The dilemma, therefore, becomes how to close communication gaps in the workplace that might stifle collaboration, reduce productivity, and harm the business's bottom line.

Step one is crucial, according to experts, is to acknowledge that members of Generation Y despise dictatorial communication in contrast to their older peers. They also require constant input from their superiors, having been raised on a continual diet of positive feedback and accolades. As a result, managers, and leaders should consider the following:

- ◆ Adopting a less terse, acidic, and aggressive style of communication in favor of one that is more courteous, conciliatory, and indirect

- ◆ Submitting requests that specify specific business objectives rather than making broad instructions

- ◆ Substituting more frequent progress reports and informal updates for annual performance reviews

Another critical step is empowering and encouraging all staff to utilize a variety of communication platforms. Even workers with technophobia can communicate with others via e-mail, blogging, text messaging, instant messaging, and social media sites like Facebook and Twitter through workplace learning opportunities. Similarly, virtual conversations and role-playing can assist employees who have difficulty conversing face-to-face or writing longer than 140 characters.

Additionally, productive intergenerational communication occurs when managers and team leaders take steps to bring the generations together. When older and younger workers are integrated into functional work teams, they can share information and collaborate on formulating corporate strategy, producing new products, and resolving service concerns. This level of collaboration fosters mutual understanding, trust, and respect.

As over 90% of Fortune 500 firms have learned, workplace affinity clubs also foster common relationships. Alternatively referred to as networking or resource groups, affinity groups bring employees together based on shared characteristics such as race, ethnic origin, gender, and sexual orientation.

Additionally, they build around common interests in literature, sports, travel, and music. Whatever their emphasis, affinity clubs can develop the types of ties that encourage meaningful dialogue and engagement among employees of all ages.

There is little question that when four very different generations coexist in the same job, significant communication barriers occur. Managers and team leaders may overcome these barriers by using practical strategies for establishing and maintaining meaningful connections across generational divides.

By empowering employees to adopt new communication methods and pursue shared interests, businesses lay the groundwork for a strong communication foundation that will last well.

MULTIPLE GENERATIONS OF MANAGEMENT IN THE WORKPLACE

In the United States, we currently have four distinct generations coexisting in the workplace. It was easier in the past when there was less diversity and a firmer set of norms. The older employee was the boss, manager, or supervisor, while the younger employees were subordinates who "obeyed" their supervisor's rules.

Older workers spend a longer duration of time in the workforce. (whether by choice or necessity). Business is becoming more globalized, technology is transforming the way people work, and the skills required are changing. These factors contribute to the amended, dropped, or adjusted regulations, highlighting the importance of effective communication, management, and leadership.

When we engage with customers, it becomes evident that generational differences can impact every aspect of business, including the how's, why's, and where's of recruiting, team building, dealing with change, motivating, managing, sustaining and growing productivity.

Consider how generational disparities in communication styles may cause misconceptions, high employee turnover, trouble recruiting and retaining staff. We know that people communicate in ways influenced by their experiential and generational histories.

The attitudes of each generation are distinctive actions, expectations, habits, and motivators. They are developing the ability to converse effectively with people of different ages. It can help avoid many significant workplace clashes and misunderstandings and great outcomes.

These distinctions can result in four strikingly diverse employee kinds. While we do not advocate for "stereotyping" someone based on their age or generational group, it is beneficial to grasp the broad generational disparities.

The following statements are accurate, according to Clemson University:

Values:

Traditionalists/Veterans survived World War II and were raised under a rigid routine that instilled an appreciation for quality, respect, and authority.

Baby Boomers embraced the value of making sacrifices to advance. They developed a strong sense of loyalty toward their employers and coworkers due to this sacrifice.

Generation X were latchkey children who watched their parents reshape the workplace; they were the first generation to grow up with computer technology. Increasing output is more important to them than the number of hours worked.

Generation Y/Millennials are technologically savvy. They multitask and are easily bored. They are more adept at maximizing and leveraging new technology than any previous generation, and they desire a balanced lifestyle.

Several of the general traits of each generational group include the following:

- Traditionalists
- Because of this, I was born and reared in a time of war.
- I grew up in a time of scarcity and a sense of deficiency
- Dedicated workers
- Priority is given to duty over recreation.
- Observes the rules
- Recognizes authority
- Money-wise, conservative
- Believes in labor division
- Correlation between seniority and age
- Work and family life are distinct.
- The distinction between supervisor and employee
- Ascend the ladder with diligence and perseverance
- Individuals have a propensity to remain in one place of employment for an extended period.

CHILDREN'S BOOMER

- Optimistic
- Dedicated to the team
- Concerned about one's health and well-being
- Constantly educating
- Loyal
- Workaholics
- Prefer direct communication
- The emphasis should be on the process and result at work, not on the consequences and outcomes.
- Job title and symbols are critical.
- Enjoys the knowledge that their management is aware of and concerned about them personally.

THE XTH GENERATION

- Self-reliant
- Children with latchkeys
- Work-family balance
- At work, I enjoy having fun and making new friends.
- Technologically sophisticated
- Approaches authority in a casual manner
- I prefer a flexible work schedule and a relaxed work atmosphere
- Concentrating on relationships, outcomes, rights, and abilities in the workplace
- Simple to recruit, difficult to retain

THE MILLENNIALS/GENERATION Y

- Optimistic
- Confident
- Diverse
- Political
- Setting goals is critical.
- Traditionalists' can-do attitude
- Boomers have a strong sense of teamwork.
- X'ers' technological savvy
- They understand what they want and are accustomed to obtaining it.
- Expect a high income upon graduation from college.
- Have difficulty connecting with baby boomers and Generation X'ers
- Additionally, various generations have varying communication methods.

TRADITIONALIST

+ Prefers unambiguous expectation
+ I despise being rushed
+ Memos and one-on-one correspondence

CHILDREN'S BOOMER

+ I enjoy being questioned to elicit information.
+ Would you like to be coached to enhance your performance?
+ Individualized communication
+ Contact me at any time (make themselves available)

GENERATION X

+ Are not scared to inquire (Even of authority)
+ Avoid office politics at all costs.
+ Respond more effectively to open-ended queries.
+ Communicates by cell phone but would prefer to be contacted at work rather than home.

GENERATION Y

+ Construct a clear picture of the workplace
+ Responds favorably to coaching by more experienced professionals, such as Traditionalists.
+ Acquaint yourself with their objectives and assist them in developing tactics to accomplish them.
+ Communicates via the internet, email, and text messaging, as well as through Facebook and Twitter.
+ Finally, each cohort had some areas of motivation that were more unique to them.

TRADITIONALIST

+ Rather than informal, formal
+ Justify your acts
+ Recognized via tradition
+ "Your expertise is valued here."
+ "Loyalty is rewarded and rewarded."

CHILDREN'S BOOMERS

+ Need to demonstrate progress toward set objectives
+ Declare the team's objectives and desired outcomes.
+ It is recognized through extensive public exposure, such as a company newsletter.
+ "Your worth is recognized."
+ "your contributions to our success are critical."

THE XTH GENERATION

+ Assist them in understanding what they should do. But not how it should be done.
+ Provide them with various duties, but enable them to establish priorities.
+ Recognized informally, such instance with a day off
+ Effective leadership
+ Consistent, candid feedback and coaching
+ "There are few regulations in this place."
+ "We're not particularly corporate around here."

Y GENERATION

+ Provide chances for ongoing education and skill development

- Understand their objectives and how they fit into the "grand picture."
- Take on the role of a coach rather than a boss.
- Informal communication via email and hallway discussions
- "You and your coworkers can assist in reviving this company."

How can you use this understanding to help your business and, more specifically, the people you lead perform better?

To begin, consider your personal style and how generational differences affect you. Then, speak with your direct reports to ascertain how much of their generational "typicals" apply to them.

Then consider completing a more extensive profile that will provide additional insight into your unique communication style and behaviors and having your staff complete one. Integrate specialized information with more broad information. There are a variety of profiles available on the market that will enable you to assess your communication and behavioral capacities.

We've used many of them and have identified and recommended one that is particularly useful for firms attempting to increase coordination, cooperation, and communication in a multigenerational workplace.

MANAGEMENT OF A MULTIGENERATIONAL WORKFORCE

If you oversee one, you are well aware that each generation brings its abilities and ideas to the workplace. However, this diversity frequently creates difficulties for managers tasked with supervising both the youngest members of the workforce, Generation Y, and the oldest, Baby Boomers and Traditionalists. So how do you efficiently and profitably manage a multigenerational workforce? Let's begin with some background information on each generation:

The Four Successor Generations

Generation Y: Also known as Millennials, people born after 1980 grew up surrounded by technology. Additionally, they want feedback on their work and performance and place a premium on both online and offline interactions.

Workers born between 1965 and 1980 are considered members of Generation X. frequently want a work-life balance that satisfies their need for a high quality of life. The Generation X generation values mutual respect and free communication.

Baby Boomers: This generation, born between 1946 and 1964, is defined by a strong work ethic. They place a premium on face-to-face engagement and are frequently regarded as loyal employees. Additionally, boomers are accustomed to the concept of climbing the corporate ladder.

Traditionalists: Occasionally referred to as the Silent Generation, workers born before 1946. They may have lived through the hard years of WWII or been raised by parents who battled during the Great Depression.

Bear in mind that these are general characteristics of the multigenerational workforce. A younger employee may have the mentality of an older employee or vice versa. The critical point is to recognize that generational disparities do exist and that you, as a supervisor, must account for them.

How to Manage a Multigenerational Workforce Successfully

Develop relationships with mentors. Gen Y was weaned on email, text messages, Facebook, and Twitter, whereas Boomers are intimately familiar with CRM and other enterprise management technologies. Utilize the strengths of each group by pairing older and younger employees to mentor one another.

Establish a productive work atmosphere. Each group may have distinct preferences when it comes to the work environment. For example, because working from home is similar to how many young professionals did in college, consider offering a work-from-home option to Gen Y employees.

While boomers and other generations are frequently content with typical office hours, they may also prefer flex scheduling, providing more flexibility in their work hours.

Utilize a variety of tools to communicate. While a Boomer/ Traditionalist may prefer face-to-face communication, a Gen Y worker is quite fine communicating by email, text message, or other electronic means. Consider releasing messages in various methods to increase the likelihood that each group in the multigenerational workforce will read them.

Create a respectful environment. Each generation adds unique abilities and experiences to the multigenerational workforce, which means that each employee deserves respect and trust. As a supervisor, you should strive to foster an environment devoid of beliefs such as "Those darn children on their cell-phones..." or "Those old people just won't change..."

Reward appropriate behavior. Reward the multigenerational workforce frequently and as quickly as feasible following the occurrence of positive action. Because each generation has its own beliefs, consider allowing employees to choose their incentives. Allow them to select a gift card from a list of local shops. This allows the Gen Y employee to select a gift card to a trendy new tapas restaurant, while the Boomer or Traditionalist may pick a gardening center or golf shop.

While managing a multigenerational workforce can be tough, you can establish a productive and profitable team by considering each group's values and preferences.

MANAGEMENT SUGGESTIONS FOR A MULTI-GENERATIONAL STAFF

Employee pools now span generations, including Baby Boomers, Generation X, Generation Y, and Echo-Boomers. Each generation may have varying expectations for workplaces and careers. How do you maintain contact with various generations? How did you go about establishing mentoring programs?

A group of CEOs offers the following advice:

To begin, let us examine some distinctions. According to experts, Baby Boomers are more regimented, have a higher level of "stick-to-itiveness," and have a greater capacity for patience than younger generations. Although not as much as younger employees, they exhibit a degree of "me" focus. They have typically had to earn recognition, promotion, and incentives.

In comparison, younger generations appear to have a different work ethic, a broader range of interests, a greater appreciation for flex time, and a greater familiarity with technology. They dress more casually, appear more self-absorbed, and believe they are entitled to more at a younger age.

They are self-sufficient and do not hesitate to request special attention or rapid gratification. Simultaneously, they will listen if you speak with them one-on-one about the realities of business operations.

According to several analysts, the generations after the Baby Boomers are becoming increasingly collaborative and team-oriented. Additionally, they expect to be involved in decision-making—or at the very least to have their opinions sought—when previous generations recognized that one needed to reach a particular level to participate in top-level decision-making.

Individuals may belong to multiple generations, but they remain unique. Inquire what inspires or drives them and what they perceive as an ideal reward for effort. Once you've ascertained their ambitions and dreams, develop incentives to address them. Consider the following examples:

* Some employers give a sabbatical after several years of employment, allowing employees to pursue hobbies, embark on adventures, or use the time they desire. This attracts and retains personnel.

* Certain personnel do not desire advancement yet are valuable contributors. They might value an additional week of vacation more than a promotion.

* One employer provides funding for employees to freshen up their work areas, giving employees some control over their work environment.

What are some helpful hints for managing younger employees?

* Teach children to communicate wisely and deliberately—rather than rashly and without regard for impact or repercussions. Younger managers may discover that articulating expectations to senior workers requires more patience.

* Because they are more receptive to coaching on working more effectively in a team context, younger employees are more receptive to coaching on how to work more effectively in a team environment.

* Due to their relatively high self-esteem, these individuals may be receptive to criticism and guidance, particularly if presented constructively. They are receptive to having more senior management sit down and speak with them.

* Create unique performance metrics for each employee and enable them to track their progress via their PCs.

* Involve them in the process rather than telling them to wait. Allow them to begin as an observer. When they have questions or suggestions, pay attention. Inquire about their opinion.

* Subdivide job tiers into new levels with increased achievement rewards. Allow them to recalibrate their expectations regularly.

METHODS FOR EFFECTIVE COOPERATION BETWEEN MULTI-GENERATIONS

"A successful guy can build a strong foundation with the bricks hurled at him." Brinkley, David

Numerous businesses now employ four distinct generations for the first time: Traditionalists, Baby Boomers, Gen Xers, and Gen Yers (also known as Millenials). Each group contributes to a unique set of values, abilities, and communication styles in the workplace. So how can senior management ensure that a company is productive and cohesive? Should they develop a culture based on their personal experiences and expect others to follow suit, or should they seek organizational "buy-in"? The difficulty with the first is that contradictory management systems can still exist, resulting in frustration and perhaps an exodus of critical individuals.

The latter can be a time-consuming procedure that could be better spent developing new products and services and responding to ever-changing competitive market conditions. Businesses must address four critical ideas to increase employee retention and favorably impact their ROI.

1. Behavior—The DISC profile is a useful evaluation tool for businesses because it offers employees a formal approach for understanding their work style and personality traits and how the two interact dynamically in the workplace. By discussing this information in a group or department setting, one might better understand their coworkers' actions and suggest more effective interaction and conflict resolution strategies.

2. Communication—Have you ever evaluated how the bulk of your staff communicate—by email, text messaging, instant messaging, phone calls, group meetings, or one-on-one meetings? Which is the most effective? The answer is almost certainly a blend of the two. By surveying staff and conducting a "communication audit," new or upgraded strategies for providing faster and more concise responses can be established or enhanced. While businesses should strive to accommodate each individual's unique communication style, individuals must understand the value of audience respect.

3. Work ethics—Traditionalists are more willing to work long hours and prefer a more professional environment. Younger generations value a more balanced work-life balance and a more relaxed work environment. By holding group meetings and indi-

vidual sessions, managers can better understand the desires and interests that are most important to each employee. For instance, the management team may decide to allow employees to dress however they choose as long as it is appropriate and does not adversely affect overall productivity.

4. Learning environment—While remuneration and growth possibilities are critical for retaining personnel, many also desire the ability to enhance their knowledge base. As a result, businesses should seek to foster an environment that values training and development both internally and externally through classes or lectures. Participants should also be encouraged to share their newly learned information with their colleagues and peers, both formally and informally, to educate, mentor, and motivate them.

These critical principles will strengthen personal connections by establishing a solid foundation for intergenerational respect. Clearly stated company objectives combined with group coaching enable employees to understand their colleagues' ideas and actions better, resulting in a more harmonious work environment and, eventually, an increased return on investment.

CHAPTER 3

CREATE AN INNOVATIVE
CULTURE

Innovation is one of the most highly valued characteristics of any organization. It keeps a firm at the forefront of its area, ensures the relevance of its products and services, and motivates its staff.

However, how do leaders inspire creativity in their teams? How can they cultivate it on the job?

'Grow' is an appropriate word to use because, in many respects, creativity is a natural process, similar to the changing seasons and agricultural cycles…

The cycle of natural innovation

Crops are grown by the natural seasonal cycle. From preparation of the soil to planting, caring, and growing the crops, and finally harvesting them, a defined sequence must occur before the products of labor are ripe.

The same principle applies to concepts. Numerous firms anticipate that employees will be naturally creative and develop ideas without preparation.'

Before they expect results, the finest leaders ensure that the ground is fertile and ready for seeds to be planted and flourish. This demands a grasp of the creative process and a commitment to fostering the conditions necessary for it to flourish within an organization.

Leaders expecting creative teams must first understand their team members' requirements, how they think and make decisions, and how they produce ideas; they must also get a better understanding of the innovation process. Then they must take immediate action to coax the finest performance out of them to foster the growth of innovative mindsets.

Seasons of invention

Extending the concept, leaders must guide their teams through the 'innovation seasons':

Spring—Seed planting

Leaders must initiate dialogues with team members to develop cohesive, agile, goal-oriented, supportive, and positive teams. They must next make real efforts to foster an environment of trust, passion, connection, and hope that fosters the development of innovative teams. This may take time, but it is critical for building a long-term mindset in which innovation occurs naturally due to a group working closely together.

Summer—weeding out the weeds that choke outgrowth

Any team must recognize what is impeding growth. What impediments to invention exist? Some are self-evident, while others require insight into why individuals believe and behave in certain ways. Overcoming these challenges is critical to fostering a long-term creative attitude inside the team, free of misunderstandings, confusion, stress, cognitive bias, and conflict.

Harvest time—enjoying the benefits of your sowing

Eight distinct attitudes contribute to the development of an innovation culture. It's critical to grasp these and establish a process for the team to follow to be innovative. This entails assessing team structure and determining ways to use individual abilities for the team's greater good.

Leadership should recognize that attempting to motivate individuals and teams to be more creative' without first establishing an environment conducive to innovation is destined to failure. Without a grasp of the innovation process and team dynamics, it is hard to promote innovation. This involves some psychology and neuroscience and a great deal of leadership.

LEADERSHIP—A CRUCIAL FACTOR IN INNOVATION

Leaders run innovative businesses. Leaders lead innovation departments. Leaders are created via innovation. How do we discover new ideas? A related question is how we can identify a leader or develop leadership skills in ourselves or our staff.

Let's examine some proposals and build a personal leadership development plan for the organization on their foundation.

To lead is to assist others in their endeavors, regardless of what we say: about developing leadership in your company or industry. By providing high-quality items, we empower those who purchase them.

The company's leader—is the head who is concerned not only with his achievement but also with the success of his staff.

The leader is continually learning and imparting knowledge to others. That leadership quality is a critical component of an innovative business. In a competitive atmosphere, leadership will assist in achieving consistent results.

Let us compare two teams: a company's team leader and a sales department team leader. A business's leader:

- ✦ The leader is adept at setting goals.
- ✦ Monitors employees' performance
- ✦ Works with high-profile clients

The team's captain:

The leader is familiar with his subordinates.

Leaders understand how to educate their subordinates and thus learn Leaders understand what qualities and talents their subordinates must grow. Leaders understand which of them will become the future leader

A leader with a training program for subordinates

The leader concentrates on assisting others in achieving achievement, not exercising control. The leader assigns talented individuals to work with critical clients.

The leader has established a development strategy for the department, enabling it to generate results exceeding expectations.

It is natural to assume that the team leader will eventually advance to the Commercial Department. Subject to the given trend, the team leader will constantly evolve, while the leader's team will remain constant, maintaining the company's level. Although, given the market's continuous competitiveness, it is most likely that leadership teams will vanish under the influence of corporations having leadership departments.

Seek out, leaders! Develop become leaders! Leadership is critical to modern business competitiveness. Through leadership, you will uncover and create variables that contribute to your company's and employees' competitiveness.

How do leaders judge their own or their subordinates' leadership abilities? Respond to the following eight questions:

Do you have a monthly, three-month, or six-month personal learning plan?

Do you have a training strategy for the following month, three months, or six months for your staff?

How many people have you assisted/trained in your organization over the last month, six months?

How is your progress tied to your employees' success?

Is your success depends on the success of your employees?

How do you determine the staff's effectiveness?

How do you evaluate your competence as a manager at work with coworkers?

What potential issues can arise while working with employees, and how would you suggest mitigating them?

Leaders are always connecting with their subordinates. A team led by a leader is constantly on the lookout for methods to improve and maximize performance.

Another critical aspect of leadership is fostering an environment conducive to creativity and work in your organization. Your workers who work in a pleasant environment provide you with various benefits: they are more receptive to customers and loyal to the firm.

A straightforward illustration. Consider two trading rooms for different corporations. The air conditioning is on in one room, and gentle music is playing, while the other room is stifling and crowded. Where will staff be most productive? Which company will they be most loyal to? The responses are logical and understandable.

The internal atmosphere is critical. We have a budget for advertising to attract new clients, but do you have a budget for creating favorable working conditions within the company?

Make your employees happy, and this includes more than simply the words in the benefits package. As a result of these actions, happy employees who aspire to work perform admirably. Employees who recognize the value of excellence in their job will have the opportunity to advance and develop within the organization or serve as mentors to new employees.

The leader's job is to assemble a team. A team focused on growth and innovation rather than a mediocre life in today's market environment. A group of individuals who are either specialists in their profession or desire to become experts in their subject.

Your staff must value their work with you:

- We work for an excellent company.
- As I progressed inside the organization, my fortune increased.
- During the last three months, we have accomplished the following objectives:
- During the next three months, others will be accomplished.

These expressions might be used to characterize employees or team leaders. Similar expressions are used by athletes, sports teams, participants, and coaches. Why? Sport is the outcome. This leadership development program is designed for solo leaders and team leaders. Business, like education, is the outcome of leadership abilities.

Discover your colleagues' positive attributes. Look for the excellent features of your employees and nurture them! Make a positive statement!

Errors will always occur, but the errors enable us to attain results.

You will be successful if you create an environment conducive to growth; your firm will succeed if you create a conducive environment! Commemorate your victory! Salute success! Assume responsibility for your achievement!

This week, who are you praising? This month, perhaps? In less than three months?

What kind of praise did you express?

Your business is your ship; it is the result of the coordinated efforts of the entire crew, according to the system that you— as a leader—have constructed. A system should be trained, upgraded, and scaled.

Leadership applies simple principles that can catapult a firm to new heights.

HOW TO BECOME AN INNOVATION ROCKSTAR

The Facts

Establishing truly innovative businesses must take precedence over the more simplistic concept of creating technically innovative firms that sustain a poisonous and destructive corporate culture. This is frequently overlooked until there are legal, financial, or public relations ramifications. As a result, brand risk management innovation has yet to go beyond this narrow framework for identifying and resolving toxic and destructive issues in most businesses.

Brand risk management is still primarily viewed through risk aversion and exposure to legal liability, and innovation is primarily understood through technological advancements. This is how glaring blind spots become institutionalized in the cultural mindset. On the other hand, those who recognize the critical role of diversity inclusion in fostering innovative organizational cultures reap the benefits.

Eighty-five percent of CEOs whose organizations have a lived strategy for diversity and inclusion report that it has boosted performance.

Organizations with a high level of inclusion rate their ability to innovate 170 percent higher.

We are enhancing organizational cultures results in decreased absenteeism.

Additionally, these organizations have a higher employee retention rate.

Intentionally promoting inclusion increases a company's likelihood of increasing market share by 45 percent.

Obstacles and difficulties

Innovation necessitates the ability to view things in novel ways. Combining distinct ideas from diverse backgrounds frequently serves as a spark for innovative solutions, and here is where diversity inclusion is necessary. Additionally, research indicates that innovation requires an environment where all ideas can be examined regardless of their source. Oppositional concerns generally present themselves through lawsuits and public shaming on social media in response to employees acting on their prejudice. Despite having policies that condemn discrimination and intolerance, corporations such as Hilton, Starbucks, and Toyota have all paid a high price this year... both financially and in terms of social capital established over decades. Simultaneously, several of the IT industry's movers and shakers have been dethroned by revelations and allegations of sexual misbehavior and prejudice.

Therefore, why do we continue to see this from companies who boast policies that promote inclusivity and respect?

Because the people within their organization, the ones who determine what the organization is, have been unable (in far too many situations) to recognize their own bias and adopt a more beneficial course of action to achieve personal growth change.

We have business cultures shaped by civilizations still battling oppressive and exclusionary traditions.

We are maintaining the status quo at the expense of fostering new ideas.

Because, in many circumstances, corporate decisions are motivated primarily by profitability and risk aversion. This is one of the flaws in that approach to brand risk management and why innovation is urgently needed.

A study found that a résumé with a black-sounding name earned half the number of calls as a resume with a white-sounding name, even when sent to firms with a strong diversity record.

Due to technology, the globe has become smaller, increasing transparency in many circumstances. Given that varied perspectives are critical for creativity, what value is gained by effectively normalizing discrimination?

"Discrimination in the workplace has a cost—$64 billion.

This figure illustrates the projected annual cost of losing and replacing the more than 2 million American workers who leave their employment each year due to workplace injustice and discrimination."

What is more difficult to assess are the consequences for the discriminating persons. The waves created continue to spread, as seen by the current condition of affairs. When it comes to the technology industry, it is often where people look to gain a sense of what is happening on the cutting edge of innovation. Beyond the obvious, there are troubling ramifications to the poisonous and prejudiced tech culture prevalent in places like Silicon Valley.

"If we do not act now, all of these biases and discrimination will be rewritten into the algorithms, artificial intelligence, and machine learning that power the future technology. Already, facial recognition technology is sexist and racist on a fundamental level. It does not recognize women or persons of color as white men are. That is significant."

The past is inextricably linked to the present. Today lays the groundwork for the future term. And because several leaders' responses are typically band-aid solutions, progress has been slow and unpleasant. The truth is that external forces cannot legislate hearts and minds; new regulations and laws will impose severe constraints on the majority. The route forward is very personal, as the outcomes discussed here all originate from a deeply personal place within the individuals concerned.

The Remedy

The straightforward solution begins with leaders. To lead by example, wise leaders must embrace personal innovation. Policy pronouncements or diversity training that exacerbate existing problems or give only a temporary fix no longer qualify as solutions. Numerous research has demonstrated that these tactics do not work. However, a courageous leader in demonstrating personal innovation can cultivate a meaningfully innovative organizational culture that appears to increase market share naturally, roll out industry-leading products and services, and contribute significantly to creating a better world.

WORKPLACE CHANGE AND INNOVATION

Making adjustments entails 'creating or becoming something different'—you are introducing something new or adjusting an existing item.

Changing something requires you to step outside of your comfort zone. You have grown accustomed to doing things a specific way and for certain reasons, and when this pattern changes, you tend to resist, claiming that 'but we've always done it this way, and it works perfectly. However, do you truly understand how or why the changes occurred? Change, when applied intelligently, can be a wonderful thing, as this chapter will explain.

We are always changing—both professionally and personally:

At work

Changes in technology influence us differently; consider how we operate now with business equipment such as computers, the internet, email, ATMs, and online conferencing.

They promised us a paperless office (which has not yet materialized!)...we now have mechanisms in place to save our information on a microchip the size of a thumbnail. Formerly, the same amount of information was stored in a file cabinet. Additionally, computers have made reserving services and keeping track of people and inventory much faster and easier.

We can save a lot of time and money by conducting business online. It saves time, effort, and money (envelopes, paper, and stamps), plus it's quick and convenient.

Within your private life

Consider the changes that have occurred in your personal life.

Attending a training session (you do this to change your prospects or your knowledge levels)

Relocating (why do you do this?)

Job changes (why do you do this?)

Graduating from high school and entering the workforce (how do you manage this?)

"You're tossing out your favorite old sneakers!!!" (How come you do this?)

How frequently do these modifications occur? Regardless of the reason for the modification, the current state of operation is altered.

To ensure that change occurs efficiently and with the least amount of disturbance or stress possible, you must address the issue methodically:

You (or your supervisors) must:

Identify the need for change—what is currently occurring and why is it no longer working?

Conduct research on what needs to be done—consider the steps necessary to get from where you are now to where you want to be (in a logical order).

Identify potential issues with the new procedure and work to resolve them.

Elicit comments and input from appropriate personnel in various departments

to implement the change—inform all stakeholders of the new plan, procedure, or system and offer any necessary training to staff.

Evaluate the change's efficacy—resolving any issues and determining whether the new process or system is performing as intended.

For instance, when you relocate;

To begin, you must determine the necessity of change;

You've had more children, and the house has become too tiny; you can now afford a more desirable neighborhood, or you've been transferred to a new city/country.

Second, you determine the type of house that would currently be appropriate for you. You:

Take a look at properties in the appropriate neighborhood

Consider the appropriate size of houses, landrace expenses, and other associated costs.

Take note of the proximity of transportation, businesses, and schools, among other amenities.

determine the cost of relocation

Thirdly, you relocate!

Finally, you settle into your new home and take care of all the tasks you were unable to complete before the move:

including more electricity outlets

removing the wall separating the family room and dining room, modernizing the kitchen, etc.

Dissatisfaction is the catalyst for change.

All changes occur due to contentment with one's current condition of being. For instance;

Individual (influenced by you). Perhaps you are disappointed with your;

Clothes Hair Partner Housework (influenced by you)

Which department do you work in?

Supervisory position (influenced by others)

Procedures for work

Equipment for the workplace

Other personnel management (influenced by others)

Organizational structure

Launch of a new product or service

New policies are implemented

New proprietors/managers (new broom—change for change's sake)

Customer specifications

Trends in the market

If you or your supervisors or managers become dissatisfied with the current state of affairs, you or managers begin looking for a better way to do things.

Reasons for workplace change

Although all changes are typically the result of EXTERNAL forces, it can be claimed that a corporation is subjected to two change motivators:

Motivators on the inside (proactive)

External stimulants (reactive)

Internal transformation is inspired by the following:

the requirement for or introduction of novel systems

extension of a company's product or service offering

the necessity of reviewing ineffective procedures and establishing new goals and tactics

diversification into new markets

The addition of new large accounts and customers results in office changes such as new furniture, equipment, and location changes.

Many of these can also be motivated by external factors, such as meeting product or service demand. Still, if the change is implemented due to significant research and before the need for the change becomes a negative business element, it is proactive and constructive.

External change is prompted by the following:

Competitors may have made beneficial improvements to their methods or enhanced their products/services, negatively affecting your firm.

The enactment of new legislation or the discovery of recent legislation requires a significant shift in how your products or services are marketed or distributed. For instance, many years ago, the government enacted new legislation imposing stringent restrictions on tobacco product promotion and packaging.

Market trends are constantly changing. For instance, individuals are considerably more health-conscious than they have ever been. This has had a significant (good) impact on various enterprises.

Numerous adjustments are pushed upon us by these external forces. If they were foreseen, researched, and addressed before having a detrimental effect on us, we were being proactive. If these adjustments are not foreseen, researched, and implemented, we will make them out of necessity or because everyone else is doing so, which is reactive. Reacting (post-hoc) to a market-driven change can be costly and unpleasant, as it typically leaves little time for retooling, communicating with consumers and personnel, and so on.

Management of Change

Managing change entails taking a methodical, well-researched, and well-thought-out strategy to integrate anything new into your organization. Consider the following while contemplating a change:

Where are you now?

We want to know what your long-term goals are.

How will you get there?

Thus, properly managing change is about

Take a good look at your current situation;

1. Your operating procedures

    Customer satisfaction levels with your products/services

    Your sales volume and profit margins determine your competitiveness.

    your productivity and effectiveness, for example

2. Determining what about your existing condition is ineffective or unsatisfactory and what has to be altered to make it more effective.

3. Determining the actions necessary to transition from the current, unsatisfactory state to the future, more efficient, and profitable state.

Much of this involves addressing issues with coworkers and eliciting their input and support. The benefits and drawbacks of making the change (or not making the change) should be reviewed with relevant staff members, as should the repercussions of each action be performed. This is critical because it can be difficult to stop or reverse direction once the ball begins rolling and things get started. Thus, it pays to be certain of your actions and that:

After consulting with and soliciting input from relevant workers, identified concerns are worked out and resolved for the change to be implemented smoothly.

Participants in innovation and change projects should ideally be drawn from a cross-section of the company's divisions, emphasizing personnel relevant to the project. Who is chosen from each department will be determined by their track record, their capacity to be open-minded and fair-minded, their ability to keep the project going forward, and their ability to convey new processes and procedures to their coworkers?

Because no two people will perceive an issue, a change, or a project identically, there is a possibility for disagreement and conflict. Keeping this in mind, management should pick a small number of employees from various departments to assist with the transformation process. This ensures the following:

All key sectors of the business influence the entire process.

Confusion is prevented by having an excessive number of opinions.

Why is Change Management Required?

Each modification made in the workplace is unique.

Certain modifications can be quite subtle, for instance:

Changing the wording or structure of a business is distinct from purchasing a new fax machine for the office.

appointing a new employee

Certain adjustments can be substantial and difficult.

Restructure of a department, or the entire company\sadding a new product or service\supgrading the company's computer or telephone systems.

Whether the change is modest or substantial, the transition from old to new will go more smoothly if the change is thoroughly researched and handled.

The goal of change management is to maximize organizational performance with the least amount of disturbance possible. It assists you in the following ways:

maintain a laser-like focus on the pertinent issues

avert any potential pitfalls along the way

Reduce employee resistance to necessary changes; increase productivity and efficiency, and plan a path toward a seamless transition.

Identify critical communication and training concerns

Modalities of change

It is critical to determine which modifications should be made and why. After all, as the adage goes, 'if it ain't broke, don't fix it!' Consider well-known product brands such as McDonald's or Coke. These brands have been established for a long period and are easily recognizable worldwide. How have they remained profitable for so long while so many other businesses have failed? They've got their pulse on the market need and have made the required adjustments.

Proactive management of why, when, and how an organization should change can be accomplished in a variety of methods, including the following:

Conducting regular research.

This is something that every firm should do annually;

keep abreast of customer demands

evaluate their efficacy evaluate their profitability

contrast themselves with their rivals

Numerous types of research exist. Two primary categories of research are as follows:

Conduct primary research.

This is information that you have obtained for yourself. You can accomplish this by;

They are obtaining survey responses from customers and personnel. These can be paper forms with a series of questions that clients or workers can complete while in your business or mailed to their homes. The questions you ask will vary from survey to survey and will be determined by the purpose of the survey.

We are inviting clients or employees to 'Focus' sessions.

This is where small groups of staff or customers meet with you (maybe over snacks and beverages) to discuss various business-related topics.

Some samples of the questions you might be asked are shown below. You could ask in your survey or focus session:

Should you continue to provide a particular product (even if revenues are declining)?

Is it time to launch a new product or service?

Are your clients and employees satisfied with specific parts of your business?

What do you excel at?

What could you improve upon?

Secondary Sources.

Secondary research is information that an individual or organization has obtained outside of yours. Secondary sources of information include the following:

Local government authorities Australian Bureau of Statistics Industry associations

Chamber of Commerce on the Internet, etc.

These sources can provide you with the following kind of information:

Demographic information about the neighborhood, such as the average age and gender of people, their employment, where they shop, and the average household income per resident, among other things.

Economic trends include the most recent job numbers, retail sales figures, etc.

governmental issues

Analyses of business.

Another way to ascertain the potential for change is to do a SWOT Analysis of your organization. SWOT is an acronym.

The areas in which your organization excels are called its strengths! They are areas where you can strengthen them and may just require modest changes.

Weaknesses; These are areas in which your organization should improve. They are vulnerable points of attack for your competition (pointing out your weaknesses to potential customers). Weaknesses should be considered as areas for growth. Once identified, a weakness can be addressed to overcome it and possibly be transformed into a strength. This is where your research will be critical;

What is the flaw?

Why is it there?

What are your options for overcoming it?

Opportunities; Thorough research and an in-depth grasp of your company environment will reveal opportunities for your organization. Typical areas of opportunity include the following:

New economic, social, or cultural developments create new commercial opportunities.

New government legislation may enable new possibilities.

New technology may boost your market reach and efficacy, among other benefits.

Threats; A threat is anything in your business environment that prevents you from accomplishing your objectives. Examples include the following:

A new competitor, a new regulation that affects your current methods of operation, a new technology that everyone else has but you...

A SWOT Analysis enables you to examine your organization in detail and provide an accurate picture of what, if anything, needs to be altered.

The issue requires resolution. Within an organization, problems can be extremely visible or concealed beneath the surface (and we've simply always tolerated them). They frequently become apparent only during your organization's analysis. After identifying the issue, something must be done to resolve it. Issues may arise;

have an effect on productivity

drive away customers

Expenses associated with personnel removal are incurred.

incur legal repercussions or penalties

Then the process of change planning begins;

What is the precise nature of the issue?

What is the source of the issue?

What needs to happen to improve it?

Dissemination of Change

After conducting all necessary research to determine what changes should be made, involving appropriate staff to discuss what should be done and how it should be done, resolving any implementation process issues, and so forth, you now need to inform the rest of the organization's staff of the upcoming changes.

You will require the following:

Describe the procedure. How did the need for change arise? Who was responsible for the planning? How were decisions made—and lastly, what is the plan?

What will the new procedures entail?

Which training will be provided to staff

What timeframes will the change be implemented?

How the implementation affects the everyday work routines of everyone, and so forth.

It is critical to be candid about your ups and downs. Given the possibility of difficult times ahead, it's vital to inform people in advance and address any concerns or questions they may have. Make the plan simple to comprehend by being concise and straightforward.

Among the possible modes of communication are the following:

Workforce information sessions in which supervisors or managers present to the entire staff—may incorporate slides and diagrams—and then allow staff to ask questions.

Papers explain the new processes and outline the specific roles of each department.

Weekly departmental meetings—Many businesses hold weekly meetings to handle broad business topics. They are an excellent platform for informing employees about new practices.

If done wisely, organizational changes can be implemented with minimal disruption and resistance while also providing a more stable and secure foundation for the company's future.

Intolerance of change.

A frequent error managers make when implementing change is to assume that the change will always be evaluated objectively and rationally. However, the truth is that change is an emotive subject for most individuals, and while they may feel apathetic toward it, they seldom experience no emotional response at all.

This is because transition entails two highly charged emotional events:

a conclusion and a commencement

An ending indicates that some aspect of your life, the way you've conducted yourself, is about to end. You are about to be yanked from your comfort zone and thrown into a strange setting, which may be better. As a result, it frequently inspires fear of the unknown, as evidenced by the following:

Will I be able to do these new tasks properly?

What will happen if I am unable to complete this task?

A beginning implies the necessity of progressing to something new. This is frequently upsetting, as it implies (ideally) fresh training and a period during which you are not quite as confident in yourself as you were previously. This damages your self-esteem and may result in unfavorable emotions.

Why are individuals so resistant to change?

The majority of people will resist change for the following reasons:

They fear losing their jobs; they do not understand the necessity of the change; they believe it will demote their position; others attempt to tell them what to do and how to live their lives; others act superior to them and make them feel insignificant; they do not trust their management; they have not been consulted about the change and its processes.

Intuitive Emotional Intelligence

Emotions can act as a delicate and sophisticated internal guidance system for an individual. Your emotional response to anything will dictate your physical and mental response to it. Emotions provide significant information and aid in decision-making. When you are uneasy about a scenario or a person, your emotions alert you and cause you to be careful, and so on.

We all have fundamental emotional needs, such as the desire to be respected and accepted. We require serious consideration. When our emotional needs are not satisfied in the workplace, we feel uneasy.

When decisions about our immediate work environment are made without consulting or informing us in advance, we become upset and resentful. While the intensity of these emotions varies from person to person—one individual may feel much more strongly about an issue than another—they all must be considered when considering big changes to a personal or professional situation.

Consequences emotionally

Feelings of being mistreated, ignored, or rejected, among other things, can have severely harmful consequences. In the worst-case scenario, the initial emotion experienced in response to a circumstance might develop into anger, resentment, bitterness, sentiments of vengeance, and the impulse to take negative action.

While management can't consult with every employee, they must keep staff informed of organizational happenings and promote recommendations.

In this manner

All employees are treated with respect. Employees are informed of concerns affecting their work area. Employees can contribute to the process by giving useful suggestions. Management can then go forward with their plans more positively.

There will always be those dissatisfied with the changes being implemented, but this is a part of human nature that must be embraced.

How you can make a difference in terms of change and innovation.

To actively contribute to change, everyone must understand the realities of change:

The change will wreak havoc on the way you currently work.

Changes may take a long time—possibly longer than initially anticipated—and will not resolve all current issues. In the short term, they may create more—until things have settled, it is normal to be concerned about proposed changes and to have some doubts there will be hiccups and glitches, and you may go off track sometimes.

Accepting that there will be hardships, the important thing is to contribute to the changes actively, strive for exceptional outcomes, be flexible and tolerant and always keep the desired outcome in mind.

Make suggestions without fear. If you can see a need for improvement or know a better way of doing a job, you should feel free to say so.

assist in communicating the change, helping others in the workplace understand the meaning of the proposed change, help with the change transition, seek and give input, offer general support

To summarize

Change entails having to perform things differently than you are accustomed to.

To implement change effectively, you must first assess the need for change, conduct research on what needs to be done, design the change process, implement the change, and evaluate the change's efficacy.

Complaints about how things are currently going are the first step in the process of change.

Changes might be motivated by internal factors such as new equipment, products, or systems, or external factors such as competitor-driven changes, government laws, or market trends.

Effective change management requires a) an assessment of where you are now, b) a determination of where you want to be, and c) a strategy for getting from a to b with the least amount of stress, resistance, and loss of business.

Change can occur for various reasons, including market trends, the need to tackle persistent problems, and a change in management or ownership.

People resist change out of concern that they will be unable to cope with the new procedures, protect their jobs, or just do not comprehend what is happening.

To contribute to change and innovation, you must assist in conveying the changes to other staff members, assist others in comprehending why the change is required and what it entails for them, and provide support and assistance where appropriate.

STEPS TO CREATE AN INNOVATION CULTURE

Effective leaders have a significant impact on the creation of innovation and opportunity. Their quest for new ways to improve and build the organization carries them well beyond the established structures, methods, and concepts. In today's fast-paced market environment, it is vital to enable members to experiment with new ways and ideas. This fosters the invention, creativity, and opportunity necessary for change.

The forces of change originate both within and outside the company: customers drive demand for product and service innovation; process innovation, on the other hand, typically originates within the organization and via its employee members. To accomplish good change and incremental transformations, specific variables are required to generate innovation—a desire to depart from established practices.

A critical aspect of the leader's position is fostering innovation and creativity, resulting in incremental improvements to the goods, services, and overall business quality. This is required to address the needs of both external and internal customers. This is accomplished by creating an empowering atmosphere that fosters and reinforces creativity.

To foster a climate that fosters complete empowerment of its members, leaders must continually influence others while maintaining open lines of communication across units, divisions, and higher management. Leaders recognize that frontline personnel is the finest resource for developing more efficient processes, generating innovative ideas and concepts for quality improvement, and executing the best solutions to solve inefficiencies.

When employees actively develop new ideas, processes, services, and products, creative innovations, new ideas, processes, services, and product improvements flow consistently within and beyond the organization. Whether this state is realized successfully is contingent upon leaders recognizing the characteristics that foster creativity, resourcefulness, and risk-taking in their workforce.

Three criteria define an environment that fosters innovation, creativity, and risk-taking. The construction of this ecosystem successfully requires leaders to raise awareness of these aspects. They include the following:

Experimentation and Dissolving Constraints

By nature, leaders are experimenters. However, they must inspire in staff a drive to experiment with novel ways to old issues and embrace the challenge of trial and error. Throughout this process, leaders actively assist people in overcoming barriers to creativity and innovation by identifying and dismantling self-imposed limitations on personal views, thinking habits, and patterns.

Observation and Insight

Because innovation depends on novel ideas, the majority of which originate outside of traditional thinking, creativity in an empowered environment primarily relies on what is referred to as "outsight." The capacity to comprehend external reality is referred to as outsight. It is the pre-requisite for insight, or the capacity to perceive the inner nature of things. Through openness and flexibility, one can develop an awareness and knowledge of outsight influences. It is up to leaders to expand employees' horizons and expose them to a greater range of events, challenges, and concerns.

Creating a 'Difficulty Factor'

Uncertainty and risk are costs of innovation that both leaders and people must pay. While leaders often thrive on unpredictability and risk, employees frequently have a different perspective. To combat uncertainty in these two domains, the question arises, "How do individuals inside the organizational unit learn to accept the unavoidable failures and associated stress associated with creative innovation and its circumstances?" The answer is found in developing a sense of grit and resilience.

When a healthy feeling of toughness emerges, it is manifested in actions and beliefs that reflect the sentiment that "uncertainty and danger are more exciting than fear." Employees understand they directly impact specific results, inspiring rather than intimidating them. Uncertainty and risk are viewed as opportunities by them.

WORKPLACE CULTURAL INTELLIGENCE

The internet and technological advancements in speedier forms of transportation have effectively transformed the world into a global village. With the press of a mouse, it is now feasible to converse across borders. Video conferencing, short message services, and email have created an instantaneous atmosphere where information may be transferred.

We have entered a previously unexplored world of human endeavor and existence in the light of this scenario. You can now communicate with someone in the remote reaches of the world from the comfort of your office or home. Additionally, many businesses and organizations are now welcoming international talent to join their ranks and contribute to attaining their objectives.

When you operate in such a culturally diverse setting, it's easy to lose sight that the people with whom you communicate have unique viewpoints and perceptions. As a result, you must develop a sense of cultural intelligence to learn how to interact productively with people from diverse cultural backgrounds.

When Howard Gardner published his seminal book "Multiple Intelligence" in the 1970s, he identified seven fundamental bits of intelligence that all humans have the potential to possess. Gardner isn't ruling anything out that further forms of intelligence have yet to be discovered. Cultural intelligence appears to be an apt addition to today's list of human intelligence in this setting.

As with many other types of intelligence, our cultural intelligence may be developed and enhanced. This will enable us to develop greater sensitivity and empathy for persons from diverse cultural backgrounds with whom we may have to interact. Additionally, as Helen Keller states, "the highest outcome of education is tolerance." Increasing your cultural intelligence will also increase your tolerance enormously.

You can increase your cultural intelligence by cultivating the following characteristics.

1. Confronting Stereotypes

It is a basic human tendency to categorize people. While stereotyping can be useful in providing a person's profile, it is also harmful because it can lead to unwarranted and hurtful generalizations. Individuals from other cultural backgrounds have their own beliefs and customs, which may contradict our own. The greatest thing to do is sympathize with the individual and judge them on their own merits rather than from a cultural standpoint.

2. Acknowledgement and Acceptance

The following step in cultivating cultural intelligence is to instill a sense of awareness and acceptance. By cultivating awareness, we can develop an appreciation for the behaviors and activities of people from other cultures. Acceptance of their methods demonstrates our sympathy for who they are and how we perceive them.

Bear in mind that your attitude toward someone from a different culture reflects how that individual perceives you. Take note that your ability to tolerate the cultures of others will invariably increase your level of compassion, which is a necessary component of developing cultural intelligence.

3. Acquire knowledge

We speak of education as a necessary component of our existence. We spend most of our time developing new skills connected to our jobs. Additionally, soft skills such as motivation, stress management, and emotional intelligence are taught. Additionally, you should make an effort to learn about other people's cultures. Today, there is no excuse for being unable to do so, as knowledge is at your fingertips and accessible with a single mouse click.

The internet is an incredible repository of knowledge. Utilize it to understand some of the cultural behaviors associated with the various types of people you interact with. This way, you may come across some interesting points that are intrinsically useful.

4. Establish a Common Ground

Although some cultures are extremely distinct and dissimilar to your own, keep in mind that humans share some fundamental characteristics and are all members of the same large family. Thus, if you dive more into another culture, you may discover some practices that are similar to your own.

Identifying such common ground enables you to understand the other person better and break down communication barriers. You can practice finding common ground by attempting to converse with members of other cultures and getting to know them better. Avoid being judgmental of others' practices, as this will breed stereotypical images in your mind, creating psychological barriers to effective integration.

Acquiring cultural intelligence is a matter of mindset. Having a xenophobic attitude will accentuate your close-mindedness and inability to interact positively with people from other cultures. The more you learn to integrate and maintain your distinct sense of culture, the more effective you become as an individual.

Additionally, keep in mind the words of world-renowned anthropologist Margaret Mead, who stated, "If we are to achieve a richer culture, one that is rich in contrasting values, we must recognize the full range of human potentialities and thus weave a less arbitrary social fabric into which each diverse human gift will find a home."

CREATING A HEALTHY WORK CULTURE THROUGH THE USE OF THE BEST INDEPENDENT IDEAS

Innovation is critical for a business's top and bottom lines, but it also helps foster a healthy and productive work atmosphere. In this age of globalization and fierce rivalry, businesses have recognized that the only lasting competitive advantage they can have is via talent. This has made it critical to retain and develop staff. Today, it cannot be accomplished solely by issuing fat pay cheques, as someone else in the market may offer a larger paycheque.

Businesses are implementing innovative concepts in the office to foster an inspirational and encouraging work environment for their employees. This is the optimal method for developing and retaining personnel. The most innovative ideas do not demand a large financial investment but positively affect employee motivation and the development of healthy work culture.

An easy and inventive technique to foster a positive work environment is to host little office contests. A straightforward contest may determine which employee has the cleanest and most organized desk. In this manner, you may promote hygiene while motivating employees with a straightforward reward system.

Another possibility is to urge employees to come up with some new ideas in response to a particular problem in the office. Employees who submit the most unique and effective ideas may be compensated. This will foster a workplace culture of creativity and innovation. Additionally, it will demonstrate to employees that their opinions are appreciated and rewarded by the organization. This is the most effective technique to motivate and maintain employees' creative abilities.

Numerous businesses have used some unique concepts in the office to make it a more enjoyable place to work. Certain respected businesses permit employees to dress informally for work. In this manner, people feel comfortable in the workplace and are not constrained by excessive constraints. This fosters an atmosphere of independence in the workplace, enabling individuals to perform better.

Another unique approach businesses use to create the ideal workplace is redesigning the physical office space to make it more attractive and inviting. For example, Red Bull's London office was designed to create a cutting-edge workplace that mixes pleasure and work. It features table tennis courts, slides, a recreational area for employees, and a roof-top conference space. In an environment like that, who wouldn't want to work there? There is no shortage of excellent inventive ideas for creating welcoming workplaces; all that is required is leadership initiative.

DIVERSITY IN THE WORKPLACE— THE IMPORTANCE OF DIVERSITY IN THE WORKPLACE

Since Thomas Cook's late-nineteenth-century advent of mass transit, the world's inhabitants have taken advantage of the ability to travel the globe. Since then, our world has become a vastly more diverse place.—a rich cultural tapestry that permeates all areas of our lives.

It has expanded our horizons beyond imaging, broadening our perspective on the world around us and instilling a sense of worldliness that previous generations lacked. It has also introduced a new set of complications where cultural, social, and economic disparities, for example, might result in miscommunication.

Globalization means that people from varied cultures, religions, and backgrounds will interact more. People no longer live and work in a closed economy; they are now members of a competitive global economy on practically every continent. As a result, organizations should foster diversity to foster greater creativity and adaptability.

Recognizing social and cultural diversity and working to resolve cross-cultural misconceptions is critical. It is improbable that we will interact exclusively with others who share our nature, background, and ideals in our daily lives. We interact with a wide variety of people regularly.

They are our customers and colleagues, and if we are to interact harmoniously with them, we must recognize and accept their right to their own beliefs and customs and, where possible, make allowances for their differences and disabilities.

We've grown accustomed to accepting and even adopting certain cultural characteristics of the people we interact with. This is reflected in the food we eat, the style of furniture and houses we purchase, and the automobiles we drive. We are all familiar with certain cultural and national characteristics. For instance, the French are renowned for their fashion and cuisine.

Italians produce perhaps the best furniture, and their architecture is renowned worldwide, but German engineering is also renowned. The Japanese are renowned for their ingenuity, the Swiss are renowned for their timepieces, and the Belgians are renowned for their chocolate! Our world has evolved into one that values diversity.

How is cultural diversity defined?

To properly comprehend and appreciate the value of a socially varied workforce, it is necessary to first define the terms social and diverse in the workplace context.

Definitions from dictionaries:

Social—Encarta defines social in the following ways:

about society: about human society and its organization

about human interaction: about the way people behave and interact in groups while living in a community: residing in or preferring to reside in a community or colony rather than alone, allowing for interaction: allowing people to meet and interact in a friendly manner to promote human welfare: concerning human welfare and the organized welfare services provided by a community of prominence in society: about or deemed fitting for a social class, particularly the upper classes

Diverse—Encarta defines diverse as follows:

Composed of many elements: comprised of numerous distinct components that differ from one another: socially inclusive: extremely dissimilar or unique from one another: comprised of numerous ethnic, class, and gender categories

Thus, the term social refers to the way individuals interact with one another and the conditions in which we feel most at ease. The phrase 'diverse' refers to how people are unique. Cultural distinctions can include the following:

how people from other cultures address one another, the degree of formality or informality with which they are comfortable, their practices and beliefs

structure and values of the family ethics in the workplace

non-verbal communication—such as eye contact, hand gestures, and physical proximity.

personal upkeep, such as dress standards and hygiene, and involvement in the local community

Frequently, diversity extends to observing specific religious feasts or other festive days due to an individual's habits, beliefs, and values. These are all critical considerations when communicating in a diverse work environment.

Cultural Prejudices

Culture is multilayered; what you see on the surface may represent only a fraction of the numerous distinctions beneath the surface, so generalizations never address the entire picture. There is no substitute for developing personal relationships, exchanging experiences, and gradually becoming acquainted with individuals.

Additionally, culture is in a perpetual state of flux; as circumstances change, cultural groupings adapt in often surprising ways, and no cultural description of a single group can ever be put into words. Categorizing ethnic groupings in specific ways, such as "Italians think this way" or "Buddhists act this way," is impractical and can result in conflict.

As we mature and develop as individuals, we gain knowledge about different cultures through direct contact with diverse cultural groups, information and perceptions from others, books, news, newspapers, and other mass media.

These encounters may result in misconceptions about other cultures or a specific cultural group. These assumptions can distort our perceptions of other cultures and are referred to as cultural prejudice. Culturally biased assumptions can be classified into two types:

Generalizations about people who are not of your ethnic origin. For instance, 'They are not comparable to us.'

A set of preconceived notions about a certain cultural group. For instance, 'Indians eat curry exclusively' or "All Dutch are stubborn."

Both of these categories affect the quality of communication and may result in ineffective work practices. When interacting with culturally diverse populations, biased assumptions result in views that can impair your objectivity. The following are the consequences:

Stigma

Stereotyping\Discrimination

Stigma refers to the social rejection of other cultural groups' personal qualities or beliefs. Stigma is frequently motivated by ignorance, illogical or baseless worries, mass panic, a lack of education, or a lack of information about a specific person or group. For instance, thirty years ago, being a single mother was stigmatized. The AIDS virus established a stigma for the LGBT community, and mental health problems can still be stigmatized today.

Stereotyping is the practice of forming assumptions about an individual's qualities based on a widely held idea about the individual's cultural background. Individuals frequently use stereotypes to describe members of a certain cultural group. For instance, "All French people are impolite and inconsiderate," or "All Germans are arrogant." While persons belonging to these nationalities may be unpleasant, discourteous, or arrogant, this is equally true of individuals belonging to any nation, not just those belonging to these nationalities.

The phrase is frequently used negatively, as stereotypes can be used to denigrate individuals based on their membership in a certain group. Stereotypes frequently serve as the foundation for discrimination since they are frequently used to explain real or imagined disparities in race, gender, religion, age, weight, ethnic origin, socioeconomic class, handicap, and occupation.

In a cultural setting, discrimination refers to expressing prejudice toward a certain group. Discrimination is frequently characterized by the unfair categorization and treatment of others and is motivated by stigma and stereotypes.

These are the most common effects; you could undoubtedly add others to the list. Within a workplace, these adverse outcomes may include the following:

Clients and coworkers from diverse cultural backgrounds harbor anger. If a worker believes that all refugees or asylum seekers are 'queue jumpers,' their attitude toward a refugee client may be less empathetic than a person who appreciates the stress and grief endured by refugees forced to escape their nation.

Inadequate service to consumers; lack of information about their wants due to stereotyped ideas about the client's ability to understand or communicate their wishes; or misinterpretation of the client's behavior as normal or abnormal.

Inability to respond appropriately to persons in distress. A heartbreaking example of this erroneous assumption occurred in 2006 at a Brisbane bus stop. Passengers and passers-by ignored and left an Aboriginal university guest speaker in a diabetic coma unattended for several hours, assuming she was intoxicated.

While race should not be an issue, the regrettable reality is that it frequently is. You will interact with colleagues and consumers from other cultures throughout your career. As a result, it is prudent to understand their cultural background to collaborate with them successfully and peacefully. In some instances, certain individuals' races (or nations) share specific characteristics with a large proportion of their members. For instance:

Australians are often thought to have a 'lax' attitude and can deal with many situations without being very offended. This frequently results in a lack of understanding when people from other cultures do not behave similarly. Australians frequently possess an innate sense of humor and mateship and prefer informality in their daily interactions with others.

Americans, like Australians, have a friendly, laid-back attitude—albeit they are perceived to be a little more conservative. Around 10% of Americans possess a passport. As a result, their worldview is relatively secluded. They are accustomed to receiving good customer service at home. When people travel abroad, they frequently expect American standards and services and are surprised to discover that this is not the case.

Germans are regarded as extremely exact, tidy, and have a strong work ethic. For instance, if you inform a German that the documents you are preparing for them will be available for collection at a specific time, they will anticipate them to be available at that time and maybe perplexed if they are not. This may drive individuals to act in an abrupt and occasionally demanding manner. Additionally, they are extremely formal in their interactions with others.

Unless you are acquainted with them, or they have taken a less rigorous approach on their own, a formal address is required. Germans who have known one another for many years continue to address their formal titles—'Good morning, Mr.

Schmitt' or 'How is your mother doing, Mrs. Schultz?' As a result, individuals often do not appreciate being addressed by strangers or being excessively familiar with their first names.

Additionally, the Japanese are believed to have a high work ethic and a strong belief in order and structure. They are team players, possess a strong sense of honor, and are acutely aware of the importance of projecting the proper image. They can easily be embarrassed in social situations by harsh or discourteous behavior and may politely but firmly stop their communication channels.

Additionally, they are rather formal in their interactions with others. Whereas in Australia, we feel that effective communication requires maintaining eye contact, excessive eye contact is regarded as gazing and impolite in Japan.

Additionally, certain civilizations have a unique manner of dealing with time. Certain cultures have a relatively casual attitude toward time and punctuality, while others are more rigid in their approach to time management. This frequently results in tension when one individual is adamant about being on time while another takes punctuality lightly and frequently arrives late for work or meetings.

Diverse ethnic groups can also exert a significant amount of influence on the surrounding community;

The variety of meals available to us, the cultural festivities held in the area, and much more.

Individuals of other races and cultures have a great deal to contribute. By interacting positively with them and attempting to understand them, we can learn about various cultures and customs, widen our perspective on life, and build our personal 'database' of knowledge. You cannot know everything; thus, polite behavior is universal when in doubt!

The intrinsic worth of cultural diversity

We've looked at some of the differences between people. However, why is this significant?

The majority of people's working lives in today's world involve frequent contact with people from all walks of life and from every part of the globe. We live in a time of unprecedented social variety. If we do not acknowledge and accept the cultural differences between people, we risk creating workplace discord and distrust. Additionally, we risk losing out on personal and team development opportunities.

Diversification has great significance in business. Through a broader basis of knowledge and experience, it can enhance teamwork, performance, and customer service. A multicultural workforce is more creative and adaptable. It exposes clients and coworkers to novel ideas, alternative methods of functioning, and decision-making. Learning from clients and coworkers from diverse backgrounds also broadens and improves our horizons and knowledge base, making us more efficient and accepting as humans.

When employees come from various backgrounds, they bring unique talents and experiences. This invariably leads to the general growth of an organization. Accepting individuals with a variety of skills and cultural perspectives enables a better grasp of the demands and wants of global consumers. Diversity in the workplace fosters a rich diversity of perspectives and business ideas. Its diverse pool of ideas and solutions enables a firm to develop the finest business plan.

Thus, the benefits of workplace diversity may include the following:

Creativity increases when people with disparate approaches to solving challenging problems collaborate to find a common solution. There is no single best answer to every subject; the more ideas you can collect from many sources, the more likely you will produce a suitable solution. Other cultures can provide you with enlightening possibilities that you may not have considered. This is a significant advantage of workplace diversity.

When people of many cultures work cooperatively toward a common motivating goal, productivity increases.

Language abilities are unquestionably necessary for today's global economy—and varied workers frequently possess them. To fully connect with the rest of the world's inhabitants, it helps to speak their language.

It is critical to understand how our country fits into the global picture. By developing relationships with people from other backgrounds, we will better understand how different cultures work and, as a result, achieve greater success in both the community and global business.

When people with disparate ideas combine, novel processes might emerge. It is no longer acceptable to believe that "we have always done things this way and cannot change in today's fast-paced society." Workers must bring a variety of abilities to the workplace, be able to think cross-culturally, and swiftly adapt to new situations.

Diverse workplaces can boost an organization's productivity and profitability. They also bring differences that must be acknowledged and embraced to realize those benefits.

Adapting the workplace

Individuals from culturally diverse backgrounds can contribute enormously to an organization's strength. Their abilities, capabilities, expertise, and relationships can help build staff confidence and enhance client service. To accomplish this, the organization must ensure that work practices consider the needs of diverse clients and employees and provide training and encouragement to employees. Culturally sensitive practices in the workplace may include the following:

The gathering and dissemination of information in a manner that is accessible to staff and customers of all backgrounds through the use of communication methods that are appropriate for a diverse workforce. This may include Braille photographs or diagrams to illustrate operations rather than text.

Translation of critical personnel/procedural manuals into additional languages and more.

Equal opportunities for employment and promotion

assistance with specific staff or customer requirements

provision of food services (in locations where a canteen is available) take cultural and medical dietary restrictions into account.

Occupational health and safety—ensuring that adequate induction and continuous training occur in a manner inclusive of a varied workforce. This may also involve the provision of disability ramps and access to restrooms.

Interpreter services are necessary since the ability to communicate and comprehend English can also affect an individual's capacity to progress within an organization in terms of processes and promotion opportunities.

Changing work practices

Work procedures may sometimes need to be altered to facilitate effective interaction with culturally diverse clients or coworkers. To determine the culturally appropriate service standards, you will need to consult with those who have a specific understanding of the cultures represented in your workplace and client base.

Conflicts between cultures

There is a part of us all that of at least one cultural subculture. The group we belong to may be determined by our country of birth, religion, physical limitations (e.g., deafness), economic status in the community, or a variety of other criteria. When the cultural groups to which we belong constitute a sizable majority in our community, we are less likely to be aware of everyday issues.

It's not uncommon for dominant groups' cultures to be taken for granted as "natural," "normal," or simply "how things are done." We are only aware of "cultures" impact in our neighborhood if they are very different from ours.

When looking at why things go wrong between people of diverse backgrounds, it is important to bear in mind the basics of human nature—that we all want to fulfill our own needs and desires in ways familiar to us. If this does not happen, conflict is inevitable. Conflict develops because we deal with people's lives, children, pride, self-concept, ego, etc.

Although inevitable, misunderstandings can be minimized and resolved by recognizing the early conflict indicators. But first, we need to grasp why disputes can and do occur.

Recognizing indications of cross-cultural misunderstanding

To preserve a healthy and harmonious workplace, we must learn to spot the signals of impending conflict and seek to redirect or resolve any concerns before they become significant issues. Conflicts and misunderstandings can emerge when two people with opposing beliefs believe they have the best viewpoint. The conflict can devolve into one of ego or regaining control.

It can also occur when individuals or organizations cannot obtain what they require or desire and act in their self-interest. Occasionally, the individual is unaware of the urge and begins acting out unconsciously.

At other times, the individual is acutely aware of their desire and strives aggressively to achieve it. Regardless of the scenario, the primary source of conflict is a misunderstanding. These misunderstandings can emerge due to several of the previously listed concerns. For instance:

Race, culture, and religion are all intertwined. Cultural influences and identities can be extremely significant to individuals depending on the circumstance. When a component of cultural identity is challenged or misinterpreted, it can escalate into a point of contention between cultural groups.

This could result in unfavorable working circumstances. In these instances, it is beneficial for the parties to the argument to speak calmly to one another, perhaps with the assistance of a mediator, to help them understand one another's perspectives and discover constructive ways forward.

Age. The 'generation gap' can result in tensions between age groups. Older generations believe that younger generations are irresponsible, and younger generations believe that the older generation does not understand them or their struggles.

Structure of the family. The influence of migration on family structures and how immigrants from other nations integrate into our communities has been significant. Family patterns evolve as each generation matures.

For instance, first-generation migrants will undoubtedly bring their homeland's traditions and customs with them, whereas second-generation migrants may have departed somewhat from the traditional methods. By the third generation, the home nation has become Australia, and many of the old traditions have been forgotten, which may result in friction between family groupings or between generations at work.

Disabilities, either physical or mental. Individuals who are deaf, blind, or have a chronic illness or condition face unique challenges and can significantly benefit from the understanding of coworkers. Because members of these groups do not usually 'publicize' their condition, it might be difficult to determine why conflict occurs.

Disputes and misunderstandings

To overcome conflict, it is vital to work for the group's benefit rather than for the benefit of individual members. This requires effective communication abilities (covered in chapter three). Among the steps that can be taken to assist in resolving a conflict are the following:

Begin by developing rapport. This can be accomplished by exhibiting an openness to listen and by being candid and forthright about issues.

Establish objectives for resolving the problem and establish a schedule for frequent communication until the matter is resolved to everyone's satisfaction.

Avoid making snap judgments. Allow the other person to speak without interfering or forcing your thoughts or opinions.

Keep an eye out for the other person's body language. They may be saying what they believe you want to hear, but they are not feeling that way. Observing non-verbal cues can provide valuable insight into what someone is truly thinking and experiencing, independent of their cultural background or linguistic considerations. Likewise, you should be conscious of your body language, ensuring that you provide favorable signals.

Remember that the goal here is to resolve the issue, and if you believe that certain points are being omitted, you will need to draw them out. How can you mend something if you don't know what's wrong?

Disagreements of opinion and culture should be discussed freely and gently, emphasizing the need to resolve the issue and achieve an understanding.

Maintain adherence to the facts and not allow emotions to cloud your judgment. Allowing emotions to surface frequently causes the communication process to break down as tempers flare and grow irritated. Keep in mind that everyone is unique! In their view, all feelings and beliefs that a person possesses or feels are valid. They have a reason for their emotions. These arguments may not be favorable to your way of thinking, but they are valid to the other person.

At all times, maintain a calm demeanor. If the other person is emotional or aggressive, you must display maturity and calmness to re-direct the dialogue. Shouting or acting aggressively will only exacerbate the problem.

Avoid blaming others. Determining who is correct or incorrect or at fault is not the goal of dispute resolution. There is an issue, and you are attempting to find a acceptable solution to all parties involved. Identifying a perpetrator will not resolve the matter.

Consider the following: 'I recognize that your principal worry is..., but what else can you tell me?' By posing this type of question, you can elicit any leftover concerns a person may have. Subsequently, ask clarifying questions. For instance, 'So what you're saying is that you're dissatisfied with your position in the accounting department and wish to be transferred to administration...is that correct?' In this manner, you will gain a thorough understanding of the issue(s) at hand.

Verify that nothing has been left unsaid. Even minor issues that are not addressed or resolved adequately can persist and resurface without warning. Therefore, an issue that you believed was handled is not! Inquire to ascertain. For instance: 'Based on what I've heard, I feel the primary source of your concern is what we've just discussed. How do you feel about the problem now that we've discussed it with you?' This way, we may ascertain whether the other party is satisfied with the resolution or if there are any outstanding issues.

If necessary, bring in an interpreter or a neutral third party to referee the debate. This should ensure that the problem is discussed civilized and peaceful. Additionally, this third party could identify areas where a compromise might be achievable.

Keep in mind that the discussion's final goal should always be to develop (or re-establish) a happy working relationship.

Show kindness and respect to the other person by enabling them to explain their case objectively.

Once again, you aim for a collaborative connection oriented around the common good. This collaborative relationship fosters a joyful and healthy work environment conducive to customer service.

In the event that nothing else works, you may need to try something new with alternative communication channels. These may include the following:

Nonverbal communication. Utilizing sign language and gestures and exhibiting or demonstrating what you're looking for.

Colleagues who may be conversant in the customer's native tongue. You may have friends or relatives who can communicate in another language and assist you if you contact them.

External organizations, such as:

diplomatic services, interpreter services

Cultural organizations on a local level, appropriate government authorities, educational institutions, and disability advocacy organizations.

COLLABORATION IN THE WORKPLACE—TEAMWORK'S DNA

The Web 2.0 revolution revolutionizes information sharing by enabling individuals, businesses, and communities to connect and share resources, ideas, and solutions in ways never seen before. Collaboration is the new critical capability for company success.

The DNA of team development fosters a work culture that values and encourages collaboration. As Ken Blanchard discovered in One Minute Manager, in a collaboration environment, employees understand and believe that thinking, planning, decision-making, and action are all improved when done together. The concept that "none of us is as good as all of us" is recognized and assimilated by people.

In America, many of our institutions, including schools, family structures, and pastimes, continue to place a premium on winning, being the greatest, and emerging victorious. Teamwork-oriented workplaces are not yet the norm.

On the other hand, organizations attempt to value diverse individuals, ideas, backgrounds, and experiences. Collaboration, co-creation, and cooperation appear to be qualities that are more readily adopted and supported in organizational development due to the worldwide social transformation.

After consulting with numerous senior managers, educators, and organizational leaders over the last 13 years, I've compiled my Ten Tips for Building Terrific Teams as a quick reference guide for cultivating successful teams, encouraging creativity and innovation, and achieving optimal results within your business or organization.

Ten Suggestions For Forming Terrific Teams

1. Communicate Expectations.

Team members must understand why they are collaborating and how their roles, functions, and outcomes contribute to the organization's overall success and the success of its clients and coworkers. As a leader, your ability to clearly explain the organization's overall vision, mission, and values will be the engine that propels the team forward.

2. Create a plan for team meetings that includes specific objectives.

Allow time for status updates, debate, brainstorming, and the development of action plans. It is especially advantageous if the meeting facilitator is trained in Cross-Cultural Awareness or Marshall Rosenberg's Non-Violent Communication methods.

These strategies can assist in maintaining a diverse team's cohesiveness and focus, encourage everyone's engagement, and readily diffuse and change stagnation. Innovation, creativity, and solutions are not born in a static atmosphere. Are relevant issues and misunderstandings brought to your team's attention and addressed appropriately?

3. Invite consultants and independent contractors to participate in brainstorming sessions.

One of the most common errors organizations makes is excluding consultants and independent contractors from staff meetings, project updates, and long-term goals and vision. You will get much more mileage out of your consultants if they are included in discussions and sessions that affect the direction and growth of your organization. Consultants are frequently natural networkers and possess an abundance of resources. They have the potential to be a significant factor in your organization's long-term success and expansion.

4. Foster an environment in which team members value the diversity of talent on the team, not just in terms of skill sets and areas of expertise, but also in the whole person. If the team is working on a lengthy project, consider investing in workplace Myers Briggs, DISC, or Enneagram training.

5. Establish a rewards or recognition program.

Giving public recognition on the company intranet, newsletter, staff meeting, or rewarding high-performers with gift certificates to a spa or event are a few low-cost, no-cost ways to acknowledge team members for a job well done.

6. Incorporate enjoyable and shared events into the organization's agenda.

Organize potluck lunches for the team and take them to a performance or cultural event. Host dinners at a local restaurant (including the families of your associates) or organize an outdoor activity such as hiking, biking, or even river rafting.

7. Promote collaborative leadership paradigms in your organization.

Reject old, hierarchical leadership approaches that stifle the human spirit and can result in division, distrust, and a competitive environment. Concentrate on cooperative team performance models. One approach to begin this transformation is to rotate facilitators at your weekly or monthly sessions. Another efficient method is to appoint co-managers to lead a project.

8. Provide opportunities for feedback-giving and feedback-receiving.

The Dalai Lama repeatedly underlined the need for dialogue and education and training opportunities during his recent US tour. How well-trained are you and your team in analyzing assumptions, active listening, clarifying, and other non-defensive communication models that enable you and your colleagues to communicate needs, be heard, and generate innovative solutions together and for one another?

9. Make materials available.

One of the surest ways to create chaos and undermine motivation, performance, and morale is to ask people to perform without the tools and resources necessary to generate results they can be proud of. Ascertain that everyone has the necessary information and tools, including healthy, ergonomic workspaces.

10. Establish a Green Team at your place of employment.

Assist your employees in increasing their understanding of energy conservation alternatives and the importance of contributing to a healthy, sustainable environment. Allowing people to assume leadership and accountability fosters enthusiasm. A green team can be extremely motivating for employees who want to make a positive difference in their workplace.

It requires collaboration to make the dream a reality!

ESTABLISHING WORKPLACE TRUST

Why is it vital to develop trust in the workplace, and how can this be achieved? Recent findings suggest that developing trust in the workplace boosts employees' level of productivity, creativity, happiness, and capacity. It fosters an environment where free communication thrives and encourages people to express their views.

When employees in a place of work feel comfortable and come together to discuss ideas, there is a better capacity for innovation within the firm. This maintains the firm alive and leading in the marketplace. Trust is the firm conviction in capacity, capability, and reliability.

Having confidence in another person is not easy, but it is a trait that should be fostered for the larger result to be obtained in the workplace. Co-workers having to rely on integrity, ability, and strength is vital to an organization's performance and a cornerstone of true company success.

In a work setting where trust exists, employees are more efficient and effective. They work better, harder, and feel good about their work. Trust is a perishable commodity; it is difficult to build but easy to destroy. Openness, comprehension, integrity, consistency, ability, and justice are critical components of developing trust in the workplace.

The best way to live your days. is to treat them like an open book; this is what it means to live a higher life. People will trust you if you live this way because you are transparent and have nothing to hide. Understanding other people's perspectives enable you to work together with others.

True personal integrity is one of those characteristics that should not be taken for granted. Maintain consistency in your words and actions; this will inspire your coworkers to contribute effectively to the firm's success.

Humans are the most difficult creatures to work with; therefore, always enhance your abilities to interact with them. Make an effort to treat others fairly, listen to them, and maintain a consistent pattern of behavior. Never forget that trust takes time to develop, so do your best to foster trust wherever you work.

Our trust in one another in the workplace affects how we operate and how we operate trust in the workplace. Trust is a result as well as a source of business traditions. It is critical in business dynamics since a workplace is comprised of individuals with varying backgrounds, and trust is the only thing that can fully unite them.

We make daily decisions based on trust, whether consciously or unintentionally. You may acquire the trust of others by being straightforward, humble, and truthful. Establishing trust in the workplace motivates employees to use their imagination, enthusiasm, and creativity.

Trust is vital to an organization's success. Office politics is a characteristic of an organization that lacks trust or distrust. Internal conflict, secret agendas, interminable meetings, gossip, and withholding of information are characteristics of this type of company. Trust in an organization pays dividends in effective synergy, increased production, and creativity. Always strive to build trust in the workplace!

METHODS FOR CREATING A GLAMOROUS WORKPLACE!

It is critical to attract and retain the brightest people in today's tough work climate. To accomplish this, you must be an 'employer of choice' that fosters an environment conducive to employment. Consider the following tips to help you recruit and retain top personnel while increasing your bottom line.

Purpose

1. Perception and Perception Clarity is the bedrock of any successful business. Businesses that explain their mission and purpose succinctly and frequently to their staff will develop a self-aware company culture. This personnel will then embody that mission in both words and behavior. This form of open communication fosters collaboration and directly affects productivity.

2. Values are critical. Once a vision has been developed, values can help guide the subsequent course of action. With enormous bailout failures, electronic and social media craze, and an average of 17 changes per minute, people are yearning for people and organizations deserving of their devotion and allegiance. Establish a values-driven corporation and watch employee morale rocket.

Passion

3. Work intelligently and with compassion. Doing something that they enjoy is a good thing. When enjoying it, their productivity and inventiveness are limitless. When individuals maintain a head/heart connection at work, they generate positive energy for themselves and their teams. They generate more, lead more effectively, and conclude the day with vigor!

4. Align individuals and positions. Most businesses' most common error is hiring or promoting qualified individuals and placing them in incompatible positions. It is critical to employ effective interviewing and evaluation techniques to match human capability to job needs. Integrate individuals' strengths and delegate their shortcomings.

Hiring the proper individuals is an art; it comes naturally when the company's mission, goal, and values are clear.

Power

5. Communicate effectively. Employees should not be required to make educated guesses about what is expected of them. Solicit their feedback and input. Employees who contribute to formulating choices or defining objectives are far more likely to enforce or attain them. Encourage buy-in and watch the performance and team spirit soar.

6. Cooperate. Cultivate a collaborative spirit throughout the organization. Businesses that designate parking for the CEO send a clear statement about who is in charge and whose voice truly matters. Employees who feel appreciated and connected will stay late to see the project through to completion.

7. Recognize and Embrace acknowledged, and affirmed Strengths will grow in depth and breadth. Capture and recognize individuals who are "doing it right." Concentrate on what you wish to achieve, not on what you despise. Bear in mind that most people learn through imitation; model what you desire rather than criticizing what you lack.

8. Assistance. Take Care of Yourself Supporting individuals during critical stages of their lives can yield significant returns in terms of loyalty and longevity. Truett Cathy, the proprietor of one of the country's top chicken restaurant chains, realizes that if he looks after his staff, they will look after his business. Employees that are content with their lives outside of work perform better at work. Encourage employees to live a fulfilling life.

Potential

9. Be receptive to change and conflict. It is critical to developing an atmosphere where change is discussed and the dispute is resolved openly and creatively. Employees are a reflection of management. Transform issues and obstacles into growth or re-design possibilities. Address issues and discuss them freely rather than issuing commands and solutions. Exclusion and secrecy shut down people; inclusion fosters creativity, ingenuity, and loyalty.

Plan

10. Make a Plan to Succeed. A well-defined vision involves a strategy for success. It might be a formal, written strategy plan or one that is frequently communicated verbally. The plan should be fluid and adaptable to the company's and wider environment's changing needs. A plan is necessary for moving forward with purpose and enthusiasm into a bright future.

Creating an engaging work environment where people want to show up each day is a natural outcome of firms that are clear about their purpose, foster enthusiasm, and enable their employees to reach their full potential. With purpose and ease, the transition from purpose to plan.

4

UNDERSTANDING AND OVERCOMING THE LEGACY MINDSET

We frequently assert that we must engage in a new attitude to effect significant behavioral changes. As a result, I'm presented with the question: What preconceived notions do we have about our relationship with work?

It's safe to argue that those of us with a few years of work experience have significantly influenced our growth through what are now increasingly outmoded leadership paradigms and mindsets. Even in the most innovative, forward-thinking businesses, much is rooted in the Industrial Age: Management is concerned with the work process, not the customers, the product, or the people, and efficiency is king.

People regard the firm as a source of labor, while the company sees them as a source of cash. Between these two, there is a stalemate, and through this tension, we come to some form of knowledge that enables us to survive and, ideally, accomplish something meaningful. This model may meet the bare minimum requirements, but it lacks inspiration and enthusiasm for all parties involved. I'm increasingly convinced that a far more elegant structure for work is conceivable now.

In many cases, there is an assumption or belief that individuals come to work, do their jobs, and then return home to live their lives. However, most of our lives, our daily hours, and most of our adult years, are spent at work!

Too frequently, there is a dichotomy between work and life, which dehumanizes work—and the office becomes a type of inauthentic place where we put on our what's-expected-of-me personas and make the best of it before escaping somewhere else for some much-needed "work-life balance."

Rather than that, what if we choose to make work a place where we bring our complete selves, where we live our lives and contribute to something more than ourselves?

Consider Roche. We have 100,000 people who spend their lives here (that is not an exaggeration); each person represents an incalculably valuable commitment of time, energy, creativity, and, ultimately, to life. That investment in life should not be lost on bureaucratic delays, hierarchical impediments, or role slicing into robot-sized bits.

When we begin with the assumption that everyone is an owner—that everyone can perceive a need or opportunity, consider it, and then act—we unleash something very powerful. A place where people may bring their ideas to the table. Their 'full selves to work, take ownership of their contributions, and find greater fulfillment through their work.

Why is the legacy mindset important?

What could prevent us from adopting a legacy mindset? In the 24-7 race that dominates our lives these days, we forget that what is important in life is a reminder of what is truly important. We desire more than just earning and consuming. We want to make a difference in our lives. Furthermore, in the lives of others. We aim to make a difference globally, not merely earn money. And to do so, we must redefine what it means to be successful.

While business leaders frequently focus exclusively on the bottom line, adopting a legacy-driven attitude positions you to take that quantum leap forward to fuel and sustain unrelenting progress for future generations.

One of the major paradigm-altering events in business and culture occurred due to a legacy-driven mindset. Businesses lament the scarcity of individuals capable of writing well and communicating in novel ways. However, in our short-term desire to believe that technology would fix all issues, we exaggerate the importance of the arts in our new digital society.

Yet the genius of the arts is that they enable individuals to think and speak differently—exactly what businesses need. Consider Steve Jobs, who was so taken with typography—and the way form followed function in such a beautiful and timeless manner—that he was on the verge of becoming a type designer. However, his ongoing passion for attractive and functional design found expression in the I-phone. He never lost sight of what inspired him.

What is so enticing about having a "legacy-driven" approach is that you are always prepared. And, in the fickle worlds of business and life, being so doggedly prepared enables you to meet luck daily. "Luck is what happens when preparation meets opportunity," Roman philosopher Seneca famously stated. People constantly refer to someone becoming an "overnight success" or reaping a windfall. Was Steve Jobs simply fortunate, or was he constantly prepared?

All substantial improvements in people's lives begin with a legacy-driven mindset. While many of us may not alter the world in the same way that Steve Jobs did, we all have a profound desire to impact others and make a lasting impression. Yes, we want to earn money, but we also want to make a difference.

Leave Your Legacy Within Individuals

What if you could change the world? Then leave your legacy in the hearts of others. Inspire people with your actions. When leaders embrace a legacy-driven approach, they leave something in their followers—and not simply for the sake of the followers. Do you want to have an impact on the world? Motivate individuals to motivate themselves. That is living your legacy authentically, continually renewed in others. Leaving people with possessions or information is insufficient. Leave people inspired.

Why Do Individuals "Undo" Their Legacies?

I'm often shocked when a firm or individual chooses to "undo" its past for instant wealth rather than the long-term success of a legacy-driven mentality. This is referred to as the candy-in-front-of-the-child syndrome. "I desire it now because I am capable of possessing it." That is the way children reason. Consider the case of Wells Fargo or Volkswagen. Alternatively, Google or Facebook.

What was Google's mission statement? Make no mistake—where did that go? However, we forgive their behavior because "they are large organizations with a bottom line and stockholders to please." However, what occurred? They had lost track of who they were and why they were there. A bottom-line driven by legacy is quite distinct from a ledger-driven bottom line. Which do you believe will last a hundred years? Any firm run by a human being will have the same qualities that a human being can undo.

How do you adopt this "Legacy-Driven mindset"? Decide what is important in your life. You are not required to complete it overnight. However, pause for a moment. Make a list if necessary. When I ask individuals what three things they would do if they could do anything in the world right now, their responses are always the same. And they're always taken aback when they receive an answer.

Your heart has already prioritized things, but your intellect is unaware. Occasionally, you must cut through the cacophony of noise and nonsense in your active mind to discover the truth that has always been there. Often, our emotions have already established the priority, but our minds just cannot—or will not—hear it.

The Four Ps's of Developing a "Legacy-Driven" Mentality

Another straightforward yet powerful method of thinking about the "Legacy-Driven" perspective is to employ what I refer to as the "4 P's!" These are the virtues of Passion, Pursuit, Humanity, and Peace.

Passion is what brings a smile to your face. What makes your eyes sparkle when you consider performing it. This enthusiasm is at the heart of living a "Legacy-Driven life."

Pursuit is how this passion becomes a reality.

Individuals exist. Make contact with them. Assemble with them. Remove the electronic obstacles that create a false reality of communication. Dance with people with whom you truly desire to dance. Additionally, do not be scared to dance in both directions. When others believe in your passion, it makes pursuing it infinitely more worthwhile.

Finding or cultivating inner peace is one of the most difficult actions in our insanely busy lives. It is conscious of one's humanity—and fully aware of one's existence. Take this modest step at the end of each day—it's a great way to wind down. Consider whether you performed a modest act of kindness that day.

Did you pause for a moment to contemplate the clouds? Do you take the time to listen to someone truly? Have you just come to a halt and ceased thinking for a moment? And if you did any or all of these things, congratulate yourself on a job well done that day. And if you didn't succeed, go to bed promising to try again tomorrow.

A legacy is not the end but the beginning of a new phase or chapter in your life. To succeed, you must first establish and assess your legacy at each stage of your life, whether professional or personal. In your drive to make a difference in the lives of others and yourself, you will learn how well this "Legacy-Driven" perspective fosters a far more robust sense of a life well lived while you are living it.

MINDSET DRIVEN BY
LEADERSHIP & LEGACY

We all want to be remembered, feel we've made a difference in the world, and leave our imprint on the future. For some, this can serve as a catalyst for great feats and amazing services to humanity, while for others, it serves as a method to make sense of their existence: "Yes, I was here. This is my contribution; this is why I hope my life was meaningful."

According to Webster's definition, a legacy is "something passed down, endowed, or transferred from one person to another, anything descendible that is transmitted, inherited, or received from a forefather."

As a leader, our leadership is not defined by the end of the road but by the moments shared, the actions performed, the contributions, inventions, and decisions made both in and out of the workplace, and the mistakes conquered throughout the many phases of your career.

We learn how to maintain a sustained impact and influence at each level of our careers. A moment in our leadership career that defines our legacy grows with each new experience and each time we inspire others to take a leap of faith alongside us. Thus, effective leadership is a process of reinvention—a continuous discovery that shapes one's thinking and aptitudes.

Consider this: If we were to retire from our current work area today, what legacy would we leave behind? What would other people define it as? Are we paying attention to feedback and how it might inform our next career phase and our ability to influence others?

How would you describe your legacy to others if you were to analyze the last decade of your career and its many stages? Would the same narrative remain true if someone else told the story? When it's difficult to define your legacy, that particular position likely had less significance and impact on your career; in many situations, it may have moved you backward in your leadership growth, necessitating an awakening and course correction to get your career moving again.

As leaders, we should devote sufficient time to considering our legacy—the imprint we will leave on the organization and the people we serve.

To aid in our long-term success as leaders and to keep us on track, the following five stages of the legacy building will define the relevance of our leadership:

1. Self-Identification and Values

We must understand and be intimately connected to who we are as individuals and leaders. What principles and beliefs shape your leadership style, behavior, and attitude? Do others understand who you truly are and what you stand for as a leader dedicated to advancing a healthier society? We must be perpetually on the lookout for our identity and value system and then connect them with those of the organization we serve.

2. Overarching Fundamental Principles

Once our identity and set of values have been established, how can we transform them into a set of guiding principles that people might begin to anticipate from us? These values should embody our most enduring beliefs and aspirations and serve as the foundation for our leadership performance requirements.

We must demonstrate our commitment to efficiency by eliminating perceived inefficiencies, reducing inventories, and deconstructing bureaucracy. Our fundamental guiding premise should be that our company should be either the market leader or a close second in its industry.

3. Courage and Taking Risks

As leaders, we must have faith in our instincts and the fortitude to take measured risks. At times, this needs you to have the confidence in yourself to confront the established quo— even if it means jeopardizing your reputation.

4. Genuine Concern for the Advancement of Others

It is crucial to understand what motivates individuals who support our leadership to be happy. We must always improve our ability to assist others and genuinely support their career growth and overall job satisfaction throughout our leadership careers. We must remember that our greatest employees will eventually depart the organization they work for. As their mentor and sponsor, we must thus ensure that we provide them with the additional time and assistance they require to help prepare them for the next phase of their careers.

5. Accountability and Responsibility

Legacy building is about being aware of the potential and duty to progress ourselves through service to others. Only you can set the tone and define the performance standards you require of yourself and others. As such, we must be extremely self-disciplined to hold ourselves accountable for meeting those criteria consistently every day, every step of the way.

Additionally, suppose the model is a family business, where history and experience are directly transferred to children and other family members to take over and grow the business successfully. In that case, it is your responsibility as a leader to uphold the legacy and traditions of those who came before you and build on those traditions to strengthen further the culture, human capital, and brand of the organization you serve.

Leaders who are dissatisfied with their careers prioritize recognition over respect. Richard Branson, the creator of Virgin Group, said clearly what he desired as his legacy: "To have built one of the world's most respected organizations." Not always the largest."

Leaving a leadership legacy does not imply leaving something for future generations. It leaves an imprint on people.

It is only when leaders aspire to be significant that they understand the actual nature of leadership and legacy building. When this realization occurs, the lens through which we view the world becomes crystal obvious; we begin to comprehend that being accountable for the growth and success of others will define how we construct, create, and grow and eventually define how we are remembered.

OVERCOMING A LEGACY MINDSET

Even though digital transformation has been around for decades, there is still widespread misunderstanding. Many believe it simply entails converting something analog to a digital format/"the cloud" and...it. that's

It is neither more expedient nor more efficient. It's simply... digital now. This kind of thinking is a significant impediment to fully exploiting the benefits presented by digital transformation:

The method itself remains substantially unaffected by this rationale. It has not been modified in any meaningful way and might be considered part of a company's heritage rather than a road ahead.

With customer expectations evolving faster than enterprises can keep up, the only option to maintain a competitive edge is to phase out a legacy attitude.

A legacy mindset does not have to exist solely in the thoughts of individuals. Additionally, it can be found in procedures, technology, or all three in the worst-case situation.

Individuals with this heritage perspective are "quite content to continue plugging away in the same way they always have, regardless of how the world changes."

Losing competitive advantage, particularly in industries undergoing fast upheaval or razor-thin margins, can be negative regardless of whether your firm has been around for ten or one hundred years.

The Constraints of a Legacy Mindset

The people behind the technology will determine the success or failure of any digital endeavor within your firm.

Consider the following scenario: As you begin to develop an internal case for a scalable process automation program at your organization, you may be up against team member trauma from previous "failed" digital transformation efforts, which may have involved their staff replicating an analog procedure, pasting it into a digital format, and then hoping for the best. Each application and process requires a unique transition plan to ensure they have all they need to operate effectively in their new environment.

How to Overcome a Legacy Mentality

Speak early and frequently

It is critical to begin establishing a cross-functional network within your firm. Beginning to end automation of a business process and converting it into more efficient and automated requires cross-departmental collaboration.

"Superheroes do not suit well in businesses." This entails seeking out partners in seemingly odd locations, depending on the nature of the project.

For example, if you're working with contracts or anything similar, you should surely seek out people in the legal/compliance field, as they'll be involved. Why not involve them from the start?

Speak about the appropriate subjects

Whatever you do, regardless of the project, avoid starting with technical details. Concentrate on the value and benefits that such a project could add to their burden. Justify how it will improve transparency and efficiency.

The critical point is that you must have a team member who can act as a liaison "between techies and suits." You require someone capable of translating technical jargon into commercial objectives and prospects and vice versa.

Evaluate a little project.

After publicizing your automation ambitions, the next step is to select a pilot project to serve as a proof of concept.

The quickest and most effective path to digital transformation is through the selection of a lighthouse and pilot project that produces results quickly. Learn more about how to select the proper project to help you get started expanding process automation at your firm.

Train after train after train. Then train once again.

Training is an essential part of achieving one's goals in this process.

Training enables your staff to incorporate new ideas into their job and develop new insight that they may layer over their existing expertise.

For example, "they gain knowledge and experience integrating with other systems, which fuels their excitement."

Present in every location

The final but most critical step in permanently eradicating the legacy attitude is to share your success story with process automation with everyone.

Celebrate your victories loudly and proudly throughout the organization. Conduct "roadshows" across departments, business, and IT, ensuring that your presentation resonates with your audience.

WHAT IS THE IMPORTANCE OF LEGACY TO A LEADER?

A legacy is valuable, such as a goal or mission, passed down from one generation to another. From a business perspective, a leader inspires and motivates personnel to strive for performance excellence and accomplish the company's vision and objective. A leader's legacy can take many forms.

It could be a method that the leader devised or created or a system for increasing the efficiency of a process in the workplace; it could also be a protocol for maintaining the employees' work decorum.

Leaders are typically long-term personnel who have grown with the organization and seen it through various struggles. Leaders remain with a company for various reasons other than the economic benefits associated with employment. Often, individuals become leaders simply because they have a passion, a belief, and a goal, not only for themselves but also for the company's best interests. Leaders that leave a lasting legacy in their organizations are referred to as "legends."

Being a legend at a firm means that long after a leader has moved on and departed the organization, his contribution to the organization's process, system, or mindset continues to be recognized and adopted by the younger generation of employees. This occurs when rookie employees see the leader's efforts and regard the leader as a role model or source of inspiration for achieving their career objectives and advancement.

Respect for a leader's legacy is critical to an employee because of what legacy means to a leader:

Attempts and Tests

A leader's legacy in a business must have been forged through repeated testing, appraisal, observation, and rollouts. It is feasible that the remaining legacy is the most effective and efficient procedure out of a dozen processes as determined by those tests. These processes are taught to new employees, who are then entrusted with carrying them out and utilizing them to increase production and efficiency.

Evaluation on an ongoing basis

While a legacy is being implemented, this does not indicate the evaluation process is complete. Procedures, systems, and standards are regularly assessed to remain competitive in today's dynamic business environment. This requires the younger generation's contribution in terms of customizing existing processes.

The new data is compared to what has worked previously or is currently working for the firm. These are then used to determine which recommendation is the most recent. To a leader, legacy means working, examining, deliberating, implementing, Repeating. The legacy will continue to be the standard until a better, more wonderful "legacy" is discovered and utilized. It leaves traces that future and aspiring leaders relate to.

A Foolproof System That Is Effective

Knowing that a process or system you created, or a procedure you implemented, is being used and producing excellent results for the business is akin to a "wow" moment for a leader. And, as the leader who enabled it all, this adds another leaf to your laurel—knowing that your contribution will benefit current and future employees adds a whole new level of enjoyment. Pride and a sense of success are instilled in those that participate. in the leadership.

To return to the original question, what does legacy mean to a leader? It translates as "pride." This entails imprinting their name on the business or firm. It knows that the work you've done and the products you've built have been successful and are being used to provide future leaders with an invisible positive procedure to work with.

A leader who has worked for a company for an extended period frequently strives to create a legacy. Achieving this instills pride in personnel and, of course, increases a leader's market value.

LEADERSHIP MEN AND WOMEN HAVE A LEGACY MINDSET

People come and go within an organization; gone are the days when an employee would spend 25-30 years with the same company to earn a gold watch and attend a retirement party after their career. Individuals leave an organization after three to five years, primarily for the opportunity to progress in their industry. When you leave a firm, what do you take with you?

At each step of your career, you learn how to continue to have a positive impact and influence on others. The best leadership legacies result from success accruing to those surrounded by those who wish to see their success continue. When you encourage others to take a leap of faith alongside you, you create a legacy-defining moment in your leadership career that ultimately defines your path to success and relevance in your profession and the legacy you leave behind for the associates and customers you serve.

As a leader with a legacy attitude, you are constantly looking for ways to produce something lasting long after you are gone. Several examples include the following:

Establishing a mentorship program for employees who have proven a desire to expand their knowledge, take on larger tasks, and advance their careers within the organization.

Another form of mentor program might pair long-serving employees with younger associates who are more in tune with how the Internet and social media are used to connect with customers, engage with the community, and conduct further industry research. As junior associates assist more senior personnel, the opportunity for 360 mentorships exists.

They are developing a program to promote diversity and creating internal groups that assist and promote the recruitment and advancement of women of all ethnic backgrounds. Often, women who work in a male-dominated workplace struggle to feel included. Creating a women's group enables the necessary connection to keep women involved inside the organization.

Consider the global picture and the future. Keep in mind the immediate and long-term consequences of your decisions. on other countries, society, the oceans, wildlife, communities, waste, and resources, among others…

Protect both the environment and humanity. Distinguish the impact of actions on people and the environment. Make decisions that will positively influence people, processes, the environment, and economies on the second and third levels.

Change the way business is conducted. Change something within your control. Develop a waste-reducing habit, such as reading an e-book or printing double-sided.

At each stage of their journey, great leaders maintain an eye on the future. Leaders with a legacy attitude have the advantage of knowing that their impact and influence are being used to effect enduring change in each capacity they have throughout their career.

THE IMPORTANCE OF A 'LEGACY-DRIVEN' MINDSET

Occasionally, a contribution can be so significant that it permanently alters the cosmos. For example, Mother Teresa and Steve Jobs are inspirational leaders who have gone down in history for their earth-shattering, worldwide offers. This degree of achievement is uncommon.

And while many individuals will not necessarily alter the world in this way, they will leave a small legacy with a lasting imprint.

It is incorrect to use the term "legacy" as a synonym for "the whole of "who" or "what" a person leaves behind, but rather for how they "walk their talk" through their own words and actions. A legacy-driven perspective provides meaning for a person's priorities. People frequently forget in the 24-7 race that occupies daily life that what is ultimately necessary is a reminder of what is truly important.

People desire more than to earn and consume; they want to make a difference in their own and other people's lives. And to accomplish so, the concept of success must be altered.

Entrepreneurs, CEOs, and other company leaders frequently prioritize profits over legacy, but adopting a "Legacy-Driven Mindset" might position them to make the quantum leap forward that will drive and maintain progress for future generations.

A mindset that is "legacy-driven" is forward-thinking and humanitarian. Additionally, it positions individuals to assist them in monetizing business success and expanding income streams. And while many people with this unique perspective will not necessarily alter the world (like Steve Jobs did), they can nonetheless seek to impact others around them and leave a lasting impression.

Why a 'Legacy-Driven Mindset' is Not an Effective Strategy or Tactic

When managing the day-to-day operations, it's natural to focus exclusively on getting through the week or even the day.

While this method is frequently necessary to get a business off the ground, it leaves little time for long-term planning.

The Legacy-Driven Mindset is about determining what matters most and then living it. Why is this crucial for long-term professional and personal success? Consider long-term success—rather than immediate gratification—to keep folks on track amid times of chaos and uncertainty.

Those who live with a Legacy-Driven Mindset typically consider the big picture of what contributes to their success in life. They also recognize that creating an effect is just as critical—if not more so—than making money. Individuals who embrace this broader perspective on life appear to be far more adept at balancing life and work dance than others.

A straightforward but powerful way to begin comprehending the Legacy-Driven Mindset is to examine the "4 P's": passion, pursuit, people, and peace.

When someone considers doing anything with passion, they smile, and their eyes light up. This enthusiasm is at the heart of living a "Legacy-Driven life."

Pursuit is how this passion becomes a reality.

Because people are genuine, you should not be frightened to communicate with or be around them. Remove the digital boundaries that create a false reality of communication.

Finding or cultivating inner peace is one of the most challenging acts in today's hectic work environment and digital world. Peace is about being aware of one's humanity and fully aware of one's existence.

Acquire a More Sensitive Understanding
of a Well-Lived Life

Adopting a "legacy-driven" approach is more critical than ever for corporate success.

Remember that leaving a legacy does not indicate the conclusion but rather the beginning of a new phase—or the next chapter.

To succeed, it is critical to first identify and assess a person's legacy at each stage of life, whether professional or personal. It will soon become clear how successfully a "Legacy-Driven Mindset" may foster a much more profound feeling of a life well-lived in the effort to impact others.

MINDSET OF LEGACY VS.
SKILLSET OF LEGACY

Without a doubt, the analytics and data science area are witnessing an extraordinary transformation. Simultaneously, many businesses have workers who continue to work the same way and have the same abilities for years. Organizations undoubtedly need to evolve beyond their historical skill sets, and the need for a skills refreshment is evident.

However, I see many organizations presuming that individuals with historical skill sets are obsolete and must be replaced. This is an error. There is a significant distinction between legacy skillsets and legacy mindsets. The two are not synonymous!

How is a legacy skillset defined?

With the proliferation of new analytical tools, methodologies, and technologies, it is nearly difficult for any individual to stay completely current. Certain analytics and data science specialists, on the other hand, are woefully behind the curve. This is true regardless of where someone works on the analytics continuum. Among the heritage skill sets are the following:

Data specialists are only familiar with traditional client-server Extract, Transform, and Load (ETL) tools that work with raw files and load them into a database.

Experts in business intelligence and reporting are solely familiar with traditional reporting suites and have never used visualization tools, open-source tools, or web-based delivery options.

Experts in advanced analytics who are still confined to the world of SAS and SQL and have never worked in a cloud environment or with open source tools such as R or Python.

It is critical to understand that I am not arguing that the talents listed above are no longer necessary or valuable. These abilities are unquestionably valuable today and will continue to be so in the future. Simply said, these abilities are vital yet insufficient in today's environment. Individuals must expand their skill set to maintain optimum influence. The fact that businesses require these historical skill sets does not negate the need for expansion.

How is a legacy mindset defined?

A legacy mindset refers to a mental state of mind and outlook. It is not synonymous with legacy skills, but the two may overlap within the same individual. A legacy mindset exists when individuals are uninterested in changing how they do things or acquiring new abilities. A legacy mindset individual is quite content to continue plugging away in the same manner as they always have regardless of how the world changes around them.

In other instances, an employee may be attempting to survive for a few more years before retiring. Generally, an employee is resistant to change and wishes to remain in their comfort zone. Having a sizable proportion of people with legacy attitudes is detrimental to the advancement of an analytics business.

To avoid declining productivity and effectiveness over time, it is necessary to jolt those with a legacy mindset into a new way of thinking. If jolting the personnel fails, it may be necessary to remove them from the organization gradually.

Management Of Legacy Skillset And Mindset

After defining the distinction between a legacy skillset and a legacy attitude, let's discuss how to cope with them. As previously stated, the worst course of action is to presume complete overlap between the two. This is not true. Making that assumption will result in an organization laying off (and then replacing) far more employees than necessary.

There are unmistakable direct expenses associated with this. Additionally, those unnecessarily pushed aside will not receive equitable treatment, and the company will lose access to its institutional expertise.

In truth, many individuals who possess a legacy skillset lack a legacy attitude. They will be delighted, if not overjoyed, to acquire new abilities and upgrade their CV. There are undoubtedly certain costs associated with the training and learning curve that this personnel must endure. However, such expenditures will be significantly less than the cost of replacing an entire team.

In the worst-case scenario, firms incur enormous expenditures by retaining existing staff to perform legacy functions while hiring new employees to modernize. Why not allow certain individuals to assist with both tasks rather than tripling the headcount?

In truth, people who lack a legacy mindset are usually already experimenting independently, whether at home or on the job. They may be nestled in a profession that primarily requires legacy skillsets today. Still, they are ready, willing, and capable of moving beyond them if given the opportunity and the charter.

As a result, the approach evaluates employees on two dimensions: their skill set and mindset. Identify people whose talents are out of step with the times but possess the necessary mindset. Then provide them the opportunity to advance their careers, develop their talents, and advance the organization's analytics and data science programs. Your present company may be capable of more than is currently recognized!

THE ESSENTIAL EIGHT QUESTIONS TO ASK TO ESTABLISH YOUR LEADERSHIP LEGACY

Successful CEOs alter their organizations in all important areas that contribute to a firm's success—financial, cultural, customer, employee, and operational. They take established foundations and transform them into a powerful new method of market leadership. They begin by asking, "Why am I here?"

The issue is determining the goal and rationale for joining something massive. Once you can confidently respond to it, you may turn the tables and leave a legacy for future CEOs.

"The trick to life is to fall seven times and rise eight."—Coelho, Paulo.

If you are a CEO seeking to establish a legacy, you must climb to the summit and begin inquiring about your life. Consider yourself 15 years from now, reflecting on yourself. What would you tell yourself if you could? What replies would you give yourself to these eternal questions?

1. Optimistic Vision

When people think of my business, they say;

Your initial step should be to ascertain the company's current perception. It is not a matter of good or negative perceptions. It's about having a clear vision and conveying that goal effectively through your products, services, and culture, among other things. As a result, you must consider how your organization will be perceived in ten years.

Consider the following:

When people think of my firm, they will immediately think of the best customer value and immediate fulfillment of their needs.

Employees and customers feel heard and acknowledged for their particular abilities and requirements.

We are a transformational firm that thrives on innovation and always doing the right thing.

As a CEO, you are responsible for shaping your brand's perception. This involves your consumers as well as your workers. Netflix is, without a doubt, the best source of original, easily consumed entertainment. As a result, when people think of Netflix, they think of "excellent original material that is simple to watch."

Looking closely, that is exactly what the company's creator, Reed Hastings, believed. He referred to linear television as "outdated" and pushed "streaming" as the future way to consume content. As a result, Netflix soars to new heights while cable companies such as Comcast flounder.

Thus, what will the public opinion be of your business?

CEOs maximize the value of their organization's talent. And to do so, they must develop personal ties—demonstrating to others that they and the firm care.

2. Magnificent Vision

The company's grand mission is as follows:

What is my company's grand vision? Your vision is a critical component of your CEO's legacy. You must focus your objective on something more definite, exact, and quantifiable.

Consider the following:

My vision is for people to work for a cause—a reason to do what they are doing in the grand scheme of life.

We develop value and the capacity to anticipate consumer needs.

Include them in the planning and execution phases to make customers and employees feel belonging to the team, mission, and vision.

For example, Amazon.com founder Jeff Bezos built a platform centered on the customer, and transparency in their dealings is their most valuable characteristic. He revolutionized the way people shop and is now providing them with one-of-a-kind transparency to provide the best possible experience.

The CEOs of Blackberry were devastated by the loss of their vision, while Apple proved to be more visionary. Making your consumers and workers believe in your purpose is a great vision for your firm. Help them realize your mindset of setting up a fresh and futuristic approach.

3. Work purpose

Our work's "why" or objective is to inspire and motivate people to achieve their full potential.

What's the point of our labor, exactly? What is the purpose of our actions? What impact do we have on the world and the people around us?

The cornerstone of a company's vision, value statement, and unique proposition are based on its employees' work purpose. Having a clear idea of what you desire is the first step. To achieve, you're ready to put all of yourself into it.

"Find your mission in life and devote yourself to it with all of your heart and soul"—*Buddha.*—

"Find your mission in life and devote yourself to it with all of your heart and soul"—Buddha.—

As a starting point, consider the following:

A values-based mentality is the "why" of our work inspires and motivates our team members.

We listen to our customers, meet their demands, and make doing business with us a pleasure.

As a CEO, the "why" of your firm and your legacy are inextricably linked. The CEO needs to be proactive to succeed. They must be able to clearly state the company's mission, have a clear vision for the future, and guide it to greatness.

Measurement of success

I will use this one metric to gauge my success as CEO.

As a CEO, the answer to this question is critical. Progress, lack thereof, or degradation may only be quantified numerically. Instead of being an overconfident leader, be realistic about your stats. You can never set the bar too high or too low if you know where you stand and what resources you have at your disposal.

People in the past had to deal with setbacks because they lacked a strategy for maintaining their achievements. In other words, keeping track of your progress and comparing it to predetermined benchmarks might help you stay on track.

For instance, Alan Mullaly (Ford) had a 15% CAGR. Customers, employees, investors, dealers, suppliers, and the community all played a role in how successful he considered his business to be. To be exact, you must establish cash flow goals that can be quantified.

5. Getting On With It

As a result of my being here, my company will take care of the following:

LG Electronics' CEO was recently replaced after the company suffered huge losses due to the digital transition. New CEO Kwon is recognized for his strong management style at LG. With Kwon taking over as LG's CEO, he'll devise new strategies to build his legacy by focusing on upcoming technologies.

The legacy you leave behind is influenced by the industry you work in., clients, and workers you work with. It should concentrate on the new products, services, financial enhancements, ways of thinking that you leave behind, and how you lead and manage them. As an example:

New approaches to learning and reinforcing ingrained habits of thought and behavior.

6. There are new ways to recover from previous losses or failures.

When it comes to having a positive outlook on life, I aspire to be and grow more as a leader;

In the end, a growth mentality leads us to an even better and more prosperous place. We get stuck in a rut if we have a fixed mindset, which prevents us from absorbing counsel and allowing for self-reflection. We can't win our legacy if we don't take the time to focus on our thoughts and those of others.

It's possible to conceive of it this way: As a manager, I'd like to become more aware of the lives of my staff and clients. For the benefit of my employees, I will do my utmost to find and develop their potential. I want to create a workplace where people aren't just waiting for their next payday. It is because they are always learning and growing that they are succeeding.

"Winning isn't something you sometimes do; it's something you do all the time. There is no such thing as a once-in-a-lifetime victory or a once-in-a-lifetime achievement. Winning is a way of life for many people." Vince Lombardi, NFL Head Coach

"Winning is a habit, not an occasional occurrence. There is no such thing as a once-in-a-lifetime victory or a once-in-a-lifetime achievement. "It's a habit to win." The legendary football coach, Vince Lombardi

Decide on a shared language for growth inside your teams. To succeed in your current position as CEO, you need to get to know the individuals in your organization and help them advance professionally, academically, and emotionally. As a CEO, you need to pay great attention to your grooming.

As an illustration, consider Bill Gates. He's still working on developing a growth mindset as a CEO. To promote a learning environment and growth in the workplace, they establish new platforms. Rather than making employees doubt their abilities, programs should encourage them to embrace the challenge.

7. Collaborating with Others and Establishing Links

In order to better me and the firm as a whole, I plan to work with and get to know the people and organizations listed below.

Consider this: Who in my network can assist me in achieving this goal? Cooperation should occur with others who can support and guide you while you work toward achieving the larger goals you've set for yourself. Nothing good comes from randomly connecting with people because they appear helpful. folks like these could be potential collaborators for you

Influencers' Investors' Institutes pursue the same goal.

People who can assist you get your message out to the public.

Involved parties in your supply chain who will profit from a financial alliance.

The proper people will be drawn to you based on the words you choose, the tone you use, and your values. In the future, mergers, acquisitions, and partnerships will result from your collective decisions.

Keeping this in mind, you should be systematic and deliberate in your decision-making when collaborating and connecting. See my essay on how to make amazing decisions when you're feeling unable to decide because of resistance, pressure, and other comparable situations.

8. Hours of Work

Based on those above, I want to use my time in the following manner:

"Time is money" is a phrase you've probably heard before. Why not turn your time into money by charging an hourly rate for it, as is common in the consulting and manufacturing industries? Multiplying by your hourly rate when dividing your salary by the number of days and hours you work. What's your hourly rate? Around 261 for the majority of CEOs.

Assume that there are 261 days in a year with an eight-hour day. When you put in eight hours a day, seven days a week for 261 days a year, you clock in 2088 hours in a year. At a salary of $1,000,000 per year, the CEO is paid. $4789.27 is the hourly rate. Do you make the most of every one of your 4789.27 minutes?

The Last Word

Set your sights on a bright future. This futuristic approach keeps the company's finances on track, helps establish strong teams, and develops the skills and discipline necessary for long-term CEO success. Prepare for the shifting standards of success. Consider your legacy and strive to be better than you ever dreamed of yourself. And;

How prepared are you for the role of a long-term legacy leader?

MINDSET DEVELOPMENT FOR SUCCESSFUL LEADERSHIP

Behind the scenes of any successful business is an excellent team leader who has embraced a growth attitude. Success in business and leadership can be judged only by how well a company and its executives are doing is whether the leader has adopted a growth mindset and let go of a fixed attitude.

A growth mindset is an attitude and conviction that individuals can enhance their abilities, talents, intelligence, and emotional intelligence. This essentially suggests that you feel that success results from persistent effort toward overcoming obstacles. Leaders with a growth mentality are more concerned with the process than the outcome.

On the other hand, we have a fixed mentality. This attitude argues that people's fundamental characteristics, such as intelligence and talent, are unchangeable and undevelopable. Leaders with a fixed attitude are obsessively focused on results. They frequently misinterpret difficulties as failures, believing that all work has been in vain rather than seeing an opportunity to learn and improve.

Let's delve a little deeper into the distinct consequences of a fixed mindset versus a growing attitude toward a business.

How a Fixed Mindset Affects Your Business and Leadership

Executives who run their organizations with a fixed attitude will foster a fear-based culture.

When issues arise—and always do—leaders with a fixed attitude immediately view the situation as a failure and hunt for someone to blame.

The leader may even dismiss or replace the individual who is being blamed. They believe a person's ability to solve a problem cannot be improved. Occasionally, you'll see the leader intervene to resolve the issue because they lack trust in others.

Leaders with this type of fixed thinking may become entangled in stressful situations that limit business progress, such as the following:

A fear-based culture in which their team fears taking risks, innovating, or expressing ideas; they fear being perceived as incompetent if they make any errors.

A demotivated team is incapable of performing at their maximum capacity or extending their capacity.

They are constantly putting out fires or micromanaging their team, resulting in overwork, burnout, and stress.

This climate produces a defensive, finger-pointing culture in which people are more concerned with their safety than with the company's growth. When a firm culture demonstrates these characteristics, scaling becomes difficult, if not impossible. Scaling up, at best, becomes a route fraught with drama, hostility, miscommunication, and stress.

How a Growth Mindset Aids to the Development of Your Team's Talent

On the other side, leaders who embrace a growth mentality will quadruple their team's potential and foster an accountable culture that will propel their firm forward.

Leadership with a development perspective sees opportunities for their employees even in adversity. They do not withdraw into a corner, convinced that their efforts have been in vain, and do not hunt for someone to blame. Rather than that, they make a concerted effort to expedite their team's growth to overcome any business obstacle.

To build your team into proactive, accountable, and motivated problem solvers, it is vital to lead with a growth mentality. As your team develops and changes, the firm will as well.

Within a short period, you'll have developed a culture of individuals who are receptive to feedback, accountable for their progress, and resilient enough to take on new challenges, fostering innovation and corporate growth.

How a Growth Mindset Increases Your Scalability Possibilities

Apart from cultivating your team's talent, a growth attitude is critical for your leadership evolution.

As your firm expands, it will progress through four stages of growth:

1-5 staff for a startup

Increase in size: 6-15 employees

Increase in size: 16-250 employees

Take control of your industry: 250+ employees

Each stage presents its own set of distinct difficulties. An entrepreneur who has grown their firm successfully through the first two phases may lack the abilities necessary to survive the third stage. This is where a growth mindset becomes vital, as the leader's skills will need to improve to address the next growth stage.

Similarly, a leader may have aided another business in its third and fourth stages of growth. However, this does not inherently qualify them to lead a start-up through its first growth stages. Again, acquiring and honing the new abilities necessary for success in these novel business stages will be important.

Now that we've established why it's critical to have a growth mentality, the next issue arises: How can a leader cultivate a growth mindset?

How Can a Leader Foster a Growth Mindset?

Modern leaders who are most effective have a development mentality to stay up with the demands of an ever-changing digital world. Here are some behaviors and attitudes you may embrace to help you and your team develop a development mindset.

1. Accept Change

Modern leaders that are most effective recognize that we live in a quickly changing digital world. By embracing change rather than fearing or opposing it, they position themselves to effect substantial change—whether it's altering themselves, their team, their organization's procedures, and structures, or even turning their business direction and vision.

2. Develop self-awareness

We must first comprehend our starting place before we can alter and progress. What are our boundaries, motives, and emotional states? As a leader, self-awareness enables you to make more meaningful decisions and explore chances for corporate growth. Additionally, it will assist you in identifying areas where you and your team can improve.

3. Create Your Disruption

After developing self-awareness, you are prepared to interrupt yourself. According to Mark Sanborn, author of The Potential Principle, leaders must disturb themselves before someone or something else disrupt them. If change comes from another source—for instance, a disruptive technology—you will struggle to adapt and catch up. However, if you become the catalyst for innovation, you become a game-changer.

Mark proposes the following questions to cultivate the practice of interrupting oneself, preparing for change, and cultivating a growth mindset:

Which of your habits, rituals, and routines may use some shaking up?

Are you continuing to do activities that formerly worked well but no longer do so well, if at all?

Are you wasting time on ineffective activities?

How could your time be better spent?

How much time do you spend "daydreaming" versus "daily doing"? What can you do to re-direct your energy toward more vital goals?

Are you circling in harmful relationships? Do you need to alter, limit, or terminate your relationship with someone who negatively influences you?

You will sow the seeds of change in your life by deliberately disrupting yourself, reflecting on your capacity to build your team with a growth mentality.

4. Recognize and reward the benefits of failure-based learning.

When it comes to owning a business, failure is unavoidable. Leaders who learn from their failures and incorporate these lessons into their toolkit are more equipped to continuously push the boundaries of their own and their teams' growth. Additionally, it is critical to foster an environment in your organization where failure is viewed as a teaching tool. In this manner, your staff will be inspired to expand and take on new challenges.

5. Maintain an ongoing focus on the process

A critical component of the growth mindset is emphasizing the process rather than the outcome. No team or business will operate flawlessly 100% of the time. At times, results will fall short of expectations. This is why it is critical to pay attention to the procedure. By concentrating on the process, you can expand your team and continue to improve execution somewhat.

6. Practise fortitude

A forty-foot oak tree does not grow overnight. The fruits of growth take time, which is why persistence is critical. Learning to push through failure, view hurdles as challenges, and persevere in the face of adversity will enable you to lead a team toward more significant goals.

To successfully lead a team, a leader must first display the proper mindset for success. This process begins with developing a growth mindset, which allows you to break free from the constraints of fixed beliefs and limited potential.

When you adopt the actions and attitudes associated with a growth mindset purposefully, you will open new doors of possibility without being constrained by fear of failure. "Only those who are willing to take the danger of going too far will be able to find out. how far one can go."

EXCELLENT CEOS' MINDSETS AND PRACTICES

A business has just one unmatched position: chief executive officer. It is the most powerful and sought-after title in business; it is also the most thrilling, gratifying, and influential. What the CEO controls—the company's most significant decisions—accounts for 45% of a business's performance.

Regardless of the glamour of the position, serving as a CEO may be exhausting, lonely, and stressful. When they've been working for at least 18 months, only three out of every five newly appointed CEOs live up to performance expectations.

Directors, shareholders, customers, and staff all hold themselves to the same high standards and expectations—a climate of constant scrutiny. A single decision can radically make or break an otherwise successful career.

Despite widespread criticism of the CEO's function, little is known about what CEOs do to excel. We analyzed performance statistics on thousands of CEOs to demonstrate which attitudes and practices are most beneficial for CEOs. We re-visited our own experience assisting CEOs in improving their leadership approaches.

To address the question, "What are the mindsets and practices of exceptional CEOs?" we began with the six primary components of the CEO's job—components that are discussed in virtually all literature on the role: setting the strategy, aligning the organization, leading the top team, collaborating with the board, representing the company to external stakeholders, and managing one's own time and energy.

Corporate strategy: Concentrate on outperforming the odds

It is the leader's responsibility to set the company's direction—to have a plan in the face of uncertainty. Ceos' attempt to mitigate strategic uncertainty prioritizes the business cases for the most viable solutions. However, research indicates that this technique results in the dreaded "hockey stick" effect, which involves a projected reduction in next year's budget followed by a promise of success that never materializes. A more realistic approach recognizes that 10% of businesses generate 90% of total economic profit (profit after deducting capital costs). During ten years, only one in every twelve businesses shifts from average to top-quintile performance. While the odds of moving from mediocre to excellent are long, CEOs can significantly boost their chances of breaking those odds by following these practices:

Reframe what victory entails.

The CEO is the final decision-maker for creating a company's vision (where do we want to be in five, 10, or fifteen years?). Effective CEOs do so by taking into account their mandate and expectations (from the board of directors, investors, employees, and other stakeholders), their company's relative strengths and purpose, a clear understanding of what enables the business to generate value, market opportunities and trends, and their aspirations and values.

The best take it further and reinterpret success as a reference point. For instance, rather than a manufacturer aiming to be the best in the industry, the CEO can set a goal of being in the top quartile of all industries. This reframe recognizes that businesses compete for talent, capital, and influence on a far larger stage than their industry. It reframes critical performance indicators such as margin, cash flow, and organizational health, dispelling the biases and social dynamics contributing to complacency.

Make audacious steps early on.

Five bold strategic moves are most strongly associated with success: resource reallocation; programmatic mergers, acquisitions, and divestitures; capital expenditure; productivity improvements; and differentiation improvements (the latter three measured relatives to the industry in which a company operates).

To move "boldly," one must move at least 30% more than the industry average. Making one or two daring movements more than doubles the likelihood of jumping from the middle to the top quintiles of economic profit. Making three or more bold moves increases the likelihood of such a gain by sixfold. Additionally, CEOs who make these moves early in their tenure outperform those who make them later, and those who make them several times avoid an otherwise frequent performance fall.

Not surprisingly, data also indicate that CEOs appointed externally are more inclined to act boldly and quickly than those promoted within a firm. CEOs promoted inside should ask and respond to "What would an outsider do?" while making strategic decisions.

Allocation of resources: Remain active.

Not only is resource reallocation a daring strategic action in and of itself, but it is also a necessary enabler of the other strategic initiatives. Over ten years, organizations that reallocate more than 50% of their capital expenditures among business divisions create 50% more value than companies that reallocate less than 50%.

While the benefits of this method may seem clear, a third of businesses reallocate less than 1% of their capital annually. Additionally, our CEO database discovered that the top decile of high-performing CEOs is 35% more likely than average performers to reallocate capital dynamically.

To guarantee that resources are quickly transferred to where they will provide the greatest value, rather than being distributed evenly across organizations and operations, exceptional CEOs initiate a continual (rather than annual) stage-gate procedure. This approach takes a granular picture, makes quantitative comparisons, indicates when to cease funding and when to continue, and is backed by the CEO's commitment to optimize the company's resource allocation continuously.

Alignment of the organization: Manage performance and health with equal rigor.

When successful investors are asked what they seek in portfolio firms, many respond that they would rather invest in an average plan led by outstanding talent than a fantastic strategy led by mediocre talent. The best CEOs approach both strategy and talent with equal rigor and focus. And when it comes to attracting and retaining top people, over half of the senior leaders say their biggest regret is delaying the removal of subpar performers from key roles or the organization entirely.

This is both practical (effective leaders give significant leverage to the CEO) and symbolic (CEOs who tolerate poor performance or bad behavior diminish their influence). Numerous CEOs also express regret for failing to retain adequate performers in critical positions and for failing to maximize the potential of their responsibilities. The finest CEOs think strategically about their people: the roles they play, the outcomes they can achieve, and the organizational structure that will maximize their effect.

CEOs that are adamant about systematically assessing and managing all cultural factors that affect performance more than double their chances of successfully executing their strategies. And they generate quadruple the total return to stockholders over the long term that other companies do.

Talent: Align talent with market value.

Numerous CEOs have confided in us that they are concerned about asking the same few overworked "usual suspects" to take on more duties due to a lack of faith in the people who would normally accomplish them. The finest CEOs are meticulous in connecting talent to the most valuable roles.

A critical initial step is determining which roles are most critical. Careful investigation frequently yields facts that astound even the most astute CEOs—only 10% of the top 50 value-creating roles in any given firm report directly to the CEO. Sixty percent are two levels lower, and twenty percent are even lower. What's more startling is that the remaining 10% are roles that do not exist.

Once these responsibilities are defined, the CEO may collaborate with other executives to handle them more rigorously and with the proper personnel. Additionally, robust talent pipelines can be built to ensure that critical roles stay adequately staffed. The greatest CEOs include their job for the board to evaluate viable, well-prepared internal candidates for succession.

Beyond employee involvement, consider culture.

Employee engagement, vendors of workforce surveys frequently assert, is the best indicator of "soft things." That is not the case. While employee engagement does correlate with financial performance, an average engagement survey covers less than 20% of the organizational health indicators associated with value generation.

A comprehensive assessment of organizational health considers everything from strategic alignment and execution quality to the capacity to learn and change. According to the largest study, CEOs who insist on systematically assessing and managing all cultural factors that influence performance more than quadruple the likelihood that their ideas will be implemented.

And they generate quadruple the total return to stockholders over the long term that other companies do. To do this effectively, it is necessary to take a deliberate approach to role modeling, storytelling, aligning formal reinforcements (such as incentives), and investing in skill development.

Combine speed and stability in your organizational design.

The term "agile" is one of the most overused and misunderstood management buzzwords of the last decade. For many executives, agility creates a sense of urgency in decision-making and execution, in contrast to the methodical pace enforced by huge organizations' fixed, regular routines.

The statistics demonstrate that agility does not necessitate such a trade-off: firms that are both fast and stable are roughly three times more likely to rank in the top quartile of organizational health than fast firms but lack stable operating practices.

Excellent CEOs increase their organizations' agility by determining which aspects of their organizational design will remain stable and unchanging (for example, a primary organizational axis, a few signature processes, and shared values) and by introducing dynamic elements capable of fast responding to changing conditions and circumstances (such elements might include temporary performance cells, flow-to-work staffing models, and minimum-viable-product iterations).

For example, a CEO of a services company improved the viability of her "one company" strategy by shifting the profit-and-loss axis from products to geographies, reorganizing the back office to an agile flow-to-work model, and establishing a new agile product development division.

Excellent CEOs boost their organizations' agility by selecting which aspects of their organizational architecture will remain constant and incorporating dynamic elements that adapt quickly to new problems and possibilities.

Teamwork and processes: Prioritize dynamics over mechanics

The dynamics of a top team can significantly impact a business's performance. More than half of senior executives believe their top team is underperforming. The CEO is frequently out of touch with this reality: less than a third of CEOs disclose team concerns on average. The efficiency and efficacy of an organization's basic management processes can also significantly impact its fortunes.

However, less than a third of employees believe their company's management processes support the fulfillment of business objectives. Why is there a schism? The issue is not intellectual but social: team performance and processes can mitigate individual and institutional prejudices and clumsy group dynamics. Excellent CEOs recognize this reality and combat it in a variety of ways.

Collaboration: Demonstrate resolve.

The finest CEOs make a point of ensuring their management team functions well as a unit. The payoff is substantial: elite teams collaborating on a common vision are 1.9 times more likely to outperform the market median in financial success. In practice, CEOs make rapid adjustments to the team's makeup (size, diversity, and capability), which may include difficult decisions like dismissing likable low performers and disagreeable high performers CEOs should also calibrate personal relationships, keeping a sufficient distance to remain objective but close enough to earn trust and loyalty.

Additionally, they commit to increasing team productivity by regularly assessing and enhancing the team's operational rhythm, meeting protocols, interaction quality, and dynamics.

Additionally, they forbid members from placing their interests ahead of the company's demands, engaging in "drama" rather than "content" talks, "keeping the meeting outside the room," backsliding on decisions, or displaying disrespect for one another.

Top teams collaborating on a common goal are 1.9 times more likely to achieve financial performance above the median.

Defend against biases in decision-making.

Cognitive and organizational biases impair the judgment of everyone. These biases contribute to frequent performance failures in 90% of capital projects, including major cost over-runs. Additionally, we understand that prejudices cannot be unlearned. Even behavioral economist Dan Ariely, a leading authority on cognitive biases, confesses, "I was just as poor at decision-making as everyone else I write about." Nonetheless, CEOs occasionally believe they are immune to bias (after all, they may reason, hasn't sound judgment gotten them this far?).

Excellent CEOs make a concerted effort to mitigate the effect of biases by implementing practices such as anticipating fail-ure modes (premortems), formally designating a contrarian (red team), discarding prior information (clean sheet), and abandoning plan A. (vanishing options). Additionally, they guarantee that their staff is diverse, which has been found to boost the quality of decision-making.

Maintain coherence in management procedures.

Typically, the CEO delegates management processes to other executives: the chief financial officer (CFO) is responsible for budgeting and, on occasion, strategy; the chief human

resources officer (CHRO) is responsible for talent management and workforce planning; and the chief information officer (CIO) is responsible for technology investment.

On the other hand, rational processes can cohere into a clunky
system, resulting in more confusion and lost effort than
accountability and value. Managers pressed to agree to stretch
expectations discover that they are held accountable for complete delivery at the end of the year; sandbagging occurs. While
long-term objectives are established, talent advancement decisions are made based on immediate results.

Urgent product concepts are approved only to be deterred by
lengthy technological queues and risk management processes.
Excellent CEOs ensure that one management process does
not obstruct another. They demand executives to coordinate
their decision-making and resource allocation to ensure that
management processes reinforce priorities and work together
to accelerate plan execution and refinement.

**Board engagement: Assist directors in their efforts to assist
the business**

The board's mission is to oversee and steer management's
efforts to produce long-term value on behalf of shareholders.
According to research, effective corporate governance policies
are associated with improved performance, including greater
market valuations. Additionally, an effective board can deter
activist investors.

Despite these benefits, many CEOs view their boards of directors in the same way that one CEO described his board to us:
as a "necessary evil." The chairperson leads the board, and even
when the CEO serves as chairwoman (as is frequently the case

in North American corporations), the board's independence is critical. Nonetheless, exceptional CEOs can take beneficial initiatives to improve the board's counsel to management, including the following:

Effectiveness: Advance a progressive agenda.

Exceptional CEOs work collaboratively with board chairpersons to maximize their time on the board to design a forward-thinking board agenda. Such a plan requires the board to look beyond its traditional fiduciary responsibilities (legal, regulatory, audit, compliance, risk, and performance reporting) and provide input on a wide variety of topics, including strategy, mergers and acquisitions, technology, culture, talent, resilience, and external communications.

Outside perspectives on these issues from board members can assist management without jeopardizing executives' authority. Additionally, the CEO should ensure that the board and management engage in related activities, such as talent assessment and strategy refreshment, at the same time each year.

Excellent CEOs champion a broad board plan beyond traditional responsibilities to include strategy, technology, talent, and resilience.

Consider relationships beyond the meeting.

Excellent CEOs cultivate and maintain a strong relationship with the chair (or lead independent director) and meet with individual board members on a meaningful basis. Establishing positive relationships and a transparent tone early on enables the CEO to build trust and identify management's and the board's roles. By developing relationships with individual board members, the CEO can benefit from their perspectives and abilities and privately discuss issues that may be difficult to handle in a bigger group.

Additionally, exceptional CEOs foster relationships and communication between the board of directors and top executives, which keeps the board informed about the business and involved in advancing its priorities.

Capabilities: Strive for balance and growth.

Excellent CEOs also assist their boards in assisting the firm by providing input on the board's composition. For instance, the CEO may recommend that particular expertise or experience—whether linked to industries, functions, regions, development phases, or demographics—enable the board to make more informed assessments and support decisions about the organization.

CEOs can also contribute to the board's performance by ensuring that new members undergo a comprehensive onboarding process and providing opportunities for the board to learn about changing technologies, developing risks, emerging rivals, and evolving macroeconomic conditions. Typically, first-time board members benefit from a systematic introduction to the responsibilities of a successful board member.

External stakeholders: Maintain a long-term focus on the 'Why?'

Every CEO should be familiar with their organization's mission and values. Effective CEOs understand that these statements must be more than slogans for office posters and that they must be used to influence decision-making and daily actions. Excellent CEOs go further: they reaffirm and act on a business purpose (the "Why?") that extends beyond profit maximization to include societal good.

The stakeholder interactions are prioritized with a fine-grained method and a robust corporate resilience plan; this posture enables CEOs to mitigate the company's exposure to customer and stakeholder-related risks while capitalizing on new opportunities.

Effective chief executives ensure that their organizations have an effective risk operating model, governance framework, and risk culture. Additionally, exceptional CEOs and boards of directors predict large shocks, macroeconomic catastrophes, and other possible disasters.

Consider the big picture in terms of social purpose.

Numerous corporate social responsibility projects are little more than public relations exercises: collections of philanthropic activities that elicit positive emotions but have little lasting impact on society's well-being. Excellent CEOs devote time to considering, defining, and supporting their company's purpose about the broader impact of day-to-day business activities.

They advocate for serious efforts to generate jobs, adhere to ethical labor practices, enhance customers' lives, and mitigate the environmental impact of activities. Visible results are important to stakeholders; for example, 87 percent of customers say they will purchase from companies that support causes they care about, 94 percent of millennials say they want to utilize their abilities to help a cause. Sustainable investing has increased 18-fold since 1995. And failing to demonstrate such outcomes is not an option—smart CEOs understand they will be held accountable for keeping their commitments.

Prioritize and influence interactions.

Excellent CEOs prioritize actions systematically, schedule them in advance, and drive action through interactions with their companies' critical external stakeholders. Typically, CEOs of B2B organizations prioritize their most valuable and greatest potential customers.

CEOs of B2C businesses frequently undertake unannounced visits to stores and other frontline operations to understand better the customer experience provided by the business. Additionally, they spend time with their company's top 15 or 20 "intrinsic" investors (those who are the most aware and active) and delegate the remainder to the CFO and investor relations staff. Other stakeholder groups (such as regulators, legislators, advocacy organizations, and community organizations) will also require time from the CEO. The effectiveness of these interactions is not a matter of chance.

Excellent CEOs are clear about their objectives, well prepared, express audience-specific messaging (always centered on their company's "Why?"), listen closely, and seek win-win solutions.

Moments of truth: Prepare for a crisis by building resilience in advance.

Effective chief executives ensure that their organizations have an effective risk operating model, governance framework, and risk culture. Additionally, exceptional CEOs and boards of directors predict large shocks, macroeconomic catastrophes, and other possible disasters. There is cause for this: from

2010 to 2017, headlines including the word "crisis" alongside the names of 100 leading firms appeared 80 percent more frequently than in the previous decade.

Excellent CEOs understand that most crises follow predictable patterns, even though each one feels unique. With this in mind, they develop a crisis-response playbook outlining leadership positions, war-room setup, resilience testing, action plans, and communication strategies.

They look for opportunities to attack to the extent that they can. 18 And they recognize that stakeholders' anger is likely to focus on them, perhaps affecting their family and friends, and prepare a personal resilience plan in response.

Personal work habits: Carry out the tasks that only you can do.

CEOs are prone to feeling overwhelmed, which is natural given the complexity of their responsibilities. "CEOs are accountable for their firms' whole operations. Their lives are consumed with numerous meetings and an onslaught of email." Numerous studies indicate that many CEOs suffer from loneliness, dissatisfaction, disappointment, irritability, and weariness. While no CEO can avoid these feelings, excellent CEOs understand that they will serve the company better if they take control of their well-being in the following ways:

Office: Time and energy management.

The most successful CEOs build an office rapidly (typically with one or two highly experienced executive assistants and chief of staff) that clarifies their priorities and enables them to devote their limited time to tasks that only CEOs can perform. For instance, a CEO's office should meticulously plan all parts of the CEO's meetings, including the agenda, attendees, preparation (including "alone time" for the CEO to ponder and prepare), logistics, anticipated outcomes, and follow-up.

CEOs should avoid getting involved in duties that can be delegated and set up a time to cope with unforeseen events. Additionally, the finest CEOs teach their office staff how to manage the CEO's energy as wisely as they manage their time, including sequencing tasks to avoid "energy troughs" and scheduling recovery periods (for example, time with family and friends, exercise, reading, and spirituality). This guarantees that CEOs maintain a speed suitable for a marathon-length exertion rather than exhausting themselves by sprinting repeatedly.

Choose genuineness as a leadership model.

Exemplary CEOs balance the realism of what they should do in their profession with their inherent humanity. They consciously pick their behavior in the role, considering considerations such as: What legacy do I wish to leave? What kind of impression do I want others to have of me as a leader? What am I advocating? What will I not tolerate? CEOs respond to these questions based on their abilities and motivations and the demands of the business and establish procedures to monitor their performance.

Additionally, by including these goals in the justification for their decisions and actions, CEOs can reduce the likelihood of unintended interpretations being magnified in detrimental ways. This cannot be overstated. "You speak through an incredible amplification device," a consumer goods CEO explained. Everyone in the system catches upon every action or statement you make and, in most cases, acted upon."

Keep an eye out for hubris.

It's natural for CEOs to become arrogant. While they must sometimes ignore criticism, they may also tune out critics as they learn to trust their intuition. Their conviction may grow stronger due to subordinates' tendency to speak only what their leaders want to hear. Soon, CEOs lose the ability to say "I'm not sure," stop seeking assistance or input, and disregard all criticism. Excellent CEOs cultivate a limited circle of trusted colleagues to deliver candid, objective advice—including that which has not been requested but is critical to hear.

Additionally, they maintain contact with how work is accomplished within the firm by venturing outside boardrooms, conference centers, and corporate jets to spend time with rank-and-file personnel. The CEO can build on this good basis and serves as a motivator for everyone involved.

Finally, exceptional CEOs maintain perspective by reminding themselves that their work is transitory and does not define or limit their self-worth or significance. While Steve Jobs urged college graduates to "remain hungry and naive," we counsel CEOs to "be hungry and modest."

Excellent CEOs cultivate a limited circle of trusted colleagues to deliver candid, objective advice—including that which has not been requested but is critical to hear.

Evaluation of CEO excellence

CEOs have numerous indicators of how well they are performing in their roles. The amount of value created by a CEO's company is a criterion utilized in practically every "best CEO" rating for public companies. Value creation enables the pursuit of other objectives to be sustained. However, financial metrics of CEO competence suffer from a significant flaw: they are significantly influenced by variables beyond the CEO's control.

Additionally, the focus on individual responsibilities that CEOs should place will shift with time. Early in a CEO's term, time spent developing the company strategy will often give way to fine-tuning and driving execution and then presenting actual results that establish credibility with stakeholders. At some time, it's important to look at the business objectively and decide on the next set of big steps, reorganize the organization, refresh the team and procedures, and so on.

Leadership is critical—and none is more critical than the leader of leaders. Appointed executives can strengthen their leadership talents by studying and embracing the mindsets and activities that define CEO excellence.

CHAPTER

5

THE TECHNOLOGY PARADIGM

Even ten years ago, the modern workplace was markedly different. It is even more dissimilar to the "modern" office of the mid-1900s, which had typewriters, smoke-filled rooms, and mounds of paper. The reality is that the workplace has evolved from an employer-driven culture to an employee-driven culture and continues to do so.

With technology enabling more people to work remotely, for themselves, or from home, employers are finding themselves competing for talent in ways that would have seemed strange to previous generations of business leaders.

As the entire workforce and workplace culture evolve, business leaders must adapt to remain relevant and continue recruiting the best personnel. Business executives must understand how their culture and potential workforce have evolved and continue to change to target, attract, and keep outstanding individuals effectively.

Technology has continued to play a role in this equation and is thus frequently the best place to start for businesses seeking to understand what the future worker wants from a profession. Employers can leverage technology to ascertain what a prospective employee desires in a job and incorporate technology into the job itself to entice potential hires.

For instance, a company may introduce the option of working from home or remotely on certain days of the week if they discover that potential hires desire greater work location flexibility.

Identifying Employee Desires

Employers can leverage technology to gather statistics on workplace culture. These figures can be valuable for employers seeking information about their employees and prospective hiring expectations from their employment and workplaces.

Employers can obtain this information in various ways through the use of technology. Numerous firms aggregate and analyze numerous trends and attitudes in the current and future workforce and deliver this knowledge to company leaders in simple and concise formats.

Executives and hiring managers can receive these reports and use them to grasp better the workplace preferences of their current and potential hires. Employers can also leverage technology to better understand their employees' desires by utilizing social media to learn about their lives outside of work.

When an employer views an employee's profile on a social media or networking site, they can learn about their interests and the types of things they value, which may differ significantly from what they know about the employee.

Additionally, companies should consider that individuals working in different areas may have distinct career goals. This is critical to note while reading journals and studies on employee mindsets. Some may be industry-specific and differ significantly from what employees in another industry want from their jobs.

Change Implementation

Change can be exceedingly difficult to implement. This is especially evident in a corporate context when a certain culture has persisted for a long period of time. There will frequently be some who seek to avoid change and maintain the status quo.

It's critical to realize that change rarely occurs overnight and that adapting a workplace to meet the needs of employees and potential talent frequently requires time and effort.

However, while executing change, it is usually prudent to begin with, the simplest aspects. This may vary according to the workplace, management, and the employees' desires. A great technique is to get employees and management together, identify what each can live with, and then implement those changes. This frequently results in each side feeling like they have a voice in how things are done.

While change is inherently difficult, it is more vital than ever now. Fortunately, businesses now have the tools necessary to comprehend and implement real change to continue attracting and retaining great personnel.

THE STRUCTURE OF THE DIGITAL WORKPLACE

Work has been revolutionized due to the improvements brought about by COVID-19. Businesses are speeding up their transition to the digital workplace by introducing innovative technology, reorganizing hierarchical structures, and identifying new methods to enhance the customer and employee experience.

"Expectations for experience have been increasing year after year, particularly in digital, and the demand for a compelling and engaging digital experience has surpassed safety as the top priority for businesses."

The digital workplace's objective is to create a pleasant employee journey focused on effective communication, collaboration, engagement, productivity, loyalty, a sense of belonging based on diversity and inclusion, and personal fulfillment. It becomes a reality when leaders promote and support a culture of transparency, open communication, continuous learning, diversity and inclusion, and flexibility.

The Paradigm of the Digital Workplace Is Constantly Evolving

The trends that have shaped the digital workplace began in the early 2000s and have continued to evolve since then. The introduction of the iPhone and Android operating systems, the availability of always-on internet service and high-bandwidth connectivity, the emergence of cloud computing, software as a service (Saas), artificial intelligence (AI), and Internet of Things (IoT) technology are all significant events.

Add the workplace's digital revolution and the development of remote and distributed workers, and you have the structure for today's digital workplace.

These changes are having a beneficial effect on the way businesses are conducted. "Undoubtedly, a new paradigm is forming due to the convergence of various business and technology developments. It takes a more dynamic and evolving approach to plan for the digital workplace."

The tendency date to 2004 when author and MIT management professor Thomas Malone highlighted the transition from "command and control" to "coordinate and cultivate" due to new information technology.

"He contended that those who enable a high degree of freedom and flexibility in a knowledge—and the innovation-driven economy will triumph."

"This marked a change toward a more fluid administrative style that encompassed a range of centralized and dispersed activity. In other words, rather than a rigid hierarchical structure and isolated teams, you would prioritize the necessary activities and then develop working relationships, teams, and projects around them."

The digital workplace's growth continues. Initially, email and other Internet-based communication technologies sparked the transition. "It now encompasses everything from project management applications such as Slack and Asana to robotics, the Internet of Things, and machine intelligence."

"The speed of communication, the availability of information, and the processing power enable the development of new organizational and business models."

"They enable a more agile digital workplace, where roles and responsibilities can vary in response to changing needs and where project rollouts can occur in a fraction of the time previously achievable. In a nutshell, they enable agility: the capacity to adapt and evolve rapidly."

Vertical Hierarchies Are Dead; Long Live Agile Horizontal Hierarchies In

The traditional top-down pyramid or "waterfall" business hierarchy, with executives at the top, managers in the middle, and lower-level managers and employees at the bottom, is giving way to a more horizontal or sideways hierarchy that fosters creativity and innovation by allowing employees to collaborate and make decisions independently of managers and leaders.

Numerous commercial firms have made agile methodology a fundamental component of their strategy for the digital workplace. "In a world molded by perpetual upheaval, businesses must be prepared to evolve."

"Businesses with rigid organizational models—highly centralized, compartmentalized departments, and static managerial hierarchies—are doomed to fail. They are incapable of adapting rapidly enough."

Agile is a management framework that prioritizes procedures and activities above static projects or departments. "You concentrate on the end-to-end process, identifying all the actions required to complete it, and all the team members need to participate."

"Then you promote information exchange across those contact points, ensuring that everyone is working toward the same goals and KPIs."

It is a steady but dynamic model. Specific objectives, measurements, and team members may vary depending on the situation, but how they vary is established and well understood.

They are referred to as "sideways organizations." They work in a way that standard vertical or waterfall hierarchies do not. "Water has no place to fall in a skewed organization."

"Because there is no upward or downward movement in a sideways organization, there is no reason to construct a career on top of others or to make decisions based on fear of falling."

This fresh perspective on hierarchy benefits everyone in the organization. "If we all played under the same rules on similar fields, using similar terminology, pursued the same goals, valued infinite-game rules above finite-game rules, and everyone playing chess rather than checkers, this whole employment thing may be a lot more enjoyable. To watch, score, and play."

"Many businesses would rather celebrate the illusion of development than actual success. Manage, not people. Manage the relationship the firm wishes to have with its customers so that it is an incredible place to work, top talent never leaves, and everyone wants to work there."

Virtual Meetings, Virtual Conferences, and Virtual Everything

Before the COVID-19 epidemic altered the business world, virtual meetings, conferences, learning programs, and consultancies existed. However, what was once considered a nicety or an additional mode of communication and administration is now considered vital and usual.

The pressing need to keep firms open and productive com-pelled CEOs to immediately begin developing approaches that would enable work to continue, albeit in a modified form. The importance of minimally invasive technology began to grow. We now live in a world where virtual conferences, webi-nars, live-streamed performances, seminars, telemedicine, and virtual events are possible.

Opportunities that were previously restricted to corporate leaders with enormous budgets become available to the gen-eral public.

"The increased flexibility enabled by digital communication has been a boon to staff and consumers. This benefit will ensure that these improvements stick, even when in-person meetings are possible."

Microlearning and Gamification as a Means of Continual Education

Education is a critical component of the digital workplace, and developing approaches to workplace learning are adapting.

"Educated customers and staff have a higher level of engage-ment and are more likely to become advocates."

"These new approaches to education are made possible by the digital revolution and can now be offered at scale. This is a clear game-changer, establishing one of the most exciting workplace creativity opportunities today."

Microlearning is a type of online education that focuses on the growth of employees via the use of short learning units.

Microlearning enables individuals to progress via smaller chunks of knowledge that are more rapidly and readily learned and recalled in today's segmented, always-on society. Microlearning courses are designed to be done on mobile devices and can be finished whenever the user has a few minutes to spare.

Gamification is a process that combines parts of game design and ideas with learning tools. According to a 2019 gamification poll, 88 percent of employees believe that gamification boosts their pleasure at work and 83 percent feel driven when they use gamified training.

Microlearning can be used in conjunction with gamification to build learning programs that contain interesting, compelling, bite-sized chunks of knowledge delivered via mobile devices. Larger learning programs can be split into manageable parts, gamified, and delivered in a style that employees can consume when they have spare moments to improve their ability or acquire a new skill.

The New Currency Is Data

With the increased emphasis on customer and employee experience, there was an immediate need to collect and standardize the data that underpins both projects. This occurred when organizations and consumers began to place a higher premium on data privacy.

Omnichannel data collection and analysis necessitated collecting data from frequently siloed sources. Email, in-store and online transactions, social media, phone and text messages, applications, polls, reviews, and interviews all added greater value. Customer Data Platforms (CDPs) are becoming the standard rather than the exception for unifying, analyzing, and personalizing data.

Customers will willingly entrust a business with their personal and transactional data if they believe they will receive something of value in return. According to a poll, 81% of 2,000 consumers surveyed responded that they would be prepared to contribute personal information to a more personalized experience. They agreed to supply the data, and the firm is upfront about how it is used.

The digital workplace generates an enormous amount of data that may be used to benefit society. Creating customer insights, teaching salespeople, and enforcing regulatory compliance are just a few examples. However, it creates privacy concerns that must be addressed.

"Instead of thinking of data as a liability on the digital balance sheet, I prefer to think of it as an asset."

"It, like the physical plane, requires investment and maintenance and depreciates over time. When paired with expertise, data can provide a sustainable competitive edge. Amazon, Netflix, and Google are all data companies who understand that data can also be used to fuel more intelligent AI-driven decision making."

Diverse and Inclusive Workplaces in the Digital Age

While efforts toward diversity and inclusion have been an element of corporate social responsibility for years, there is a greater emphasis in 2020.

Numerous corporate leaders have recognized that prejudice is not just unethical but also bad business. Businesses' benefits from a diversity and inclusion culture include enhanced innovation, resilience, problem-solving, retention, productivity, and a greater sense of belonging and connectivity.

The new digital workplace paradigm entails the application of cutting-edge technology to combat prejudice and intolerance.

"At the moment, there is a significant disparity between what businesses say and what they do to address discrimination."

"Despite the platitudes about eliminating discrimination and promoting equality, employees continue to withhold information about misconduct out of fear of repercussions."

This ability to speak up should be ingrained in the organization's principles and culture, beginning with the onboarding process and continuing with periodic reminders that employee concerns will be heard and addressed. Business leaders set the standard.

"In today's world of diversity and inclusion, employees can easily discern between change agents and window dressers."

"With recent social uprisings, businesses can no longer hide behind words. Real action must be taken, and it must be taken immediately."

Platforms for Digital Experiences Are Changing

Numerous companies, including SAP, Adobe, Salesforce, Sitecore, Liferay, and Progress Sitefinity, are selling all-in-one digital experience software, referred to as digital experience platforms, or DXPs, to assist in spreading the word.

To be regarded as a full-fledged DXP and not merely a collection of digital experience technologies, a DXP must include the following elements:

Native content management features include a textual, visual, online, mobile app, chatbot, and voice content. Native support for rich, extendable, and interoperable production/consumption APIs is also included.

Support for multichannel presentation and experience delivery native to the platform

Functionality for native account services: administration of registration, login, and passwords/authentication and access control

Capabilities for client data management using a customer data platform

Mapping the customer journey

Capabilities for personalization, analytics, and optimization

Artificial intelligence in practice

AI is used to make instantaneous decisions based on real-time data collected from various sources, enabling enterprises to understand better when and how to devote their resources to problems and experiences. "Within five years, the difference between firms that have made AI a core skill and those still searching for the appropriate business case to justify an investment will widen considerably."

Another strategy for DXPs is to leverage hybrid headless Content-as-a-Service (CaaS) systems such as Sitecore's Content Hub. These platforms enable content deployment on websites, digital assistants, mobile applications, wearables, and Internet of Things (IoT) devices. Although not included in DXPs yet, when used in conjunction with a DXP, this type of digital asset management enables better control over the digital experience.

The new digital workplace encompasses a range of technologies, including traditional technologies, agile horizontal hierarchies, virtual communication and collaboration, and DXPs, as well as an increased emphasis on diversity and inclusion, microlearning and gamified education, and an emphasis on improving the customer and employee journey.

"With the change to digital experiences, it's critical to remember that businesses are made up of people and exist to serve them. The greatest digital technology, including AI, enables those people to interact, thereby establishing trust and humanizing the experience."

TECHNOLOGY'S IMPORTANCE IN THE WORKPLACE

The value of technology in the workplace is evident in the collaborative work environment that it has fostered. Rather than being limited to large organizations, contemporary technology assists small business owners in accomplishing large goals.

Business owners have never been more self-sufficient with various hardware and software solutions at their disposal. Technology has simplified and expedited the process, whether conducting a face-to-face interview via video conferencing or delegating duties to many staff.

The introduction of technology into the workplace began with wheels and sails, enabling humans to travel to distant regions and barren seas.

Today, technology's roots have permeated considerably deeper into our professional lives.

Tech-savvy millennials and Generation Z personnel dominate today's workplaces. Technology integration becomes even more critical to meet their needs. As a result, computing has become ingrained in today's workstations.

The steady flow of modern technologies has impacted a large portion of the workflow in today's businesses. Businesses rely on technology more than ever to survive and prosper in today's competitive economy. And this has resulted in a shift in the dominant human work nature.

Additionally, with the advent of cloud-based tools and technology, the workplace no longer remains static. Professionals can now participate in office activities through the internet from any location. And this arrangement allowed the emergence of "Telecommuters" and "Remote Workers."

Additionally, with the advent of cloud-based tools and technology, the workplace no longer remains static. Professionals can now participate in business activities through internet access from any location. This resulted in the emergence of a new type of labor known as "The Remote Workers or Telecommuters."

In short, the employment of technical tools has affected human resources within enterprises. Not only have technology-enabled industries kept up with today's fast-paced work culture. However, it has enabled companies to address certain critical workplace challenges.

The Advantages of Automation in the Workplace

Around 40% of workers reported leaving a company due to a lack of access to cutting-edge digital tools.

Automation is a term that refers to any task that does not require significant human interaction and is performed by pre-programmed machines.

For instance, with file management systems in place, locating a document within a jumble of files is no longer a problem.

Automation is a necessary component of a twenty-first-century workplace. Unlike the 12-hour workday of the past, work schedules have become more unpredictable in recent years. Globalization of business has created opportunities to cater to millions of people simultaneously worldwide at any given time. And this transformation has necessitated the urgent need to automate a large portion of job activities.

This process encompasses everything, from monitoring employee performance on the job to assuring the delivery of services to clients worldwide.

The availability of multiple SaaS technologies has simplified and accelerated recruiting training and engaging staff.

The Following Are the Critical Points at Which Workplace Automation Becomes Necessary:

Improved Communication

Tasks are more effectively completed when employers and employees communicate openly.

Whether a video conferencing meeting or a status update via instant messaging, numerous commercial communication solutions have enabled seamless communication, including desktop and mobile applications. As a result, improved coordination leads to the greatest results in the workplace.

Enhanced Efficiency

Utilizing technology enables organizations to address difficulties such as file management, report generating, and growth tracking that frequently impedes employee productivity.

Modern workplaces rely heavily on computer-assisted tools to maximize efficiency. These tools assist in reducing the amount of time and money required to complete a task. By providing employees with cutting-edge technologies in the workplace, they may be more creative and efficient. Additionally, having a real-time system for providing detailed feedback on their work may assist your employees in achieving the intended result.

Increased Workforce

Enhancements occur due to the correct decisions being made and implemented based on accurate, scalable metrics.

Employing technology in the workplace enables individuals to accomplish more with fewer resources. This saves them both time and energy, which they can invest in other endeavors. Additionally, cloud-based solutions enable employees to stay connected to their job abroad. These elements contribute to employers' ability to manage their workforce's productivity.

As a result, they can make sound decisions that result in an increased workforce.

Significant Areas for Technology Involvement in the Workplace

Modern technology enables individuals to tailor any product or service to their specific requirements. This critical aspect has facilitated the adoption of technology-driven tools in the workplace by a large number of business owners.

Employers' management of numerous workplace tasks has changed due to technology usage.

Some of the Workplace Functions Affected by Technology include the following:

Recruitment

Recruiting the best people for a position can be a daunting endeavor. And it's not likely that the businesses will discover the proper talent just next door. However, cloud-based solutions and social media have suitably answered this challenge. Employers can now look for and engage the perfect person for the job from across the horizon. The introduction of social media has also played a crucial impact in this regard.

This has not only helped firms to diversify their staff but also grow their presence abroad.

Related: Best Recruitment Tools—A Comparison with What, Which, & Why\Onboarding

Onboarding is the process of making the new hires familiar with their work. It takes a lot of engagement from both the employers' and employees' sides. In huge organizations, it may not always be possible to provide each new employee with the same level of attention.

The employment of appropriate instruments in the workplace, on the other hand, speeds up this entire process. Conducting onboarding sessions online is far more convenient than individually contacting each employee. This helps save critical time and resources, which has a favorable effect on the workplace's overall productivity and standard of living.

Engagement

Employee involvement has become a must for today's businesses. In this regard, the influence of numerous SaaS solutions similar to Vantage Circle's employee engagement platform package is significant.

Employers may now engage their staff on the go, regardless of geographical constraints.

Most working-class members are members of the tech-savvy age, so engaging them via mobile has become the only viable option. Additionally, implementing a cloud-based platform enables organizations to save a significant amount of their tangible resources.

Management of Performance

This is the main area in which the benefits of technology are readily apparent. Thanks to technology, monitoring workplace productivity has never been easier than it is now. Numerous performance management solutions enable businesses to obtain precise data about their employees' work actions.

Decision-makers can now take the appropriate action at the appropriate time based on this information.

Surveys of the Workplace

Employee surveys are a necessary component of today's workplaces. They provide significant insight into any subject and aid in decision-making. In the case of a large workforce, surveying and collating data may become tedious. On the other hand, using automated survey technologies simplifies this process considerably.

It significantly speeds up collecting data and synthesizing useful information compared to the more traditional methods requiring pen and paper.

Utilize Vantage Pulse Employee Benefits to Conduct Effective Workplace Surveys and Increase Engagement

Providing benefits to employees is a critical component of an organization's employee engagement policies.

These benefits could include employee discounts, a wellness program, or a rewards program. These can now be distributed quickly using a cloud-based platform such as the one offered by Vantage Circle. By incorporating such a platform, employees can customize their benefits. As a result, you're laying the groundwork for a successful employee benefits program.

Management of Projects

Project management is another critical sector that makes extensive use of technology. The incorporation of such tools into the workplace streamlines the process of managing a large number of projects concurrently. Project management software enables teams to keep a close eye on their progress on a daily basis.

Additionally, a project management application enables team cooperation.

As a result, the output is increased while effort is reduced.

Abandoning

Technology has fundamentally altered work culture in today's highly competitive industry. Businesses thrive for the top spot by incorporating cutting-edge technology into their workplaces.

Issues that previously concerned business owners are no longer a concern, as technology has resolved most of them. Involving technology in the workplace has streamlined the workflow, resulting in superior outputs in less time. Additionally, as businesses increasingly rely on cloud technology, the responsibilities involving numerous tech-enabled products and services have expanded.

THE PARADIGM CHANGE AND PARADIGM BUSINESS IN THE WORKPLACE

A paradigm is a shared way of thinking within an organization or a group of people. Businesses, organizations, and individuals build paradigms to comprehend how the world works and manages it. While paradigms can be beneficial, they can also be incredibly restrictive, preventing us from innovating and discovering new and better ways to succeed as businesses and human beings.

Joel Barker discusses some well-known paradigm shifts in his infamous film, The Business of Paradigms. In each case, a paradigm was held sacrosanct by individuals, groups, or even countries. Change is exceedingly difficult, and in many of these instances, individuals refused to adapt and were left behind as the paradigm altered.

Barker discusses the Swiss Watch business and their decision to forego digital technologies in favor of mechanical designs. Within a decade, their market share had been halved, and the Japanese had consolidated their hold on the sector. The Swiss were slow to notice the paradigm shift and paid a high price.

Why are individuals so resistant to change? For one thing, change instills fear. It's a plunge into the unknown. However, change is a reality of life, and businesses that do not accept it as the standard will wither and die. Individuals and organizations must have the bravery to look beyond their constructed perspectives. While a paradigm shift requires courage, it is a choice that businesses and individuals can make.

Diversification is one of the best indicators of paradigm shifts. We develop such strong attachments to paradigms that we simply cannot see anything that does not suit the paradigm. Organizations miss critical information due to their inability to see outside the paradigm. Bringing in "outsiders" or diversifying opinions within an organization enables the organization to notice paradigm shifts and see beyond the conventional paradigm. An "outsider" or fresh employee in an organization is not immobilized by established norms, making change simpler.

The world is in constant flux, and each individual and organization must adapt. If we remain trapped in the same old paradigms, nothing changes, and the world continues to pass us by. Avoid the Swiss Watch Industry's demise. Every business must be aware of paradigm shifts to innovate and remain competitive in an ever-changing global environment.

MODERNIZING INNOVATION PARADIGMS

"How do you define innovation?" "Is it truly about introducing new technology to a big audience?" These, I believe, are the ones that pique your interest the majority of the time!

Indeed, innovation trends have shifted dramatically during the last few decades. Previously, businesses launched sparkling new technology and abundant communication channels to satiate the appetites of wide segments of the audience. However, as of now, these tools are insufficient to spur innovation. The reality is that true technological advancement occurs nowadays in underpants.

Innovation entails transitioning to something unique and novel to provide value and worth in the broadest sense. We are about to enter a new era of innovation. In terms of services, new technology tools, enhanced modes of communication, and ever-richer software may just be sufficient to complete the purpose. However, do these technologies truly foster innovation?

Consider the relationship between TechCrunch and AOL. Following this transaction, innovation will become even more critical as the corporation faces population-related growth limits. Innovation does not require the application of technology or technological tools in this state of circumstances. Any form of knowledge can be used to create a successful innovation, as long as it adds value to the business.

That is the essence of the concept of modern innovation. A small application of knowledge can significantly enhance the value of the company's procedures and methodologies. Even the most intricate methods and technology instruments may not be adequate to achieve innovation.

Second, innovation is not synonymous with invention. It does not even necessitate the development of novel information or tools. Rather than that, it demands the application of current knowledge in such a way that it adds value and riches. As we further detail, innovation does not occur exclusively within research units. Rather than that, it spans all facets of business and encompasses a diverse range of functions.

In terms of technology's role serves as an enabler, not a driver, of corporate innovation, the successful application of which can result in increased value. Indeed, innovation is primarily concerned with the effective application and management of the skills and competencies of every employee.

To summarize, a trained workforce, enhanced internal relations, effective communication, and increased management levels all play a crucial part in fostering an innovative culture.

DESIGN AND TECHNOLOGY OF WORK

Organizations use technology to revamp occupations and work schedules to boost employee satisfaction and productivity. Technology alters how a business works and how people evaluate its performance. Technology is not merely a means of converting input to output. This word refers to complex machinery and instruments that generate output using computers and other electronic instruments. This technology pervades industrial areas, and cloth can now be made considerably more quickly and efficiently.

Electronic money transfer and financial management instruments facilitate dynamic growth in the banking and finance sectors. Technology affects the workplace culture and works lives of employees. Continuous improvement is displayed in any organization to increase production and efficiency concurrently.

This approach of continuous improvement necessitates changes to all organizational activities. The word re-engineering refers to the process of creating a more advanced electronic version. Reengineering requires fundamentally modifying how we do things in any company.

Its fundamental rule is, to begin with, a plan sheet to rethink and modify the current management system. This makeover entails modernizing the process by eliminating outmoded aspects from any job design.

Management is responsible for comprehending the critical parts and fundamental processes that contribute value to an organization's specific competencies. Since the early 1990s, process reengineering has been popular, and virtually every large company in Europe and America has implemented some improvements to enable work redesign.

Employees who retain their positions following the organization's redesign process discover no longer performing the same work. The process of work redesign may include increasing employee service excellence, customer interaction, cooperation with suppliers and colleagues, increased responsibility, creativity, follow-up, and rewards.

It is primarily difficult on personnel and takes between three and five years to finish the entire re-engineering process. Workers become apprehensive during this period due to increased duties, tasks, a new work style, and the inherent risks. Individual and group implications for process reengineering are designed and selected.

Individual actions address employee motivation and reinforcement, cyberloafing, and ethics-related issues. Along with decision-making, communication and coordination and organizational politics are examined in greater detail, with an eye toward group-level consequences.

Job regulations and interpersonal connections are also altered due to the introduction of new technology in the workplace.

Before examining job activities, it is necessary to grasp their features. Collectively, these task qualities influence various jobs and influence employees' performance, motivations, and relationships.

The features of tasks primarily include the range of knowledge required, the task's identity and relevance, the degree of independence granted, and feedback. With these task features in mind, it is possible to evaluate an employee's growth requirement strength for a certain job; based on key job dimensions, critical psychological state, and personal and work outcomes.

Additionally, technology enables establishing an optimal work design to boost overall performance. Organizations are exploring the possibility of offering employees flexible work schedules. Employees require flexibility in an ever-changing work environment and work schedule possibilities, as they serve as a strategic tool in enterprises.

THE AGEING WORKFORCE AND TECHNOLOGY

Working parents, caregivers of elderly parents, and persons with special needs have pushed for years for flexible work schedules or telework hours to balance work and family. Still, the graying workforce will finally force corporate America to embrace flexible hours, job sharing, and telework.

Around 20% of workers are already eligible for retirement, and another 30% to 40% will reach retirement age during the following decade.

While no one knows for certain, AARP estimates that approximately 69% of baby boomers intend to remain in the labor force if possible. However, older workers will be unwilling or unable to remain on the payroll unless their employers solve the issues inherent in older bodies; as a result, job-enhancing technology of all types is predicted to grow in most industries.

Workers with deteriorating vision will require large-screen computers, while those who are hard of hearing will require assistive gadgets. Most significantly, video communication technology is projected to increase as older workers find it more difficult to travel for business meetings, training classes, consulting professionals, or just to report to the regular workplace daily.

Even if an employee must remain on-site, technology exists to handle worker health concerns, such as automatic external defibrillator programs and Phonoscope's Health Services, which connects workers to medical professionals via video conferencing by dialing a four-digit number.

Employee benefit options such as onsite medical support, rapid access to a physician, prescriptions and refills, health profiles, preventative screening, and chronic disease management are available through this service.

Telework, also known as telecommuting, flexiwork, and flexiplace, addresses several workers' diminishing health concerns as they age and is predicted to experience a significant increase in the next five to ten years. Face-to-face meetings with supervisors are already being phased out in favor of more realistic communication options, and 1-on-1 or small-group 'teams' with clearly defined objectives can collaborate wherever convenient. Thus, teleworking has the potential to attract a whole new group of individuals to the labor market, such as those with disabilities, who frequently face barriers to employment due to public transit and building adjustments.

There will always be jobs requiring a human connection, such as teachers. However, even in these instances, technology enables an increasing number of duties to be performed remotely. The Phonoscope high definition Video Conferencing System, which includes equipment and maintenance as part of the monthly service, provides T3 Internet access, allowing video conferencing to be transmitted via fiber optics.

However, the true value of Phonoscope's technology is found in the video communication apps, legal services, corporate training, health care, and education that the company offers, all of which provide vital flexibility for the post-retirement worker.

TECHNOLOGICAL TRENDS

Technology is the outcome of scientific and engineering investigations into the natural environment. It is the process through which humans modify nature to satisfy their desires and requirements. It examines the use and knowledge of tools and crafts and the impact on one's ability to manage and adapt to one's surroundings.

It is derived from the Latin words "technologia"-"techne" (craft)-"logia" (knowledge) (saying). Despite this ambiguous definition, "technology" can refer to material things of human use, such as utensils, machinery, or hardware, and broader concepts, such as procedures, systems, or organizations. The phrase can be used broadly or narrowly, for example, "medical technology," "space technology," "construction technology," or "state-of-the-art technology."

The technological developments reflect a market that is undergoing rapid and ambiguous evolution. Contemporary technological trends are continually evolving, and new advancements always enhance computer components. A computer's fundamental components include hardware, software, and peopleware.

The term "software" refers to instructions or programs, such as an operating system, utilities, compilers or interpreters, and any other software packages. Hardware refers to the computer's physical components.

A personal computer's hardware includes, but is not limited to, the monitor, keyboard, system unit, formerly known as the CPU, mouse, printers, and webcam. Peopleware represents the personnel involved in system analysis, operations, and maintenance. In some sectors, innovation is inevitable.

Vendors of software and hardware are undergoing profound changes to their business models. It intends to climb out of the commodity bin with new items and a marketing campaign. Microsoft, Oracle, First Data, SAP, Accenture, Google, and Yahoo are just a few examples of large software companies. Others include Computer Sciences Corporation, Electronic Data Systems, SoftBank, Symantec, CA, Fiserv, Affiliated Computer Services, Adobe Systems, Capgemini Group, ASML Holdings, Electronic Arts, Advantest, Intuit, Autodesk, VeriSign, Check Point Software, DST Systems, The Sage Group, Dassault Systemes, CSK, and Ak

Businesses that sell operating systems such as Windows, Office Applications for creating professional documents, financial reports, and presentations, IT security (anti-virus, internet protection, and the like), and other programs spring to life, transforming a marketing blunder into a witty field that could transform your work and even your life.

Electronic payment systems lure many consumers and merchants, establishing themselves as the silent stars of e-commerce. Businesses that conduct business online do so to generate additional revenue. We understand their business cycle and are devoted to assisting them in succeeding.

Printers, scanners, speakers, headphones, modems, fax machines, and copiers are just some of the peripheral devices available for personal computers. They come in various styles, colors, sizes, and impressive features that enable consumers to manage better their growing collection of documents, photos, music, and videos.

Cable television companies are transforming millions of televisions worldwide at a breakneck pace.

Nowadays, computer gaming is attracting the attention of individuals of all ages. It is one of the fastest expanding segments, contributing to the industry's multibillion-pound size. It has entirely new entertainment that has never been seen before.

Now that most commercial operations and knowledge work are undertaken in the digital arena via computers and a worldwide data communications network that does not impose restrictions on the sort of data that may be transmitted, technology is undergoing another transformation. And it will continue to grow indefinitely as long as the world requires it.

LEADERSHIP AND THE ARTIFICIAL INTELLIGENCE ORGANIZATION

Business writers and experts have supplied business executives with various concepts, theories, and methods to assist them in managing and leading change in their organizations for decades. While these prescriptions were important at the time, they may present difficulties for leaders planning and executing AI advances today.

The distinction is that corporate executives must be able not just to implement change, although continuously, but also seek opportunities to transform their organizations.

According to Merriam-Webster, transform means:

...to alter the composition or structure of; to alter the external appearance or shape of; to alter the character or state of a convert.

For leaders, this entails fundamentally altering the way their firm operates. Strategic transformation is required in a workplace where AI applications coexist with human capabilities as implementation instruments. As authors Rohit Talwar, Steve Wells, and Alexandra Whittington state in Fast Future,

As AI grows more prevalent, the importance of employees' soft skills will increase. As corporations increasingly rely on rule-based thinking and automation, soft talents such as sensitivity, creativity, verbal reasoning and communication, empathy, and spontaneity may become increasingly valued.

Human resources or a new Department of Humanity can promote this aspect of personal development, ensuring that firms maximize the interaction between human and machine intelligence.

If these writers are true, what behaviors might we anticipate from leaders on this journey with their organizations?

Motivated to acquire new knowledge continuously

In light of the unrelenting acceleration of artificial intelligence (AI), cognitive technologies, and automation, 86 percent of respondents to this year's Global Human Capital Trends poll feel they must reinvent their learning capacity.

Despite nearly a decade of economic prosperity and a ubiquitous corporate focus on digital transformation, 84 percent of respondents indicated they need to rethink their employee experience to boost productivity. And, in response to increased challenges to move faster and adapt to a considerably more diverse workforce, 80 percent believe companies must rethink how they create leaders.

As the workforce demographics change and the baby boomer cohort retires, there is a significant need for leadership skills transfer. When AI is introduced, the leader's skill challenge multiplies. Leaders must continually improve their abilities while providing constant training and development for their staff.

Exposure to problem-based learning will present leaders with game-changing experiences that will help them develop their capacities and strengthen their flexibility and agility.

Leaders should continue networking, investing in educational opportunities, conducting research to stay current on trends and new advances in their respective fields of expertise, and trusting that younger team members may know more than them is critical. These behaviors are critical for developing relationships both internally and with external AI contacts and coworkers.

A disposition to share

Dynamic leaders recognize the value of collaboration, recognizing that when some team members' skills deteriorate, others improve. This occurs in the world of artificial intelligence. Technical skills that were once thought vital may become obsolete, but the requirement for emotional intelligence skills will be a strength of the leader and team. While AI lacks empathy and compassion, human abilities require leaders to show concern for their teams and coworkers.

Chatbots must be accepted as new team members and can be used to onboard and teach new team members and assist them with certain processes and activities. This frees up time for team members to apply critical thinking, creativity, and innovation to more complex situations.

Leaders must demonstrate their enthusiasm for AI by committing to new processes and practices and communicating effectively with all stakeholders to ensure that everyone advances together.

By acting courageously as change agents, they develop trust in and reliance on others and continue to encourage team members and colleagues from various disciplines. These leaders broaden their team to encompass a greater range of abilities and participants, minimizing existing organizational silos.

A passion for inventing and creating

Leaders must be adaptable, flexible, and agile to build an innovative culture. Adaptable leaders are not hesitant to choose a different path when the situation requires it, and their versatility enables them to overcome obstacles.

This is necessary when tactics incorporate AI technology. Leaders must maintain engagement notders must maintain engagement not only with their teams but also with other members of the business, consumers, and the community

As leaders develop their innovative capabilities and expertise, they guarantee that their teams do the same.

Agile organizations require adaptive leaders. When leaders stay informed on changes in the competitive landscape and community, value chain trends, and customer or client base trends, they teach their people how to be agile.

Confidence in challenging established assumptions.

To be successful in the era of artificial intelligence, leaders must constantly question/change their mental models, challenging assumptions about the business, its customers, and the future. They accelerate performance by focusing on purpose and strengths.

They must concentrate on the behaviors and processes that maximize the team's creative potential and, consequently, the AI's power. This will bolster decision-making and problem-solving abilities when confronted with difficult scenarios dictated by client needs and desires.

A capacity for identifying and overcoming impediments

This is about retaining everyone's attention

What is impeding their progress? It is critical to tie the team's talents and strengths to the company's vision and mission. By including them in collaborative decision-making, introducing them to creative methods like brainstorming, establishing pilot groups, project teams, and member rotation, teams will have additional possibilities to participate. Humans may spend less time on repetitive and non-value-added jobs by utilizing chatbots and virtual feedback platforms.

What remains constant with the arrival of AI is the critical nature of well-defined goals. Leaders and their teams should collaborate to create performance objectives, which they should then be free to fulfill or surpass.

Without the proper setting, this leadership development will have a negligible effect. Transformative acts require the correct environment; organizations must also 'change in composition or structure.'

Organizations must be staffed with varied teams; cross-functional, multi-skilled, interdisciplinary teams that collaborate. There are no silos. All members of these teams must be engaged and actively participate in the design of new processes, procedures, and practices within a culture that values front-line decision-making and problem-solving. These teams are encouraged to be original and creative by using a continuous cycle of try-test-measure-review-learn. Organizations staffed by leaders that understand and recognize the benefits of AI will be able to reshape their cultures, a culture built on a foundation of complementary AI applications and human strategic skills.

HOW ARE WORK AND ORGANISATIONS CHANGING AS A RESULT OF TECHNOLOGY?

Several possibilities have been brought to the forefront due to growing technology. Technology growth and advancement have also significantly impacted work and organizations.

1. Expanded and altered modes of communication

The advent of email, internet calling, and video conferencing has made communication between employees easier. Earlier forms of communication included telephone calls, letters, and face-to-face encounters. The development of smartphones, talking apps, video calling capabilities, social media, email programs, and communication strategies have revolutionized the way connections are formed.

2. Cost Savings

Profitability is the primary objective of any organization. Whether it's an educational institution or a workplace, the emergence of many new and advanced software technologies has aided organizations in reducing expenses through reduced staffing. This has resulted in cost savings and the reputation of being progressive and adapting to evolving technologies. The overall cost of utilizing these software solutions is far less than what was previously paid to employees.

3. Customization Options

Many website design tools have made it easier for users to construct their web addresses and personalize them according to their preferences. Numerous online businesses allow clients to customize their experiences and express their preferences. For instance, various internet platforms assist students in obtaining homework assistance. Given that we are discussing technology let us consider a student who requires assistance with a programming project. He can begin with his service provider and work his way up to the structure and language utilized in his task. Technological advancements have made it easy for everyone to pick and do things their way.

4. Telecommuting

Another way that technology has facilitated job performance is through the proliferation of the 'work from home' mentality. There is no need to report to work if you can complete the task using resources other than the office facility. There are numerous technologically advanced reasons why the work-from-home culture thrives in the modern era.

Among these are online meeting platforms, tracking tools, and so forth. You may also be interested in learning more about employee productivity tracking, which is in great demand now that many people work from home.

We've tested numerous solutions, and that's certainly the best one, so if you need to monitor your staff, that is the service to use. The same is true for educational institutions that provide online classes, where students do not need to be physically present in the classroom; instead, checking in via the program suffices.

5. Significantly Reduced Security Risks

With the passage of time, technology has also overcome security issues and data theft. Previously, it was difficult to maintain track of each employee's activities, but technological advancements have enabled organizations to keep track of their employees' communication and work activities. Certain tools also assist in monitoring the data stored on the organization's various servers.

6. Establishment of online services

Numerous internet portals offer various services, from drafting legal documents to purchasing a needle. One can obtain professional assistance or purchase the most expensive items without physically procuring them. Employees and students can get assistance from service providers and have their presentations, assignments, and other materials delivered with the push of a button. A student specializing in technical courses such as information technology might approach an academic services provider for IT assignment assistance simply by paying a small fee and completing his job more easily.

7. Enhanced Collaborations

Without the need to be physically present in every location, and because of advancements in communication techniques, enterprises have become extremely easy to work with one another.

Thanks to technological advancements, people may now connect anywhere and at any time. For instance, online training in the workplace and audio-visual lectures in educational institutions have aided firms in growing with a larger perspective.

Technology has made life easier at work, businesses, and practically everyone who utilizes it. However, the fact that technology is continuously advancing at a rapid speed necessitates considerable effort to ensure that you keep up with the changing technology or risk falling behind. In a nutshell, technology benefits an organization or work by enabling them to maintain its position and compete effectively in the market.

FOR A DIGITAL WORKPLACE, THESE ARE THE ESSENTIAL TECHNOLOGIES

Today's workplaces are accustomed to purchasing digital technologies to solve business problems. While this may be the progressive course of action, you will eventually wind up with many tools that do many of the same responsibilities.

As an example of a digital workplace, suppose your finance department makes use of a particular technology for invoicing. The app automatically updates all spending and keeps the information structured. A few months later, your sales staff will require a method for tracking the costs associated with obtaining a customer.

While new technology may fix the problem for the sales team, the finance team is now in the dark regarding the department's spending. Due to the fact that one necessity arose at a different time, the requirement for the other was overlooked. You have two distinct tools that must be monitored, maintained, and paid for separately.

Always take a step back and consider the big picture when investigating the arena of digital tools. Your entire organization functions as a single unit, utilizing various tools and personnel. These instruments are distinct and must work in unison to benefit your business.

These tools should not be viewed as short fixes for specific situations to get the most out of these tools. Investments in new technologies for your digital workplace are called tools.

Rather than playing whack-a-mole by hurling a new digital tool at every difficulty, consider how technologies may assist you in achieving your bigger objectives. Which technologies are easily available on the market as tools? Which ones do you require immediately? Which ones are still in the works? How are they going to address cross-functional requirements? Sorting through these issues will help you navigate your way and save you money in the long term.

Several digital workplace technologies form the backbone of the majority of enterprises. Numerous products have been on the market for an extended period and have reached a point on the innovation curve. Others are considerably more recent and will require a considerable strategy to integrate across the firm.

The Top Six Essentials of Workplace Technology

1. Management of documents

Each day, the amount of data created increases. Your organization may create dozens to hundreds of thousands of new papers, spreadsheets, forms, and videos every day. Employees, companies, customers, operations, and marketing information should be organized for simple access and timely insights.

A cloud-based document management system may be the optimal solution for data management. They also serve additional uses in addition to data management. They can serve as adaptive learning platforms for employees, allowing them to obtain the information they require in the order they need it.

These platforms' powerful search capabilities have made it simple to locate any file across the business. Additionally, employees may cooperate effortlessly on various types of data.

Document management systems have evolved into powerful products capable of analyzing all structured data.

2. Management of work

Automation of processes is a fundamental requirement for firms seeking to improve their agility. You may save a lot of time and resources by identifying and automating routine operations in each department. Automation technology should provide maximum flexibility to assist you in designing workflows while maintaining control over visibility permissions.

The second criterion for a workflow tool is the capacity to construct user-driven workflows on an individual basis. As with repetitious procedures, each department has its own set of unpredictable workflows that must be monitored. Customized case and project management solutions can assist virtually any department in managing ad hoc requests that require human interaction at each level.

Employees should be capable of planning, organizing, coordinating, managing, and executing tasks. You can no longer expect employees to be effective just by providing them with email, word processing, PowerPoint, and spreadsheets.

Management of projects and processes has become critical to completing tasks.

Work management tools should be intuitive and allow teams to convene before a project, collaborate effectively during execution, fix faults, and evaluate results. These criteria can be fulfilled through various functions such as chat, email, audio and video conversations, meeting solutions, and file sharing. The tools should simplify staff to manage assignments, projects and collaborate internally.

Obtaining maximum functionality may also require the use of various tools. Decision-makers should carefully select tools that combine most essential functions into a single package. Along with cost savings, it also increases employee productivity by decreasing tab switching and facilitating contextual talks.

3. Collaborative and interpersonal communication

Enterprise social networking is a critical component of an organization's long-term success. Apart from allowing employees to communicate news and other pertinent information, it can be an excellent tool for analyzing team and individual participation in the digital workplace.

Additionally, thoughtfully built workplace social networks can assist in avoiding distractions by displaying algorithmically appropriate messages and refraining from constantly ringing notification bells. Individuals can cultivate a healthy digital culture by comprehending and appreciating their digital capabilities and restrictions.

Chatbots are gaining traction in both internal and customer-facing environments. They can be straightforward algorithmic answers or sophisticated artificial intelligence-based algorithms with a broader scope for understanding language and discussions.

When implemented internally, chatbots improve the employee experience by allowing employees to self-serve HR and service desk functions. It alleviates the burden on IT teams by boosting resource accessibility.

The majority of its potential is in chatbots for customer service. They can cut customer service expenditures by 30% while improving the client experience. Automating routine questions reduces response times for requests, and support staff can spend more time addressing unique difficulties.

Team collaboration is becoming an increasingly critical technology as an increasing workforce is distributed via remote work and flexible work hours. In contrast to a hierarchical structure that prescribes work to individuals, teams are now more connected and have a broader network. Today's leaders are accountable for creating this environment and working tirelessly to improve its efficiency.

4. No-code solution development

Nowadays, employees are increasingly empowered and given responsibility for their work. However, to genuinely empower employees and mid-level executives digitally, they should be empowered to build solutions for their requirements.

When IT teams are required to develop tools, deadlines lengthen. They must first analyze and comprehend company requirements before beginning to develop tools and applications. Skill reliance can be decreased if the person who has the business knowledge and the authority to build solutions is also the person who has the ability to build solutions.

You can deploy low-code platforms throughout your organization to assist departments in developing their applications for any business case.

5. Information security

Since data breaches have become a greater worry, IT leaders have been working to strengthen security while allowing employees to flex their digital boundaries more freely. All cloud-based applications include a built-in layer of security. Cloud storage has advanced to the point that it is now more secure than on-premise storage.

A breach occurs on both internal and external sides of the wall. Internal data breaches can be avoided by identifying and restricting access to sensitive data (data policies) and establishing network, device, and application monitoring solutions.

External malware attacks are most frequently launched via email phishing. Educating employees on best practices and instilling a sense of responsibility for data security can significantly aid in the prevention of breaches.

6. Analytical data

Most program providers now offer analytics features as an add-on. Data analytics can reveal insights on an individual and a broader organizational level (workers and customers). Without presuming any prior knowledge of data sciences, end users can be empowered with the power of analytics.

When used individually, it can provide information on each employee's area of competence. When leaders understand their team members' abilities and interests, they can manage them more effectively. Additionally, with a bit more visibility, they can identify talent gaps.

With analytics tools becoming increasingly powerful, leaders must properly pool data provided by each business process. It is an excellent strategy to ensure that data remains organized by grouping data into fewer tools. This will also save significant data movement costs when more sophisticated technologies are required.

Additional control and knowledge provided by new technologies

The following technologies are gaining traction in the workplace IT sector. They are not immediately necessary, but they should be on your radar so you can begin planning their use.

The next level of artificial intelligence

Sentiment analysis is a rapidly growing field of study finding uses in marketing, customer service, and even internal objectives. Analyzing text using natural language processing can make precise predictions about a person's feelings. Thousands of reviews can be accumulated in marketing to understand how buyers feel about the products.

Customer support personnel can utilize sentiment analysis to decide which tickets require quick attention by segregating irate clients from ordinary inquiries. Additionally, sentiment analysis can examine employees' behavior on digital apps based on data like anger clicks and the frequency with which certain buttons are pressed. It may be an excellent tool for analyzing and improving employee experience.

Employees can use virtual assistants (VAs) to aid them with daily chores. They are the equivalent of personal assistants in the digital age. Virtual assistants observe users' habits and recommend relevant actions at the proper moment.

They can act as the employee's/power customer's handler by automating chores and retrieving information. The most useful talent is visual data manipulation and visualization. Numerous software vendors offer virtual assistants as an add-on to their products.

IoT

IoT is largely concerned with integrating disparate devices and networks to automate everyday tasks in the workplace. The Internet of Things (IoT) can help ensure that all activities run smoothly and on time.

Multiple systems can be combined to create a self-contained workplace. Employees are relieved of the burden of manually interfering in a variety of tasks such as scheduling meetings, setting up facilities, and managing supplies. They may just go into the business and use one device to manage items like printers and air conditioners.

Technology is only the beginning.

Having a framework of technologies in which to invest is the first step in developing a more robust system capable of advancing company objectives and empowering people. The following stage assesses and chooses the appropriate tools to complement these technologies.

After acquiring the necessary digital workplace technologies, your focus should be on developing a program that aligns all employees with your digital workplace goal. Leaders should direct efforts toward developing a strong digital culture that fosters an environment conducive to employees working toward the company's future success.

THE NEW WORKFORCE PARADIGM SHARING THE BUSINESS FUTURE

The future of business can be murky at times, all the more so as the world continues to move at a breakneck rate that many are unable to keep up with. Recently, business experts have frequently expressed concern about their inability to foresee future trends, whether economic or labor market-related, which has resulted in a slew of problems: talent shortages, under-or unemployment, and even profit losses.

Without a clear vision for the future and understanding of how things will continue to evolve, many businesses are unsure of what to do or where to go. Fortunately, many of those changes are due to a single reason.

Changes in technology have impacted every aspect of life over the last decade—how we communicate, have fun, work, and even our personal lives—so it's only inevitable that the face of business would alter substantially as well.

As a result, adjustments have been made to human resources and how we deal with our staff. Traditional methods and processes have begun to dwindle, being replaced by a business environment rife with new factors.

How do we adapt to a changing global marketplace without jeopardizing our objectives? How can we respond confidently to an uncertain future? And, perhaps most significantly, how do we fill newly created and unexpected personnel gaps?

The Temporary Workforce

This is where contingent labor comes into play. A contingent workforce may consist of individuals from any industry, ranging from arts and design to engineering and technology. They are independent contractors, consultants, contractors, temporary workers, and other non-permanent workers rapidly gaining prominence. According to some estimates, 40% of America's employment—60 million workers in the United States alone—will be freelancers by 2020. Why is this? Efficiency, efficiency, and the independence that individuals and employers enjoy are significant draws.

Contingent workers are employed to fill workforce gaps, areas where full-time skilled professionals are either unavailable or unqualified. While some businesses may be hesitant to hire these types of personnel, a growing number have embraced this new paradigm.

Flexibility

Flexibility is sometimes cited as the primary benefit of contingent labor. Companies working on specific projects may consider employing people with highly specialized skill sets to work on the project for the duration. Alternatively, a full-time employee with the same skill set may find themself unemployed after the project is over, becoming a cost burden.

Certain routine but critical jobs within a business may only require a few hours per week, yet devoting a full-time employee to them may be a waste of their time and abilities. Hiring a freelancer to undertake those chores, on the other hand, frees up your employees' time and can save you a lot of money in the long run.

Contingent labor can also be targeted at certain areas within a business. It can take the form of payroll specialists, human resource reps, social media gurus, content developers, or other positions for which hiring a full-time employee would appear excessive.

Providers of Contingent Workforce Management

Numerous agencies have sprung up in response to the rise of contingent labor, providing you have access to a wide pool of dependable, highly skilled people for when those situations arise. They have extensive networks of vetted workers and can provide invaluable guidance on utilizing your newly acquired contingent staff best. Agencies can help you navigate the relatively new and choppy waters surrounding freelancers, ensuring that you can trust your hiring and attract the best talent.

TOMORROW'S DIGITAL WORKPLACE

The digital workplace notion encompasses characteristics of people, processes, and technology. An ideal digital workplace prioritizes employees, is constantly evolving technologically, and is organized and managed in such a way that seamless coordination between people, processes, and technology is possible.

Human beings are sociable animals. They yearn for interaction (some more than others). Google, Salesforce, and Twitter have all successfully expanded their work-from-home policy. Certain knowledge workers will never set foot in another physical office facility. As a result, businesses are examining the future of communication, collaboration, and employee engagement.

To sustain this path toward virtual employment, we must increase our ability to keep knowledge workers motivated while they remain separated. Whether through virtual work rotations, sharing forums, training, and development, or software that connects and shows individual efforts as a percentage of total corporate success, daily employee engagement will be considerably more valued than in previous years.

Future Digital Workplace Technology Requirements

We are all familiar with the essential features of digital workplaces: intranets, collaboration tools, and knowledge sharing repositories. From my vantage point, I see new analytical technology requirements emerging to support the future digital workplace.

Today's technologies, such as Microsoft's Workplace Analytics, track staff productivity, process efficiency, and pattern of collaboration. Additionally, the service is touted to assist in accelerating cultural shifts and diversity and inclusion activities. These types of solutions are geared toward organizational optimization.

On the other hand, MercuryApp or TinyPulse monitors staff morale and emotional responses, primarily via employee questionnaires. These are qualitative solutions that are centered on employee mood.

Organizations will require comprehensive, extensible, analytics-driven quantitative systems in the future to track employee engagement, morale, and inclusiveness. I envision these systems recording and analyzing employee behavior patterns at a granular level to make recommendations to both the employee and the business regarding virtual work enhancement.

These strategies for combating virtual weariness may include exercise breaks, engagement activities with coworkers, and workplace adjustments. It's critical to note that these new solutions must consider privacy and trust. Employees will be reluctant to reveal detailed work patterns to firms that may use that knowledge against them during organizational restructuring.

Always put others first

Organizations will need to prioritize the following: work rotations, sharing forums, training and development programs, and possibly employee engagement tools. People first means that businesses actively participate in monitoring employee engagement and morale and then acting on the data.

The objective is to assist the individual worker in developing and maintaining self-esteem, self-health, and levels of engagement.

Develop Processes That Increase Productivity, Employee Engagement, and Employee Health

Individual staff should also develop their processes. It includes simulating a commute to and from work to allow for preparation and decompression. Additionally, I partition my day to provide structure: designating meeting and work hours, lunchtime, and time to network and socialize. Additionally, it entails having a separate workspace apart from the couch where you relax. By establishing repeatable routines, you can plan for and react to your workday.

Technology

As we all agree, the best technology is one that works. Provide your employees with the greatest technology available to assist them in completing their assigned tasks. Consider flexible, analytics-driven, and well-integrated systems, such as those listed previously. Similarly, the workday improves when employees invest time and effort in their technological setup. Consider alternatives to the laptop at the dining room table: design a comfortable workspace in your virtual office that enables you to work outside of normal business hours if necessary, a place where you can concentrate and produce.

Individual and organizational innovation and adaptation will enable us to not just manage with change but to reimagine the workplace of the future as a more productive environment.

LEADERSHIP WITH A SPECIALIZED FOCUS ON TECHNOLOGY AND ADAPTABILITY

Evolution is a synonym meaning 'adapting to change,' flourishing, and progressing to the next level of accomplishment.

Diverse industrial workers have seen more change or evolution in the last five years than their parents did in their entire lives. Technology has enhanced the speed at which we perform our tasks and has resulted in a rise in the pace at which we perform our tasks. The workplace is changing as a result of Generation Y's (those in their twenties) and Millenials' values shifts (those under 20).

Generational values vary significantly among generations and contribute to the rapid speed of change. Zoomers (baby boomers who refuse to age and those in their early 50's to late '60s) and Gen X (those in their 30's to early '50s) are under pressure to develop a new and more evolved workplace from Gen Y and Millennial employees and customers.

As we approach an altering 2020 workplace, several themes include changing behaviors impacted by social media and a sizable population of Gen Y and Millenials.

Consider the following:

50% of the world's population is under 30 years old.

Kindergartners are now taught using tablets rather than chalkboards.

Britney Spears has more Twitter followers than Sweden and Canada combined.

And...What occurs in Las Vegas is broadcast on Facebook, Twitter, and YouTube...

There is no doubting that technology and social media have had a significant impact on business over the last decade.

Therefore, what came first? Is it a case of generational values shifting, or is it a case of technological advancement?

The answer is technology. Since the postwar era of the 1950s and 1960s, when the workplace was dominated by authoritarian leadership and command and control, and employment was mostly task-oriented and repetitious, the workplace has evolved.

The 1950s workplace was characterized by people who did as they were told, leaders who expected to be respected, and monotonous employment. For individuals working at that age, the values were thankfulness for their occupations, and workers would frequently begin early and work for the same company for the remainder of their lives.

In the 1970s and 1980s, the workplace was a place where structures were created, exceptions to rules were formed, and leaders were promoted based on their ability to 'do.' Training was a novel notion, and the resulting lack of structure necessitated continual reorganizations and modifications to the workplace.

The leadership style was more akin to that of a manager,' but with the autocratic edge associated with the preceding era of leadership. In this era, customers followed what businesses established, and employees followed the organizational structures established by leadership.

The workplace began to evolve in the 1990s and 2000s in favor of stronger leadership. Visionary and inspirational leadership came to be regarded as valuable. This was the era of strategy, lean work environments, visionary leadership, and mentoring people to success. This was the beginning of workplace culture, and employee engagement and motivation became a big topic.

This was also a time of layoffs, mergers, and reorganization inside enterprises. During these decades, employees, especially Zoomers, realized they would have multiple jobs or careers throughout their lives and that retiring from a single workplace was not as likely as it was for Traditionalists (those in their late 60s and older).

The decade from 2010 to the 2020s saw the introduction of enormous technological development. The workplace began to evolve into a place where the capacity to adapt to change rapidly was highly valued. This includes generations cooperating more effectively and adapting to a workplace in which leaders are not 'better than their employees and possess the ability to innovate, collaborate, and synergize.

Additionally, the world has shrunk in the last two decades due to technological advancements and commerce being global rather than local. With the entry of Gen Y into the workforce, a renewed emphasis on having fun at work, working smarter rather than harder, leveraging technology to accomplish tasks, and collaborating as a team began.

Whereas in the past, the workplace would have had the luxury of a few weeks to complete a project or conduct a performance assessment, we now live and operate in a real-time' world. The rapid evolution of the workplace necessitates that leaders and their teams modify their mindsets in order to boost their agility and focus on a 2020 vision.

When we consider the impact of technology, we must also consider the impact of social media and how it is altering the way we communicate as a society. Generation Y and Millenials are continuously connected via Twitter, Facebook, YouTube, and Instagram, which has heightened their need for rapid recognition, a voice, and democratization of the workplace.

Social media has a greater impact on Generation Y and Millennials than any other mode of communication. Eighty-seven percent of Gen Y and Millenials surveyed place a higher premium on peer ratings than advertisements.

Let's fast-forward to the workplace in 2020--what will it look like with the influence of technology and the increased presence of Gen Y's and Millenials?

The future and growing workplace will feature increased enjoyment, position flexibility, and collaborative teams working on 'parachute projects.' To keep Gen Y's and Millenials interested, the workplace will be a creative setting with a work environment that facilitates work and personal life integration. This contrasts with the Zoomers and some Gen X, who emphasized keeping 'work and personal life apart.'

Nick Shore, senior vice president-strategic insights and research at MTV, stated at a briefing with MediaDailyNews, "[Millennials] have a strong work ethic and integrate their professional and personal life even more than Boomers do."

According to the study, 93% of Gen Y and Millennials are looking for work that fits their lifestyle. It is a reality that a fast-paced, social culture surrounds today's youth. Is your workplace harnessing such vitality? Eighty-nine percent of Gen's and Millennials said they desire a "social and entertaining" workplace. To emphasize the significance of the statistic, only 60% of Baby Boomers share that mindset.

The future workplace will premium on a leader's capacity to engage, coach, and circulate high-performing individuals. Employees who stay on the job for five years or longer are shrinking.

Gen Y and Millenials want to continue learning and growing by working in various industries and jobs. According to research, the average Gen Y/ Millenial will change employment up to 15 times throughout their career, compared to Gen X, who would change jobs 5-7 times during their lifetime, and the Zoomer, who will change jobs 1-3 times during their lifetime.

This means that organizations and leaders must develop the ability to manage an employee base that is continually changing and cycling. Hospitality and restaurant industries attract Generation Y and Millenials. It is critical to understand that the leadership style must evolve from managing a set employment base to managing a continually changing and dynamic team of individuals. Generation Y and Millenials are always seeking opportunities for learning and advancement, which forces leaders to adapt to this reality.

Earls Restaurants is an example of a company that performs an excellent job of reacting to its Gen Y and Millennial employees. They look for students because they understand that most Gen Y/Millennial hires will not stay in the food sector for the long haul. Rather than viewing this as a barrier, Earls focuses on providing flexibility, enjoyment, and educational opportunities to Gen Y and Millenials. Earl's, surprisingly, has a greater percentage of Gen Y employees that make a restaurant work a vocation than other comparable restaurant companies.

The newest generations of workers are constantly looking for new opportunities for engagement, improvement, and advancement. Seventy-five percent of Generation Y and Millenials would value having a mentor at work. This is not simply someone who trains them to drive a bus or wait tables; this is a mentor who actively assists people in developing their careers.

The employee and mentors must establish a social connection to establish an engaging foundation in their work lives. This relates directly to Gen Y's belief that they require explicit instructions from their supervisor to perform at their best. This generation does not lack independence or desire; rather, they seek a way to succeed. Indeed, 89 percent of Generation Y and Millennials believe it is critical to learn on the job constantly.

Gen Y and Millenials' effect on performance evaluation will shape the developing workplace.

Historically, many firms across various industries have glossed over performance appraisals. However, the study found that eight out of ten Gen Y and Millennial hires desire regular feedback from their supervisors, with more than half desiring feedback at least once a week, if not more frequently.

With high turnover rates, not every employee receives an annual evaluation, and those who do are presumed to be competent. During his interview, MTV's Shore said, "Millennials and Gen Ys are like, 'Can you give me daily reviews?' Their desire to develop themselves is incredibly strong, reflecting the culture in which they grew up, as they are always in a feedback loop."

Indeed, real-time performance assessments have been pioneered by Gen Y with the website work.com, formerly ripple.com, where leaders may deliver daily feedback, acknowledgment, and coaching via text and group text for increased recognition.

Generation Y and Millenials will continue to embrace technology to boost their productivity and performance.

Technology is a significant distinction for Generation Y. They are the first generation to have consistently had access to high-speed Internet, social media, e-commerce, and interactive digital media throughout their lives. 85% of Gen Y and Millennials believe that their understanding of the technology enables them to work faster than their elder peers. And two-thirds of this age believe they should mentor senior coworkers on workplace technology.

It is no longer a matter of "should" technology be used in any business; rather, it is a matter of "how" technology may be used to expedite processes. Gen Y and Millennials are infusing the workplace with a technology-infused work mentality. Innovative and competitive businesses will look to this generation for guidance in updating methods.

The future workplace will also include evolutionary human resource practices, but the emphasis will be on human resourcefulness rather than human resources. In other words, Generation Y and Millenials will focus on assisting people in becoming more resourceful, flexible, and adaptable to change. Every part of the company is touched by the changes brought about by technological advancements and generational mindsets.

There can be no doubt about the impact of technology and Gen Y/Millenials on all industries.

The growth of the workplace necessitates new mindsets, new abilities, and, most importantly, the willingness of each individual to evolve.

TIPS FOR IMPROVING YOUR BUSINESS'S PRODUCTIVITY THROUGH TECHNOLOGY

You're in business to profit from your efforts. When you waste important time performing routine office duties, you are not developing your business or improving your bottom line. Entrepreneurs who embrace productive technology ahead of the curve concentrate their efforts on their enterprises, which thrive. Here are eight pieces of technology that may assist your business in becoming profitable.

1. Cloud Computing Services

You've heard about cloud computing but remain suspicious. I was as well, but a little understanding has proven beneficial. Cloud computing enables remote access to data, programs, and other resources from any electronic device.

When data is stored on a remote Internet server rather than a local server, it can be shared, updated, developed, and authorized by a group of individuals in different locations while keeping everyone on the same page. It saves time, money, storage space, and money on individual apps because they are kept in the cloud and accessible to everyone. Security and encryption are maintained at a high level, exceeding what the average small business can afford in-house.

2. Notes Written by Hand Make the Switch to Digital

Occasionally, we need to record something, but it is complete by the post is published. With the help of technology and software such as Evernote, Penultimate, NoteTaker, and Notability, handwritten electronic notes may be created, organized, and searched, saving time on the tedious task of locating that location dang yellow square.

3. Small Business Robotics

Once reserved for large industrial duties, robots have reduced in size and are now available with interchangeable hands, a tiny height, and limited tasking capabilities, making them an attractive option for repetitive activities required by some small firms.

Packaging, palletizing, material handling, simple assembly, and machine burring can now be handled by robots that operate 24 hours a day, 7 days a week, except for software upgrades and routine maintenance.

Food and beverage manufacturing procedures, battery manufacturing processes, dairy manufacturing processes, paper goods manufacturing processes, and corrugated cardboard manufacturing processes favor this dedicated personnel who do not require 401ks, raises, or sick days. It may be precisely what countries like the United States require to gain an edge against inexpensive international labor.

4. Accounts Receivable Management That Is Fully Automated

Receiving payments on time is one of the simplest ways to enhance operating capital. Receivables are automatically managed using software such as ZenCash and the Receivables Dashboard. There is no need to assign people to follow up, as this application is equipped with status and update information to keep everything current. Allow the machines to do the work while you continue to conduct business.

5. Conversion of Voice to Text

Siri is fantastic, but this assistant can assist Siri with some of the translational challenges she may encounter when dealing with your Southern drawl. Spoken to text conversion services from companies such as Dragon Dictation, Evernote, and Voice Assistant can convert your voice message to text with astonishing speed. It saves time from your mouth to their displays. Additionally, time is money!

6. Alternative Payment Methods

Numerous transactions that previously required invoicing occurred outside the confines of an office due to the delivery of goods or performance of services. Mobile payments conducted via a cell phone equipped with a sliding credit card attachment can transfer payments more quickly than invoicing and provide automated recordkeeping.

While this is advantageous for high-value, low-volume enterprises, the per-transaction costs may be crippling for those with a huge low-profit transaction.

7. Leasing of Software

If you're in the cloud, everyone who uses the service has access to the program. If you require specialized software, such as Adobe Creative Suite with its expensive price tag, leasing it may benefit you. Adobe's CS rentals start at less than $40 per month, which is far less than an expenditure of more than two grand for something that may become obsolete in months.

Your creative personnel will appreciate having the most recent versions and constant access to all programs without worrying how many PCs have downloaded the programs.

8. Refurbished Offices

Are you still using incandescent lamps and a massive coffeemaker that burns continuously throughout the day, with nearly full pots discarded at 5 p.m.? Are your visuals out of date, uninspired, or simply boring? Increase staff inspiration by adding LED lighting, single-cup coffeemakers, and leased art that is replaced with something fresh every month. Newer appliances save money on energy, provide a current trend vibe in the office, and increase morale, contributing to motivation and productivity.

CHAPTER 6

YOU CAN'T DO IT ALONE: TEAMWORK AND EMOTIONAL INTELLIGENCE

Employers and employees alike should model teamwork. Working cooperatively toward a common goal is critical for a successful team. When projects are given, each team member is assigned specific tasks. Though individuals will work independently on some of these duties, there will almost certainly be significant collaboration, hence the term 'teamwork.' This is when each member is obliged to choose the team's goals over their own. It's critical to remember that everyone is working toward a common goal, and it's up to all team members to collaborate to get the job done.

Collaboration is critical. Teamwork is a collaborative endeavor, and everyone involved must do their fair share so that no one person is left to complete the job that is left over. The project must be completed regardless of the number of people involved, and this is usually much easier to accomplish when everyone pitches in to do their share.

Businesses use teams for several functions, ranging from problem-solving to manufacturing. Each team member must have a clear grasp of the team's purpose or aim and the numerous tasks assigned to each member. This is especially true when one person cannot do a specific activity. If the other team members understand the task and how it is to be completed, they will be able to step in for the absent member.

Teamwork is an idea that will continue to increase in popularity in the workplace. More and more businesses are finding it necessary to form teams to handle various critical duties. Knowing how to collaborate with people is critical while looking for work since it is a skill that employers look for during interviews.

THE CHARACTERISTICS OF A SUCCESSFUL TEAM

If you lead a team, you are well aware that the road to great performance is never-ending. It is a rare team that achieves peak performance and maintains it. Throughout my professional career, whether managing a team within an organization or running my firm, it has been uncommon to keep the same team together for more than a year. Team members come and go as the organization's needs and personal, professional ambitions dictate. And if a team's composition changes, the squad must regroup and concentrate.

What is the role of the team leader? To begin, consider the following seven qualities of a high-performing team (what we refer to at NetSpeed Leadership as a Total Team):

Commitment to a Common Goal and Direction

Motivating Objectives

Individual and Team Commitment

Communication in Multiple Directions

Decision-Making or Acting Authority

Dependence on a Diverse Talent Pool

Mutual Assistance and Trust

Commitment to a Common Goal and Direction

Every member of a high-performing team is devoted to the team's mission. They precisely understand that mission because the team leader continuously communicates it during team meetings and regular updates. The team leader assists each team member in meeting their unique requirements while also serving the team's general mission.

Motivating Objectives

The team leader is responsible for ensuring that everyone on the team has well-defined goals and objectives. Senior management determines the strategic and departmental objectives of various firms. In that instance, the team leader ensures that these objectives are shared openly. Team members should understand how their occupations contribute to attaining established goals and, if possible, be allowed to develop personal goals and action plans outlining how they will contribute to the organization's success.

Individual and Team Commitment

On a Total Team, team members have well-defined expectations and understand how their jobs relate to one another. Team leaders ensure that members are cross-trained in additional roles so that they can assist one another when necessary. The team leader ensures that individual job obligations are met while also assisting employees in developing a shared language, processes, and techniques that enable them to work as a team.

Communication in Multiple Directions

The best teams solve problems, interact with one another, and keep the team leader informed of developing concerns or challenges. Communication is either one-way (from the team leader to the team members) or two-way in low-performing teams (between the team leader and individuals). Skilled leaders place a premium on building multidirectional communication, avoiding the trap of talking exclusively with team members.

Decision-Making or Acting Authority

Without a doubt, new teams will need to earn this power by demonstrating an understanding of the team's mission, methods, and priorities. On the other hand, effective team leaders work to delegate authority for the team's outcomes to team members.

Team members understand when and how to obtain approval for decisions and, in the best-case scenario, are tasked with making on-the-spot decisions when confronted by a customer. On low-performing teams, team members must constantly

seek clearance before acting, dramatically reducing their efficacy and affecting their sense of team engagement.

Dependence on a Diverse Talent Pool

Astute team leaders focus on assisting team members in identifying their skills, talents, and flaws. No single team member
can be excellent at everything. The finest team leaders support
their members in developing an appreciation for their unique
styles, natural abilities, and personal experiences.

Teams are urged to speak in acceptance and gratitude rather
than judgment and criticism. Team leaders purposefully
employ individuals with complementary skill sets, unique
experiences, and opinions.

Mutual Assistance and Trust

The seventh feature is perhaps the most critical and, honestly,
the most elusive. The team leader cannot coerce a team into
being supportive and trustworthy; it occurs naturally due to
shared accountability, shared success, and mutual respect.

The high-performing team develops mutual support and trust
due to their history of collaborating to accomplish lofty goals
and objectives. They have surmounted barriers and supported
one another in both good and bad times. The Total Team has
earned the trust of one another.

Developing a high-performing team is a difficult task. However,
if you are a capable team leader, you should deliberately focus
on cultivating these seven characteristics. Bring them to your
next team meeting and solicit feedback from team members.

How do you determine whether your team possesses or lacks these characteristics? What is the team prepared to undertake to cultivate these seven characteristics? Then, have each team member commit to three to five specific actions they will perform over the next 60 days. Revisit these commitments regularly to observe how they evolve. I guarantee a pleasurable path to peak performance.

TEAMWORK, LEADERSHIP ABILITY, AND SUCCESS TOOLS

Most new team leaders state that they need to improve their leadership skills and expand their ideas and strategies for interacting with others. When they assume a team leadership role, they gain power merely by the authority conferred upon them in their newly allocated position. They must make judgments and coordinate the work of others.

Management Of Others

Leaders must have well-defined objectives and the ability to communicate them effectively to others. If it were so simple, we would not have so many books on leadership. Technically, we are all capable of performing our jobs, so we are hired. Dealing with people, their expectations, and their needs makes teamwork and leadership difficult.

Some people require frequent pats on the back and recognition for their accomplishments; others require a sense of competence and constant challenge, and still, others prefer to play it safe for security reasons and avoid taking risks or sticking their necks out for fear of having them chopped off in another workplace.

By being concise, consistent, and fair, you may maximize performance by focusing on measurable objectives. By doing so, you are completing your assignment. If you put your need to be liked ahead of your standards, you will fail.

If you become defensive when someone challenges your approach to the task, you will fail. Your team's productivity, the quality of its results, innovation, and construction initiatives determine your efficiency and effectiveness. This is never more true than when dealing with team conflict.

Conflict Impacts Teams

At some point, every team will experience disagreement. As an effective team leader, it is vital to confront it, resolve it fairly and constructively, and demonstrate to your team that everyone is taken seriously and that results are critical for all team members.

Allow any upset on your team to serve as a reminder that you have something to handle, but never address a team member out of anger. Allow the anger to register that you have something difficult to say or something that may be difficult to hear. Additionally, keep in mind that it is merely content and cannot harm you; however, your reaction to it can!

Dealing with disagreement effectively builds a team where more people are willing to take chances, resulting in increased creativity, innovation, and synergy. This results in increased production since everyone is engaged. When a team's creativity flows, you as the team leader will be seen as a competent, if not exceptional, team leader.

Share Your Strength

You are comfortable with power as a great team leader since you are not scared to share it with others. When you share power with others, the power your team bestows on you is the power you have earned.

Success Methods

The following are the tools that can help you improve your success rate as a team leader:

Remember to communicate your team's mandate in advance—establish clear goals.

When collaborating with your team on a new project, make careful to break it down into "baby steps" and solicit their input to ensure buy-in.

When expressing aims and expectations, incorporate as many open-ended inquiries as possible to ascertain their thoughts. Continue to inquire until you have a firm grasp of the subject.

When coaching and training others, inquire about their preferred learning technique and then instruct them using that method—not yours. They may be visual learners who prefer to get an overview first but are also interactive learners who want to talk about it with you, work on it a little bit, and then discuss it some more; or they may be hands-on learners who prefer to work on it and learn about it as they go. Alternatively, they could be a combination of two or three of the above.

People are motivated for various reasons, so make an effort to understand their motivations and the best way to engage with them.

While many of us dislike conflict, you can use it to grow, coach, challenge and develop your team. Never attempt to subdue someone out of defensiveness. That is more about retaining your authority and position. Never make others feel tiny or insignificant or subdue them into conformity.

Never stifle innovation by following the rules to maintain the status quo and avoid change and dynamism. And certainly never throw problems under the rug in order to avoid conflict simply because you dislike tension.

When there is more engagement, trust, respect, and confidence between you and your team, you will know you have succeeded as a team leader.

WHY TEAMWORK IS A CATALYST FOR SUCCESS

Without strong teamwork, a firm or organization will never achieve its full potential. You can probably think of dozens of successful people off the top of your head, from entrepreneurs to inventors to political leaders.

Although the leader's name may be displayed prominently, or they may be publicly honored for their accomplishments, very seldom, if ever, has anyone achieved any level of brilliance on their own or without the assistance of an effective team.

A leader's potential is decided not only by their abilities but also by those closest to him. You may have heard that you are the average of the five people closest to you. If you have a goal that is larger than yourself, you must recognize that it is better to form a team than to go at it alone. Additionally, it makes sense to assemble a team that will, in a sense, increase the standard. To do more than you could alone is precisely why cooperation necessitates a strong inner circle.

We cannot be all things to all people, and everyone surely lacks the skills necessary to do everything in business. Collaboration is critical, and success demands a strong inner circle led by trustworthy leaders. You want your inner circle of elite players to possess various traits, abilities, and talents that you may lack. When we consider business, most of us start a firm searching for freedom.

Perhaps the goal is to be your employer, financially independent, or have the freedom to do as you please and when you please. Regardless of how lofty your ambitions are, they will necessitate players capable of exceeding the demands of your fantasies. It does not end with the team's formation; it is vital to continue growing the team's leadership.

The critical factors for forming the ideal inner circle and fostering unstoppable teamwork are as follows:

1. Developing your leadership abilities first enables you to recruit high-quality team members. The first stage is identifying a mentor who has already achieved success and can teach you. World-class athletes are well aware of this principle. As you can see, while the winners of a race may not always finish first, they are always among the first group of racers to win on any given day.

Simply put, surrounding oneself with individuals who achieve at a higher level than you force you to work more. When you meet mentors who are more capable and capable than you are, it might act as a spark for you to attain your full potential.

2. Invest in developing established leaders. We can develop individuals inside our organization, within our team, so that they can step into those higher-level leadership responsibilities. Personal development is critical. Prioritize your development first; then, lead by setting an example and setting the pace for the team. By raising the bar within your organization, you also raise teamwork and leadership.

When you raise the bar, you'll discover that people adapt to meet the challenges. The reality is that no one enters leadership as a great leader. Great leaders evolve on a daily and continuous basis. People emulate their role models, so you must first become one to develop strong leaders.

An excellent rule to follow while assembling a great leadership team is to look for individuals who add to the team's worth. This requires forthrightness. You want members who will tell you the truth, not just what they believe you want to hear. To operate well as a team, each member must be able to communicate openly and honestly.

When we communicate candidly, we determine what we are doing well and where we need to improve. You may grow your business and team more quickly if your leaders can communicate when something does not make sense, rather than being frustrated after something fails, and the team believes it was doomed to fail in the first place.

A team's mission is to bring together diverse minds and ideas to accomplish a shared goal. Finally, remember that nothing great has ever been accomplished without assistance, so cooperation demands a strong inner circle.

Teamwork is essential!

In the workplace, we do not act independently. We must interact and work collaboratively in the office. We rely on coworkers for insight and feedback. To execute jobs, we rely on one another's skills. To get assignments started, we create teams. Collaboration is critical and pervasive. Collaboration enables us to synergize. That is, to generate output far greater than the sum of its parts.

There is a well-known adage about synergy: $1+1=3$. (instead of the mathematical 2). Teamwork benefits everyone since it compensates for one another's limitations or capitalizes on one another's abilities. You may argue that you can complete the task on your own. However, if you can focus on something else that you are more familiar with and competent in, and allow another person to take command of what you are doing in pursuit of a common goal, don't you believe you can accomplish your goal more quickly?

Teamwork compensates for our shortcomings. Remember the Me factor and the quadrants of personal awareness? We are aware of our limitations and desire to overcome them. The straightforward solution is that we leverage the expertise of others. To put it in a more dignified tone, tap means leverage. And utilizing one another's knowledge is a form of collaboration.

When faced with a task that you cannot complete, you assemble coworkers to supplement your weaknesses with theirs.

However, before finding the appropriate coworkers, you must first determine who complements you. And this knowledge is contained within your consciousness regarding the You element. By incorporating a person who balances your weaknesses with his strengths, you can increase productivity by forming a well-balanced team.

Teamwork necessitates mutual respect and accommodation amongst team members. Let us acknowledge that neither you nor I am perfect. None of us are. And, as imperfect beings, we rely on one another. To work well as a team, members must be willing to accept one another's differences.

Distinctions in terms of working style, habits, and mental model. For instance, your team member may be meticulous in handling the report and spend some time proofreading it before the management review. On the other hand, you believe the report is adequately polished and ready for review by management. There is a misalignment of work styles in this instance.

You want it sent quickly to management, whereas he wants it provided slowly to ensure no errors are made. If you do not appreciate and compromise his working style, you will become frustrated. Consider it from a different perspective. He may be sluggish to deliver, but he does verify that everything is in order and points out any errors you made.

There are two distinct styles of teamwork: dynamic teams and balanced teams. The supercharged team may include persons who share similar skill sets. It is comparable to a double-loaded cannon with greater rapid-fire capability. Scientists and engineers are excellent examples of dynamic teams.

The disadvantage of this team is that it comprises similar types of people who may overlook commonalities. As the name implies, a balanced team comprises members who complement one another. The advantage of such teams is that they can build on one another's strengths. The downside is that they do not always provide a direct boost to a particular talent.

Teamwork is ubiquitous and critical to productivity. While a person may achieve this far on their own, with the assistance of others, the individual can achieve far more. Teamwork is about capitalizing on one another's strengths. Before you can utilize another individual, you must first respect and accommodate their differences. With an understanding of your team members, we are confident that you can exceed your expectations for productivity.:)

TEAMWORK IN BUSINESS AND THE EMPLOYEE'S ROLE

The telling component of corporate cooperation entails the management or leader notifying the staff of the outcome of a decision. Staff employees will receive thorough direction. Informing employees is beneficial when they require information on safety concerns, government laws or regulations, or decisions that do not require or necessitate employee input. Telling does not require any coordination and is most effective when information has to be communicated, but no choice needs to be made.

'Selling' is a necessary component of corporate teamwork that the manager or leader must excel in, or else enmity would be formed. If a manager is competent, the selling portion will be effortless. When an idea or choice is sold to employees and employees commit, the selling process begins.

Employees must be convinced of the decision's benefits. However, one thing to keep in mind is that employees cannot influence an already-made decision. The objective is to persuade personnel to perceive the positive aspects, hop on board, and be motivated. The employee's function in selling is to be influenced by the manager's new decision.

'Consulting' is another aspect of corporate teamwork that involves the employee. This step enables the leader to get opinions from the staff. Bear in mind that while employees are providing feedback at this level, the manager or leader must retain the final decision-making authority.

The key to successfully counseling employees using this teamwork approach is to communicate to the team that you value their input but retain final decision-making authority at the outset of the session. If you do not communicate to employees that you have the final say, they may become irate afterward.

Inform them that you would appreciate their feedback while you retain ultimate decision-making authority. However, as a leader fostering teamwork, you mustn't enter the dialogue seeking opinion until you have concluded. Simply convince the employees of your decision. Never make your staff believe what they believe matters when it truly does not.

When a manager applies the 'join' strategy with their workforce, the employee's part in corporate teamwork is maximized. When a manager joins, they will encourage personnel to assist in making a choice. During the decision-making process, all voices are heard equally. Joining successfully establishes consensus on the choice and ensures equal influence.

An employee's position differs depending on how you approach specific decisions with the employees. Whichever method you use as a manager is entirely up to you. Among the several strategies are telling, selling, consulting, and joining. If you want employees to be engaged and take ownership of choice, joining is the most effective method.

A BUSINESS CASE FOR COLLABORATION

Numerous benefits accrue from assisting individuals, managers, and departments in cooperating more effectively. Rather than viewing team development in the workplace as a one-off intervention, it should be viewed as assisting the business in reaching its full potential. At its core, teamwork is a collection of individual behavioral decisions made by employees in their own best interests, for their satisfaction, security, and survival.

Improved teamwork is virtually free, and the benefits of enhanced synergy, collaboration, communication, and dedication can result in tangible outcomes, including increased profitability, performance, and organizational competitiveness. However, utilizing this 'free resource' is a highly skilled procedure that is frequently mismanaged, poorly delivered, inaccurately monitored, or completely ignored.

Consultants and trainers are frequently brought in to provide a quick fix, teach employees how to work better, provide a 'feel good' team-building experience, or attempt to resolve long-standing conflicts and animosities between departments that are causing serious breakdowns process or production.

Often, these band-aid solutions are too little, too late, and provide no long-term solution.

The stressors associated with a lack of teamwork in an organization are numerous; insecurity and mistrust, dishonesty, failure to share knowledge or resources, willful non-cooperation,
a lack of communication, and general subpar performance in
comparison to what is achievable. Whether deliberate or not,
the complexities and interconnections of any firm with more
than 50 people are certain to generate friction and misunderstandings when humans attempt to work together. That is
why teamwork is one of the most critical elements to consider.

Teams and Identities within the Department

Each department develops its own identity, culture, and standards. Without intentional guidance, natural competition
between departments will develop ad hoc. According to research,
small units benefit the most from teamwork growth and can
adopt positive teamwork practices to get the quickest outcomes.
Regarding the potential benefits of improved teamwork, the
departmental team is 'where the rubber meets the road.'

Teamwork Culture in the Organization

On a macro level, the entire organization should exercise
caution in its communication regarding teamwork. Clearly
defined expectations for departments and divisions to collaborate effectively should be highlighted continuously in top
management remarks, corporate communications, and sym-
bolically throughout each plant and office.

Dismantling Barriers and Silos Collaboration is critical
amongst internal customers in the value chain who conduct

the organization's fundamental functions and contribute to critical processes. Collaboration can act as the lubricant that keeps all of the machine's components running smoothly.

At Work, Human-ness, Fun, and Enjoyment

When individuals are at ease and secure, they function at a significantly greater level. Employee happiness, turnover, and organizational climate difficulties are all highly associated with fun and enjoyment at work. The warmth of relationships can boost morale and break down barriers that prevent individuals from approaching one another and cooperating effectively. It is always preferable when employees love coming to work and getting along with their coworkers.

Effective Leaders Lead More Efficiently

Leaders may more effectively share the load through efficient cooperation, eventually training their employees to be more self-directed. This also provides an opportunity for employees' development and fosters respect for leaders. Leaders that effectively lead their teams receive increased support and credibility inside the organization. Leaders with a strong team are better equipped to fulfill specific demands that necessitate more work.

Evaluation of teamwork

With the reliable measurement of teamwork elements and longitudinal analysis of attitudes, the success of teamwork training and other activities can be directly linked to them and recognize downward trends before they become problematic. Measuring teamwork should be a key metric on the business dashboard.

Collaboration Skills Result in Increased Productivity.

Teams that invest in problem-solving, group processes, continuous improvement, and other advanced teamwork behaviors outperform teams of comparable size and composition. Meetings will be more efficient, objectives, strategies, and tactics will be more clearly defined, critical collaboration relationships will be emphasized, and teams will have a clearer direction.

New organizations, mergers, new leaders, and change are all part of the process. Spending time and energy developing new teams and relationships is crucial for integrating the cultures of disparate businesses, integrating new managers and leaders, and establishing a new set of norms and behaviors conducive to high performance.

There is no substitute for the integration phase between companies after a merger or between managers and employees during a leadership transition. Still, it may be managed efficiently and pro-actively from the start, emphasizing improving teamwork. When all parties are on board with the new path, inefficiencies associated with change can be reduced.

Invest in lubricating long-distance or virtual relationships

Any gathering in which ties are maintained digitally or at a distance should place a premium on teamwork. When the group is physically together, time spent developing greater collaboration and deeper relationships serves as insurance for the lion's share of the time when team members cannot meet face to face.

Customer Satisfaction Impact

Customer satisfaction is one of the areas most affected by ineffective interdepartmental collaboration. This could manifest in different client experiences when dealing with one department versus another. It could be a failure of production to follow through on a vital commitment made by sales or engineering.

It could be the unpleasant customer experience of being ignored because no department inside the supplier's organization appears willing to accept responsibility. Every one of us has been there. A significant subject for teamwork training and development should demonstrate the immediate influence on the external customer and the possible costs if the organization cannot collaborate effectively.

Consequences for Strategic Alignment—With strong teamwork, it is easier to gain buy-in and support for ideas, especially as they become more complex. When a company is confronted with multi-dimensional complexity, demanding clients, or the requirement for extremely precise and particular quality standards, far more thorough interactions and collaboration are required.

The significance of effective teamwork increases as projects get more complex. Employees who perform well in teams are more eager to accept individual responsibility and participate in a positive culture of mutual assistance and support to help shoulder the load. Only naturally strong teams can respond to change, achieve bigger goals, and implement more complex plans.

Employee Self-Actualization Requires Teamwork.

Excellent teamwork paves the basis for freely shared initiative, the emergence of innovation, and the application of extra effort when necessary. Every employee aspires to a higher sense of involvement, ownership, and participation. Teamwork satisfies fundamental human desires for group participation and acceptance while allowing individuals to express themselves and their gifts to their full potential.

A proactive commitment to cooperation is a strategic need for organizations, not merely a token gesture at the annual company picnic. When fostered responsibly in each department and across the business, cooperation may be vital in ensuring targets are met, initiatives are implemented effectively, and greater competitiveness is attained. When high levels of cooperation are in place, various quantifiable indicators improve, from staff turnover and stress-related absenteeism to departmental improvements and efficiencies and increased customer satisfaction.

Additionally, your organization will be a happier place to work.

IMPLEMENTING TEAMWORK
IN YOUR BUSINESS

For over a decade, it's been astonishing how many businesses openly utilize the term "team." Teamwork is beneficial, correct? Many business corridors include stunning

photos of sportsmen paddling a kayak beside the slogan "Teamwork" inscribed in bold letters at the bottom. It's an excellent reminder, but once employees enter their work areas, they are reintroduced to the reality of individualism, such as the prospect of receiving a bonus based on individual performance or the announcement of the next employee of the month—complete with parking space. Of course, there is always the politics of associating with the right people to advance.

Unfortunately, by designating their organization charts as "absolute proof" that they are joking about "teamwork," the majority of businesses unknowingly demonstrate that they are joking about "teamwork." The most common organizational chart consists of boxes with names inside or below them that begin at the top of the page and descend in a pyramid-like fashion.

It's clear from these charts that some people are "above" others, which sparks debates about "who outranks who." I've even heard folks holding an organizational chart up to their eye and scanning the page to determine whether they are a "little higher" than another. How can a business foster teamwork when evidence exists that management does not encourage a team environment?

And I've seen some astute CEOs arrange their organization charts "inverted," with workers at the top and leaders at the bottom. The objective is to illustrate that management's role is to work for employees and provide them with the resources they require to serve consumers. While this is an excellent idea, it still falls short of clearly defining the duties and connections within teams.

Rather than that, visualize an organization chart as a collection of concentric rings. When organized in this manner, the business resembles a true "team of teams." Like concentric circles, each team is connected to the others. For instance, the Client Services Team may be a subset of the Operations Team, a larger organization led by the Executive Team.

The Executive Team's role is to "see the big picture" and establish business objectives. The remaining teams are responsible for establishing "how" to accomplish the company's objectives as expressed in their respective "team objectives."

Although an organization chart is simply a piece of paper, it wields great influence over how a company's culture is defined. A "team of teams" organizational chart can be an excellent starting point for businesses that desire true collaboration. Consider transforming your incentive program into a team-based compensation plan as a highly effective next step.

People experience a sense of belonging in a true team culture. Once individualism is eliminated, people will be far more likely to join their teams than pursue personal gain. And, perhaps most importantly, the enhanced teamwork will begin to manifest itself in the company's performance.

Establishing this type of culture demands modest executives to "live the talk" for a lengthy period. However, it can serve as a secret weapon against competitors who have "top-down" cultures in which employees do the bare minimum to avoid getting into trouble. As your business differentiates itself from the competition, your competitors will wonder what you're doing!

Teamwork is critical since it aids in uniting and coordinating the group's various members. Because a corporate organization comprises numerous individuals accountable for a distinct job, they must operate effectively together. This ensures that your business's processes run efficiently and smoothly. Additionally, you can be certain that you will meet all of your objectives when there is strong teamwork and spirit in the office.

Developing and promoting collaboration inside your organization is critical if you want all of your members to be efficient and contribute to the business's success. There must be someone responsible for initiating teamwork and leading the members. If you are the president of this business organization, you will need to set a positive example for your group.

The group's members must first recognize that participation is required. This teaches them that work must be shared with others and that everything done in the group is a collaborative effort. When team members understand this, they will be more receptive to other members' recommendations, ideas, and assistance.

If you are a leader, you must set the standard for teamwork. You must exemplify teamwork in your interactions with other team members. If you do not practice collaboration, your members will revert to their old methods. It is always preferable to set an example.

The members of the group need to understand the value of teamwork. Once they know that they are a part of every process that makes up the organization, they feel valued. They will also realize that their presence is important in reaching the success that the organization is aiming for. This, in turn, will help them do quality work that will make a great contribution towards reaching success.

Moreover, the members of the team need to share their experiences. They need to reinforce and encourage one another in getting their share of work done. This way, the less experienced team members are also learning, which will lead to a more efficient workday.

When fostering a culture of collaboration within a group, it is necessary to reward it. Not a single individual gets honored here, but the entire squad. Rewards and incentives should be provided in recognition of accomplishments and hard work.

Additionally, it is critical to inject some humor into developing a culture of teamwork. This contributes to a more relaxed work environment and injects a little humor into a professional and serious environment. This encourages employees to relax a little and helps them feel more at ease in their professional positions.

Finally, it should be stated that all of these teamwork ideas must be followed consistently. You do not simply create a culture conducive to teamwork for a year and then abandon it. It must be cultivated and maintained indefinitely to be entirely successful. Additionally, teamwork must become more developed and robust. This will ultimately increase profitability and success for your team and the overall organization.

THE IMPORTANCE OF SUCCESSFUL COLLABORATION IN THE WORKPLACE

Why is collaboration critical in the workplace?

Effective teamwork is critical in the workplace for various reasons, but one of the most critical in achieving success.

Frequently, organizations will form and utilize teams to perform tasks or projects that require more than one person to complete. A successful outcome with high-quality standards is ensured when a team works effectively together.

When a team works together, diverse individuals contribute innovative ideas and solutions to issues. A team that works effectively can also motivate one another as they progress through a project or assignment, accomplishing their objectives efficiently.

Five Essential Components of Effective Teamwork

Leadership

When selecting a team leader for your organization, you're looking for someone who exhibits great leadership abilities. Your team leader should be someone who will listen to each team member's unique perspective while still maintaining the team's overall positivity and motivation.

Responsibilities

When each team member is allocated defined roles and tasks to perform within a project, it assists everyone in remaining focused on the ultimate goal. When it comes to allocating responsibilities, you want the 'best person for the job'; therefore, be sure to allocate roles and obligations to each team member based on their area of expertise and level of knowledge.

Communication

It is critical to have an open communication channel when working as a team. When you have effective communication, you also can address conflicts collaboratively. Effective communication enables a team to bring diverse perspectives and points of view together for productive and healthy brainstorming.

Resolution of Conflicts

Conflict can occur within every team or business, so it is critical to have a plan of action in place in the event of a conflict amongst team members.

If a conflict occurs, it is critical to resolving it immediately, or it will escalate unnecessarily.

Positivity

Always endeavor to have a cheerful attitude and inspire others to do the same. Demonstrate that we can and will. A cheerful attitude can help teams overcome numerous obstacles. Additionally, it might help a team develop trust and excitement.

Effective Collaboration Produces

Numerous benefits accrue from effective teamwork. These include a strong team spirit, enhanced productivity, the accomplishment of high-quality work, and the achievement of objectives. Effective teamwork ultimately results in success.

Does your team exemplify these characteristics?

PERFORMANCE OF TEAMWORK

In a team-based organization, teamwork performance must be obvious. This could be accomplished in a variety of ways. For starters, there should be an effective monitoring and reporting system in place. This could aid organizational leaders in tracking project progress and evaluating group performance. While individuals may collaborate on various tasks, teams have evolved into the backbone of modern organizations.

Productivity

How effective has the team been in terms of productivity? Did it make effective use of the time allotted? Was the time squandered on interminable meetings? What about personal productivity? Did they give the project they're all?

Productivity is a critical indicator of performance. Given two teams tasked with similar duties, the team that completes the task the quickest and highest quality might be regarded as the superior performer. However, from a leader's standpoint, it is critical not to jeopardize the quality of work. You will not be compensated if you finish sooner but produce sloppy work.

The cohesion of the team

Team cohesiveness is another critical component of teamwork performance. How well-balanced were the relationships? Were there any unwarranted clashes and frictions? Did the team members get along well? If the response is no, teamwork performance is likely to be lacking. One could argue that individuals rather than a team obtain the results.

Objectives attained

The team's accomplishments must be compared to the stated objectives. At times, it is more vital to hit the target perfectly with a few darts than to have an abundance of darts that miss the target entirely. Thus, the output's quality is critical and may override all other considerations. The team can readily accomplish these objectives if they are started early on.

Measuring teamwork performance is not difficult. On the other hand, managers frequently measure the quantitative component of teamwork. Always, performance is data-driven. However, some statistics are qualitative as well. As a team leader, you must be sensitive to two factors: your team members' situations and the demands of the duties assigned to your team. You must work to safeguard the team members' interests while producing exceptional results! That is a surefire technique to achieve superior teamwork performance.

Teams have an incredible ability to boost an organization's productivity. However, collaboration performance must be monitored regularly to guarantee that these teams function for the organization's advantage.

Have you ever been evaluated on your teamwork performance? How was it determined? How would you rate the performance of your team?

EMOTIONAL INTELLIGENCE
AND TEAMWORK ROLES

Organizations increasingly find that hard skills testing and personality assessments are inadequate methods for picking new personnel. As businesses recognize the value of social abilities such as collaboration and teamwork, they are also seeking those "emotional intelligence" characteristics in new hires and existing employees. Emotional intelligence is critical for team development, and here are seven reasons why.

1. Awareness of One's Self

It is exceedingly difficult to comprehend the feelings and motivations of others until one first understands oneself. Individuals with a high level of emotional intelligence can swiftly understand their emotions, which is the first step in controlling or managing them. Self-awareness is a fundamental component of emotional intelligence.

2. Self-regulation

Recognizing your emotions is one thing; controlling them is another, particularly in difficult situations. A person with a developed EI understands why they feel the way they do, enabling them to assess and control their emotions objectively.

3. Biologically determined motivational tendencies

Motivation is critical to team momentum, and each member contributes to that motivation. A positive attitude, persistence, and a natural ability to encourage others are all signs of developed EI. In a nutshell, it is contagious, and others will follow suit.

4. Compassion

A person with strong emotional intelligence is capable of comprehending and empathizing with the feelings of others. They are conversant with people from all walks of life and the influence of various cultures on decision-making processes. Understanding these distinctions enables an individual to accept variety without posing a barrier to good collaboration.

5. Superior social abilities

A strong sense of social skills is critical for team members. Managing problems mutually agreeable is crucial to the team's overall performance. Social skills that are well developed can significantly contribute to collaboration and cooperation, increasing productivity.

6. Interdependence on society

When a team is formed, it establishes an environment of social interdependence, which can be beneficial or detrimental depending on how it is managed. If the team leader explains that the group's focus will be on team goals and that success will require the contribution of all team members, the effect will be an increased effort to collaborate.

On the other hand, if the team is structured as a competition, e.g., "the first person to sell 100 widgets receives a large prize," you have a team of individuals with distinct aims.

7. Emotional intelligence and teamwork

Positive and successful interactions among team members have been shown to be the optimal emotional environment for achieving objectives. Members that have built a professional and personal bond will work harder to ensure the group's success than a team that has not developed similar bonds. Through activities and training, developing emotional intelligence can significantly increase the likelihood of good team performance.

If you manage a team, you truly set the tone. If you want to get the most out of your team, aim to create an environment that fosters relationship development rather than tearing them apart via competition.

EMOTIONAL INTELLIGENCE CULTIVATED IN THE WORKPLACE

Over the last two decades, our human resource functions have evolved from being purely administrative to making strategic judgments about the future path of our firm. Identifying and strategically aligning our people is critical for this new function. The critical nature of this responsibility cannot be overstated, but how do we go about identifying the appropriate individuals?

Historically, new hires and promotions were made based on technical aptitude or education and experience. If someone has the necessary abilities and experience, it was expected that they would make effective leaders capable of imparting information to others. That was occasionally true, but as we all know, an employee can possess the necessary degrees, be an absolute genius at his profession, and still "be cancer within the firm."

Let us discuss Carl. Carl is an excellent employee. His telephone numbers are perpetually at the top of the list. He's been an employee of yours for years. He never misses a day of work and is always on time. He frequently works late into the night to complete tasks. Carl is a committed and self-motivated individual. On the other hand, Carl is a hard charger, and no one wants to be near him.

Carl will never win a popularity contest. Carl is never invited to lunch. His leadership style is characterized by intimidation and insult. He is arrogant and abusive. He browbeats his subordinates. Carl appears to be unable to convey his message without resorting to insult. He holds himself to a high level, and he cannot fathom others who do not.

He is unaware that he is a contributing factor to the situation. When members of Carl's squad are assigned, their numbers inevitably decrease. Carl transforms a productive employee into someone resentful of coming to work. Carl is poisonous, but how do you deal with Carl?

How did Carl progress through your company's levels if he is such a bad leader and communicator? That is simple. He was an expert at his work. Many firms promote solely based on performance, with little respect for the soft skills that contribute to a person's strength as a leader. Carl's bad habits have been reinforced. After all, he is constantly promoted. He must be performing all of his duties correctly.

When outcomes are the only consideration, you end up with results-driven personnel whose approaches may not be sustainable or scalable. Dr. Daniel Goleman pioneered a new method of predicting success in the 1990s. Rather than focusing exclusively on technical skill or IQ as predictors of success, he urges for a greater emphasis on Emotional Intelligence (EI).

Emotional Intelligence focuses on four critical aspects that great leaders must possess: Emotional Perception, Emotional Reasoning, Emotional Understanding, and Emotional Management.

Perceiving Emotions—This refers to an individual's capacity to perceive and understand the emotions of others. It entails reading others' body language and interpreting their verbal and nonverbal messages.

Reasoning with Emotions—This element refers to an individual's ability to pay attention to and disregard certain stimuli selectively.

Understanding Emotions—This entails understanding what motivates others and your emotional responses. What causes people to behave in certain ways?

Managing Emotions—Perhaps the most critical part of Emotional Intelligence is the ability to manage one's emotions. It entails manipulating your own and others' emotions to accomplish a purpose. Human beings are emotional beings. Managing such emotions for positive outcomes is a critical component of being a successful leader.

Since its introduction into business, the impact of Emotional Intelligence has been studied in both clinical and real-world contexts. Each time, it was a breeze. Employees with a high EI positively affect others rather than negative ones and make better employees. Businesses with a high proportion of emotionally intelligent personnel outperform those with a low proportion of emotionally intelligent employees.

This is not to say that businesses should indulge in daily hug therapy. Employees with a high EI have also been shown to have the superior technical ability. They make better use of their own and others' abilities than those with a low EI. It is possible to prioritize technical skills while also considering EI when hiring, firing, and promoting.

Okay, Emotional Intelligence is fantastic, and you need more employees with a high EI. How are you going to accomplish that goal? Setting that objective is the first and most critical step, and here are a few fast ways to incorporate EI into your existing organizational structure.

Employ Individuals with a High Emotional Intelligence

The simplest approach to alter your company's culture is through new personnel. A successful business will always have turnover, which can be viewed as a chance to develop the corporate culture. You can concentrate on hiring new employees with a high EI throughout the interview phase.

This can be accomplished in various methods, which rely significantly on the interview process. At first, there is no reason to employ EI experts or to run a battery of comprehensive tests. A simple adjustment in emphasis during the interview process from professional experience to Emotional Intelligence is a significant step in the right direction. Examine a candidate's emotional response to challenging events during the interview. Ascertain the candidate's specificity. Allow them to get away with a generic response.

Evaluate Current Employees

While hiring is one strategy to boost your company's Emotional Intelligence, you cannot simply fire everyone and start again. Your business already has personnel in place. This entails conducting employee assessments with a view on EI. Numerous tests exist to assess EI.

The instrument is secondary to the act of assessing and anticipating EI. The act will communicate to your employees that this is now a priority. Additionally, it will assist you in identifying individuals who may be fit for a higher job within your firm.

Stress Rather than the Results themselves

The outcomes are pertinent. While you want your staff to perform well, their tactics to accomplish that goal are critical. Your employees must be aware of this. When doing your assessments, ensure that you emphasize the significance of communication, teamwork, and flexibility.

Promote the Correct Individuals

When it comes time to promote someone to a position within the organization, ensure that they display a high EI. Before promoting, you should ask candidates pointed questions about what they believe is required for success in their new job. Then inquire about how they have exhibited those abilities in their current roles. Again, by emphasizing EI during the promotion process, you communicate to the rest of your firm that these are desirable characteristics.

While you know how to incorporate EI into your company's human resource processes, is the effort worthwhile? Not every employee is Carl, and you have done rather well for yourself over the years. What results can you anticipate as a result of these changes? Consider some hard numbers.

American Express, the world's largest credit card company, incorporated EI into its training courses. Employees that got EI training increased sales by 20% compared to the control group.

When assessing whether airmen would make good recruiters, the United States Air Force analyzed EI. Individuals with a high EI were 300 percent more effective than those with a low EI.

L'Oreal Cosmetics began selecting agents based on their emotional intelligence (EI) rather than their technical aptitude alone. These agents outsold their competitors by an average of more than $90,000 in their first year.

Emotional Intelligence is a success predictor. Whatever line of business you are in, emphasizing emotional intelligence and technical skills will help your business develop. Employee productivity will increase, as will employee retention. A corporation with a high rate of EI is a terrific place to work, and skilled workers will resist leaving. Successful businesses retain high-performing personnel.

As an HR professional, you aim to assist your company's other employees in reaching their full potential. You are aware that your business will continue to thrive and grow by doing so. Among the ways to reach these aims is implementing programs that stress Emotional Intelligence. There are numerous solutions available to assist you in increasing the overall intelligence of your business.

The most critical factor in building Emotional Intelligence inside your organization is your dedication. Once employees understand EI's critical to the company and their overall success, they will explore ways to improve their performance. All that remains is to lay the groundwork.

HOW HIGH IS THE EMOTIONAL INTELLIGENCE (EQ) OF YOUR TEAM?

Emotional Intelligence (EQ) is frequently defined in terms of individual characteristics. It refers to an individual's capacity for recognizing, managing, and effectively utilizing their own emotions. A high EQ is necessary to effectively manage one's behavior and develop and maintain healthy interpersonal interactions with others.

Individuals, teams, groups, and even entire companies benefit from EQ. While most people understand what a person with a high EQ looks like, clear indicators can help determine your workgroup, team, or entire business's EQ level.

How a High EQ in Teams and Groups Contributes to Improved Performance

Teams with a high EQ are easily identifiable because they exhibit a high interpersonal skills in various day-to-day interactions. These groups collaborate to build trust, use conflict to generate smart judgments, and hold each other accountable for producing exceptional results.

Members of a team with a high EQ are not "divas" or "lone wolves." They are equally committed to the success of each team member as they are to their own. They understand that team members' success is contingent on one another. One of the most obvious characteristics of a group with a high EQ is that difficult topics are brought to the surface and resolved.

Conflict is viewed as a natural and important component of the problem-solving process. While significant subjects are vigorously argued and addressed, clear ground rules are in place to prevent unwelcome emotional outbursts or personal assaults. Rather than that, critical issues are addressed through candid discourse and debate.

Additionally, high-EQ teams demonstrate a strong sense of commitment, which results in an alignment focused on accomplishing goals and outcomes. If team members become diverted or derailed, other team members either utilize accountability to redirect the errant member or bring the matter to the attention of the rest of the team or leadership for assistance. However, they do not allow prestige and ego to obstruct teams from producing results.

Signs of a High Emotional Intelligence in Groups, Teams, and Organizations

* Team members have enough trust in one another to openly discuss their strengths and faults.

* Sincere dispute is regarded as required, if not desired, for effective decision-making.

* Passionate debate and discussion are utilized to produce various ideas and approaches from which the best course of action can be chosen.

* Senior organizational leaders are self-aware of their power and influence and exercise proper self-control to communicate effectively with others. For instance, they may reserve their opinions till the end of a meeting to avoid suffocating a more complete and open conversation.

* Supervisors and managers exhibit integrity and are trusted, even when others disagree on specific acts or decisions.

* While negative criticism is not avoided, it is presented to members to protect their professional dignity and self-esteem to maintain employee engagement and motivation.

* The process of achieving an outcome is just as significant as the outcome itself. Producing superior achievements while engaging in unacceptable behavior falls short of the required level. Neither the ends nor the means justify the means.

* Members readily accept responsibility for their actions and are aware of the repercussions of their conduct, decisions, and reactions on other team members.

* Team members set unambiguous ground rules for undesirable behavior and ensure that the standards are widely understood. For instance, problem-solving is about learning from mistakes rather than apportioning blame.

* Team members are accountable to one another, confront inappropriate behavior, and share credit for team success and accomplishments.

Why Low EQ is a frequent saboteur
of team and group success

Additionally, low EQ teams exhibit their distinct characteristics and methods. However, these attitudes frequently
obstruct teams and organizations from efficiently resolving
difficult situations.

Teams with low EQ frequently experience fits and starts of
success and emotional outbursts, especially during times of
crisis. As a result of this dynamic instability, teams frequently
deliver inconsistent results.

Members of low-EQ teams frequently feel uneasy, lack management competency, and view conflict as a symptom of dys-
function. Team members frequently fear meetings, and their
group interactions are marked by an aggressive avoidance of
conflict, leaving members with high levels of stress resulting
from unresolved critical issues.

Team members are unlikely to take calculated risks or urge
others to do so. Team members with low EQ become skilled at
inventing "pre-emptive" reasons so they can easily deflect criticism when the team frequently fails to achieve results.

Often, members have an unspoken agreement not to hold one
another accountable, allowing team difficulties to be external-
ized to external forces or unforeseen occurrences. This safe-
guards everyone's ego and position and prevents team members from examining how their interactions contribute to low
performance and failure to produce the intended results and
goals.

Signs of Low Emotional Intelligence in Groups, Teams, and Organizations

* Team members are hesitant to publicly admit their shortcomings or errors and rarely seek assistance, even when needed.

* Team members are hesitant to hold one another accountable for their commitments and responsibilities for fear of jeopardizing interpersonal connections and so exposing them to accountability from others.

* Senior leaders' fragile egos result in "off-limits" or "forbidden" problems that need to be addressed. Still, they cannot because team members feel unsupported in confronting key players' unsuccessful pet policies.

* Individual competition and the desire for high individual success frequently obstruct the collaboration and teamwork required to generate win-win solutions.

* Members are unwilling or unable to engage in a heated debate over key subjects unless a crisis looms, the conflict turns personal and unproductive.

* When powerful external players are present, artificial harmony occurs between team members. When the regional vice-president pays a visit, everyone gets along swimmingly.

* Time and energy are expended actively to avoid conflict and deflect blame and responsibility to others.

To protect status and egos, "pre-emptive" excuses and other methods of evading accountability are commonly used.

* Fear of making a "wrong" decision frequently results in "analysis paralysis" and continual delays, preventing team members from acting decisively. The pursuit of a "perfect" answer obstructs the development of an "effective" solution.

* Negative feedback is frequently offered inconsistently and in an unconstructive manner. Emotional outbursts occur, and team members are made scapegoats for ineffective leadership.

* Team members frequently feel humiliated or embarrassed, while senior management views them as too sensitive and in need of a thicker skin.

* Organizational leaders absolve themselves of responsibility for concerns of culture or morale. The issue is always with the individual or group, never with the institution or culture.

What Should You Do If Your Group's EQ Needs to Be Raised?

If you are fortunate enough to be a team member with a high EQ, you already understand what it means to be a part of a successful group, team, or organization. On the other hand, if you observe your team exhibiting Low EQ behaviors, you must decide what you can do to improve things.

It is critical to understand that raising the EQ level of an entire group or team is a considerably more difficult process than working with a single underperforming team member. This is because you deal with group dynamics, varying levels of interpersonal functioning, a jumble of egos, and individuals who are likely to be scared of change and mistrust their abilities to grow.

After all, they have evolved various ineffectual methods for evading responsibility and accountability, so don't expect them to welcome the chance to resolve the disputes they have been intentionally avoiding.

To begin establishing a higher group EQ, determine where your team is already performing effectively and where there is an obvious need for professional development. Do not attempt to complete this task alone—enlist assistance. Locate either internal or external specialists with expertise working with EQ and groups.

Collaborate with your expert to determine which behaviors contribute to team success and which obstruct team goals. Then devise a strategy for advancing team development around the fundamental concerns of trust, conflict resolution, commitment, and accountability. Bear in mind that change is a process, not an event. Professional assistance may take six to twelve months of sustained effort to achieve meaningful progress.

From personal experience, I can attest that it is possible to boost a team's EQ. However, it is extremely necessary to have a strong and secure team leader capable of recognizing the indicators of low EQ and its detrimental effect on performance. Additionally, the team leader must be willing to seek assistance, accept outside advice and guidance, and encourage continual transformation.

The expert and team leader must collaborate to build mechanisms for team members to hold one another accountable and to let go of established modes of interaction. Conflict avoidance must be abandoned, and teams must be taught how to incorporate conflict efficiently into routine issue solving to obtain better results.

The team members must be educated on giving and accepting candid feedback in ways that address genuine concerns. Finally, all team members must feel empowered to confront teammates who lose focus or fail to follow through on commitments.

Not many teams can make the transition from low to a high EQ. It's difficult, requires effort, and disrupts the conventional engaging manner. However, teams who successfully enhance their EQ frequently discover that they are capable of significantly more effective problem solving than they ever imagined possible.

Team members with a high EQ are more engaged, deliver higher-quality results, and are dedicated to their team and organization. Finally, high EQ teams frequently operate as talent magnets, attracting great people across the organization.

ESSENTIAL TEAMWORK SKILLS

As more firms adopt a team-based approach, assessing the skills required for effective teamwork is critical. The following are six skill categories that team leaders and members could consider developing further.

The team's vision and purpose must be crystal clear for good teamwork to exist. Teams should consider the following: What is the team's purpose? Why are we here? Why is it critical to work as a team rather than as individuals? What is our vision for the future? Is this vision truly coordinated and universally shared? Is every team member aware of the impact of their job and work on this vision, purpose, or mission?

1. Communication—Efficient cooperation requires effective communication. Communication is composed of multiple components: listening, our words, our body language, and our pace. A reminder that communication does not have to be limited to what we say. Indeed, body language accounts for nearly 55% of face-to-face communication messages, followed by words at 7% and tone, tempo, and pitch at 38%. These figures change when we make telephone calls and lose the clues provided by body language. The balance swings again in an email when the tone is gone. Our comments carry weight when sent by email.

   Communication is not only what is spoken on a team; it is also what is not said. What is the team not discussing? What might unpleasant conversations be necessary?

   Listening is closely related to communication. What is the team's listening ability? Are our team members truly paying attention to what others are saying and non-verbal cues? In comparison, our team members are so anxious to "get a word in" that they fail to listen to what the other person is saying and instead focus only on what they want to say?

   What are your team's communication strengths? Where is the potential for further development of these?

2. Flexibility—Adaptability is more critical than ever in today's corporate environment of accomplishing more with less and constant change. The capacity to pivot frequently, think critically, and be resilient is crucial for teams who wish to compete at the highest level.

   In general, how adaptive is your team? Who makes up your team? How critical is an adaptation in your situation?

3. Appreciation of differences—Any team can contain a great deal of diversity. Effective teams value variances in everything from working styles to professional backgrounds, priorities, and even generations. A component of this appreciation is examining how team members are similar and dissimilar.

   Learning more about the interests and styles of each team member can foster understanding rather than cause conflict. For instance, one team member may be extremely detail-oriented, but another may be a "big picture" thinker.

   Understanding our particular preferences and styles enables us to be more aware of our prejudices and how we must alter our approaches while interacting with others. This topic is inextricably linked to the team's emotional intelligence.

   How does your team value and operate with diversity? What are the team's differences, synergies, and strengths?

4. Trust and Respect: A vital component of any collaboration is trust and respect. If no team member has the other's back, the team members will work in their silos. Similarly, getting things done is greatly dependent on

the team developing trust in one another and sharing the resources and knowledge necessary to complete tasks.

What is your team's degree of trust and respect?

5. Emotional Intelligence—These days, leaders are paying more attention to Emotional Intelligence, EI. Emotional intelligence is defined as "the aptitude for identifying our own and others' feelings, motivating ourselves, and effectively managing our own and others' emotions." (Harvard Business Review, Daniel Goleman).

    Individuals and teams with a high level of emotional intelligence demonstrate self-awareness (knowledge of oneself), social awareness (knowledge of others), relationship management (ability to build strong relationships), and self-management (the ability to control emotion).

6. Accountability, Commitment, and Follow-Through— Teams exist to accomplish goals. Commitment to the goals required to accomplish the results (both shared and individual) is vital. Many teams struggle with accountability and follow-through.

    What are you committed to doing or undertaking as a team, collectively and individually, to drive the team forward? How are you establishing responsibility and conducting check-ins? Is there a point of contact for following up on action steps, or is it expected that everyone has followed through? High-performing teams agree on how actions will be tracked and consistently focus on this.

Teams—Obstacles To Team Successfulness

Highly productive teams have the potential to accomplish amazing things for the organizations they serve. They are achieving organizational success results in increased personal success and achievement. However, team success is not a given. Thus, what are the five most prevalent impediments to team performance, and how can you prevent them?

1st impediment: ambiguous outcomes

If a team is to thrive and produce results, it must be crystal clear about the results or outcomes that the team is expected to produce. Too frequently, teams are assigned ambiguous and imprecise outcomes, which results in little in the way of results. Make your objectives explicit and quantifiable. For instance, the goal of reducing waste from product X by 10% by 31 December 2008 is both explicit and quantifiable.

2nd Obstacle: Ineffective conflict

All successful teams require friction and challenge; else, everything becomes too cozy. On the other hand, it is critical to maintaining productive conflict rather than harmful or unproductive conflict. Proactive conflict occurs when a lively and heated debate results in a more favorable end or solution. A challenge that focuses exclusively on the problems without proposing solutions is ineffective.

3rd impediment: Playing it safe

Teams and team members must take calculated risks and venture outside their comfort zone to significantly improve performance or turn things around. This will only occur if the organizational culture encourages and rewards this imaginative and balanced risk-taking. For instance, if the culture encourages people to hunt for scapegoats when things go wrong, they will remain inside the confines of safety rather than taking a chance.

4th impediment: Individual agendas.

To thrive as a team, all members must first sign up for and commit to the team's aims. This is particularly difficult for many because, in business, we are accustomed to being concerned about our unique circumstances. Developing a group-based compensation system can be a beneficial first step toward encouraging teams to prioritize the team schedule.

5th Obstacle: Leadership

Someone must assume the role of leader in teams. Without a leader, a team is analogous to a ship without a captain. The team may elect a leader, or, as the team matures, a natural leader may emerge. Any effective team, however, requires a leader.

Bottom Line—Teams can achieve great things, but it is critical to identify and eliminate the impediments to team success. Thus, what impediments are impeding your team's success?

TEAM COOPERATION: EIGHT INDICATORS THAT YOUR TEAM IS NOT COOPERATIVE

We've almost certainly all been a part of teams that were a big success and teams that accomplished nothing. I am confident I have. If you're a team leader, what are some indicators that your team isn't working or is operating at a level below its true potential?

Indicator 1: No One Trusts Anyone

Trust is a critical component of a team, similar to the foundations of a structure. Establishing trust requires a significant investment of time, effort, and energy. It may appear to be an uphill battle, and it frequently is. Simultaneously, you will always receive sub-optimal results unless you can establish and retain trust.

Indicator 2: Individuals Are Working Alone

One of the reasons teams succeed is that they are very dependent on one another to provide the desired result or conclusion. Occasionally, teams are formed when none are required. Individuals working in isolation rather than collaboratively suggest a problem with the team or that there is no need for a team to achieve the desired objective.

Indicator 3: Individuals Are Not Held Accountable

Accountability is one of those areas that is frequently misunderstood. Accountability entails setting expectations with others and then allowing them to account for their accomplishments. Occasionally, leaders do an excellent job of creating expectations but fall short of following through.

Indicator 4: Decisiveness Is Slow Or Non-Existent

To derive any advantage from a team, choices must be made, and those decisions must be implemented. Too frequently, particularly in more senior teams inside larger organizations, people dither or entirely avoid making decisions.

Indicator 5: No One Is Listening

Communication is unquestionably a critical component of teamwork. People, in my experience, are excellent communicators and writers. On the other side, listening is much more spotty and challenging. Yet, in reality, listening can yield the greatest benefits from teamwork.

Indicator 6: Free Expression Is Suppressed

At times, issues inside teams must be discussed and brought to light. What frequently occurs is that to avoid conflict, individuals are encouraged or convinced to keep their mouths shut and remain silent. This serves to increase dissatisfaction, bitterness, and detachment. Recognize that disagreement is a necessary component of effective teams.

Indicator 7: Suffocation of Creativity

To do something novel or distinctive, a different way of thinking is required, as is an element of risk-taking. Occasionally, creativity is stifled by the mistaken belief that being safe is the best course of action. To avoid this, begin by determining the worst-case scenario if you took a chance.

Indicator 8: The Most Loud Voices Receive All Attention

Individuals are unique. Some individuals are extremely gregarious and extroverted, while others are more introspective and introverted. You need all of those varied characteristics on a team, and as the team leader, you must find a method to ensure that the voices of everyone, not just the loudest, are heard.

The Bottom Line: Teams can accomplish extraordinary achievements, and frequently, modest tweaks can significantly improve the outcomes achieved as a team.

Collaboration begins with you!

That's correct; you are crucial in bringing your team together and ensuring its success! If everyone in your organization adopted this approach, imagine the impact! Collaboration has the potential to be amazing. Teamwork is a state of mind, a mode of thought, and a mode of operation. These straightforward tactics give a blueprint for fostering team harmony within your firm. Commit to being a team player today!

Concentrate On Your Strengths

Contribute to the development of solutions within your organization. Concentrate on what is right. Those that focus exclusively on what is wrong with your organization are rarely those who provide value. These individuals expend all of their efforts whining and bickering. Maintain a good attitude and give your all!

Reach out to others to learn about their strengths. Concentrate on others' strengths and assist them in maximizing their inherent potential. A key component of being a successful team player is your ability to focus on others' strengths rather than their flaws. As you accomplish this for others, they will reciprocate by focusing their attention on your strengths.

Consider how you can collaborate with people in your organization in a complementary manner. Thank goodness not everyone possesses the same set of skills. Consider how you can assist others in ways that maximize the benefit of your strengths. If you possess unique abilities that others lack, assist them by bridging such gaps. For instance, if you are quite adept at Excel spreadsheets, a skill that others in your department lack, step up and offer assistance whenever the opportunity presents itself.

Consider areas in which your strengths can be enhanced. We are not always able to perform what we do best all day. Nonetheless, seek ways to strategically position yourself so that you may accomplish what you do best the majority of the time.

A Shared Vision

Identifying and communicating a clear vision is one of an organization's most critical assets. A vision is a mental picture of the business's future. The vision articulates who and what the business is, why it exists, and where it is headed in the big picture. To comprehend or define your organization's vision, you must first define:

+ The basic purpose for your business's existence beyond profit maximization
+ The business's ageless, unchanging core principles
+ The business's "big picture" objectives for the future. What fuels your organization's passion for what it does?

Determine your organization's vision and how your function fits into that vision.

A shared vision exists when every company member accepts it, comprehends it, takes ownership of it, and most importantly, aligns their behavior. Assure that you contribute value to this vision and are part of your organization's broader picture.

Equality

Individuals keep a close eye on the checks and balances in any social interaction—what they offer vs. what they receive. This is also a regular occurrence in the job; we monitor relationships in the same way we do outside of work.

Ascertain that everything you do contributes to your team's strength. Every opportunity you get to add value. Distribute workloads fairly—volunteer to do your fair amount of labor and be open to increasing your contributions.

Make collaboration the norm. At times, "doing the bare minimum" becomes the standard, and individuals grow enraged when they believe they are doing more than everyone else. When numerous people are cautious not to do more than their fair part, you have a significant problem! We can alter these norms by embracing a spirit of complete participation, assistance, and hard work. Consider your coworkers to be equals and do everything possible to aid them if necessary.

The allure of this line of work is that genuine connections are reciprocal. What you get out of a relationship is proportional to the amount of effort you put into it. You will almost always win in professional relationships and teamwork if you follow this straightforward rule. Always give first and disregard what you receive! This is a straightforward rule with huge beneficial consequences. If you adopt this as a way of life, you will be astounded at the benefits to your professional and personal relationships.

Trust & Transparency

Building trust in your business is not an easy undertaking, and there is no magic formula for doing so. However, there is a hidden first step to trust-building. This key phase entails developing an ability to trust others. When the phrase "Watch your back!" is frequently used within an organization, a lack of trust is unavoidable. You must shift the norm to frequently stating, "I've got your back!"

As with any other aspect of relationships, you receive what you give. Therefore, you must first demonstrate trustworthiness if you wish to be trusted. Similarly, if you desire a large circle of friends, you must be outgoing! That's not rocket science. Therefore, resolve to be trustworthy. If you commit to completing a project by a specified deadline or if you agree to cover a shift for a coworker, etc. Do it! Keep your promises! Trust is eroded when individuals talk the talk of collaboration but are unwilling to walk the walk.

Demonstrate your reliance on your coworkers. Inform them that they may rely on you and that you, in turn, must rely on their support. Such expressions of trust and confidence might create opportunities for trust development.

Acceptance of Distinctions

Diversity in the workplace is frequently discussed in terms of ethnicity, gender, religion, or other facets of one's ethnic identity. Consider the following: two individuals may share a large list of ethnic characteristics (i.e., African American, female, Christian, married with three children, each with a household income of $75k per year), but they may have markedly different ways of thinking and behaving. Diversification boils down to having a varied perspective.

Diversity in the workplace has always been a part of our world and will always be. We are lucky to deal with individuals that think differently than we do. Recognize this as a strength for both your organization and yourself. Make use of the distinctions of others. Accept others' points of view. Individuals with narrow minds believe their path is the only way. Avoid falling for this trap! Allow them to be themselves, just as you want to be yourself at work, and enjoy your differences.

Great firms seek internal innovations and solutions to market conditions that are challenging to navigate. This is an excellent approach that is underutilized. By soliciting new ideas from your staff, you will offer them a voice, empower their perspectives, and engage them in the company's growth and achievement of its goals.

Participate in such a program if your organization has one! You may have ideas, but they are worthless until you communicate them publicly and systematically for your "higher-ups" to become aware of your brilliance.

Communication

Communication is frequently blamed for failing teamwork. Rather than that, the absence of communication is frequently blamed. You know what's odd, but I'm sure you can recall a moment when this happened in your company... Communication is frequently blamed, even though it is only a subset of the more significant and complex underlying issue.

For instance, you might hear someone say, "We're having a serious communication problem." You realize that nobody trusts the boss and that a newly enforced policy results in a decline in sales. Surprisingly, neither of these situations is truly a "communication issue," even though both could readily be classified.

Thus, what constitutes a genuine communication issue? What is the essence of effective communication? Make the following commitments, and you will be considered an excellent communicator in your workplace.

1) Be candid, forthright, and forthright. Maintain an authentic relationship with others. Communicate the facts and avoid sugarcoating problems.

2) Assume the best intentions of others. Maintain a pleasant attitude toward others and concentrate on what is right. Communicate what is correct.

3) Educate the public. Keep people informed regardless of your position in the line of command. Communicate horizontally and vertically, left and right. The more individuals are aware; the fewer stories will need to be invented.

4) Avoid all forms of drama. That is correct; I stated drama! Keep your mouth shut about rumors at your workplace. If conversations are going on at the water cooler, avoid approaching with your ears and interest pricked up. Keep your distance! Drama, rumors, and gossip are all detrimental to an organization's health and, more specifically, to teamwork.

Altruism

Finally, cultivate a generous spirit by displaying an unselfish concern for the well-being of others. Selfishness, or the act of boosting one's ego, has become far too prevalent in the workplace. Enhance your self-esteem by enhancing the appearance of others. Prioritize the needs of others.

Teamwork's strength begins with you! The key is in your hands. Demonstrate superior team abilities, and you will see a big improvement in your reputation and true character. Others will regard you positively as a team player. They will emulate your example and allow you to continue achieving long-term success and sustainable personal progress.

CONCLUSION

When you glance around your office, do you notice that everyone is the same as you? Most likely not. Over the last 50 years, the demographics of the workforce have shifted considerably. In the 1950s, white males constituted more than 60% of the workforce.

They were typically the household's sole breadwinners, expecting to retire at 65 and spend their retirement years engaging in leisure activities. Today's workforce is a more accurate picture of the population, with various genders, races, religions, ages, and other demographic characteristics.

Any business's long-term success requires a wide pool of personnel capable of bringing new ideas, viewpoints, and perspectives to their work. The difficulty that diversity presents enables your managers to leverage the diversity of genders, cultural backgrounds, ages, and lifestyles to respond more quickly and creatively to business opportunities.

A benefit of a varied workforce is the capacity to tap into the diverse talents brought to the workplace by people with varying backgrounds, viewpoints, abilities, and disabilities. This is demonstrated admirably on the staff's business cards of a Fortune 100 technology company. At first sight, the business cards of this company's employees appear to be standard. A closer examination reveals the raised Braille characters containing personnel details.

Many businesses, however, continue to experience difficulties in creating a diverse work environment. A factor contributing to this is the inclination to pigeonhole employees, categorizing them according to their diversity profile. Which category of diversity does an employee fit into if he is male, over 50, English-speaking, and atheist? Is it a matter of gender, generation, globalization, or religion? Diversity cannot be readily classified in the real world, and enterprises that respond to human complexity by using the talents of a diverse staff will be most effective at developing their businesses and client base.

When considering ways to boost corporate earnings, consider expanding into new markets or strategically partnering with clients. Consider how a diverse staff will help your business achieve those objectives. Consider unconventional solutions.

If senior management supports a diverse workforce, diversity should be visible at all levels. If you do not, certain employees may rapidly conclude that they have no future in your organization. Make no apologies for using black, white, gay, or lesbian terms. Demonstrate respect for diversity concerns and advocate for succinct and positive responses. How can you exemplify your organization's dedication to diversity?

As baby boomers retire and more minorities enter the workforce, managing a multigenerational and multicultural workforce will become the new business norm. Additionally, there is a multitude of specialist equipment available to assist people with impairments in successfully contributing to their work environments.

If your corporate culture does not encourage broad diversity, you risk losing talent to competitors. How can you ensure that your recruiting efforts reach all qualified candidates?

Eliminate artificial impediments to achievement. The interview style—behavioral or functional—may work against some job prospects. For example, older employees are less experienced with behavioral interviews and may not perform well unless your recruiters specifically request the types of experiences they seek.

Employees from nations other than the United States and non-Caucasian populations may exaggerate their accomplishments or emphasize "who they know" rather than "what they know." Educate your recruiters on the cultural aspects of interviewing. How can your human resource systems ensure that everyone has an equal opportunity?

At all levels, maintain variety. The term "diversity" encompasses more than color and gender. Programs that address work and family challenges—such as flexible work schedules and resources and referrals for child and elder care—make sound financial sense. How can you retain your most valuable employees?

Employing real examples to teach small groups of employees how to handle conflicts and value varied perspectives benefits businesses significantly more than huge, abstract diversity seminars. Additionally, training should emphasize the value of varied viewpoints.

Workers are more concerned with whether their supervisor appears to value their ideas than whether they are part of an all-white male group or an ethnically diverse workforce.

Additionally, develop leaders' capacity to see beyond their cultural lens to exploit the productivity potential inherent in a varied population fully.

How can you implement diversity training in your organization?

Include your supervisors in a mentoring program where they can coach and provide feedback to employees who are unlike them. Some of your most important mentors may be strangers. Locate someone who does not resemble you. Identify someone from a distinct ethnic group, race, or gender. Find someone who has a different perspective than you. How do you locate a mentor who is unlike you?

Conduct periodic organizational reviews on compensation, benefits, work environment, management, and promotional possibilities to determine your long-term growth. Continue doing what is effective and discontinue doing what is ineffective.

Any business's long-term success requires a broad pool of individuals capable of bringing new ideas, insights, and attitudes and a corporate mindset that values those perspectives. Additionally, it is a well-known fact that a lack of diversity might impair your ability to communicate successfully with a diverse clientele.

Connect your diversity strategies to specific objectives, including morale, retention, performance, and profitability. Build your firm with everything you've got, with your workforce's complicated multi-dimensional talents and personalities, and leverage diversity.

Printed in Great Britain
by Amazon

83412427R00220